Practical and Theoretical Reason in Modern Philosophy

Edited by

Paniel Reyes Cárdenas

The University of Sheffield

Roberto Casales García

UPAEP University

Daniel R. Herbert

The University of Sheffield

Series in Philosophy

VERNON PRESS

www.vernonpress.com

In the Americas:	*In the rest of the world:*
Vernon Press	Vernon Press
1000 N West Street, Suite 1200	C/Sancti Espiritu 17,
Wilmington, Delaware, 19801	Malaga, 29006
United States	Spain

Series in Philosophy

Library of Congress Control Number: 2023949183

ISBN: 979-8-8819-0015-1

Also available: 978-1-64889-736-8 [Hardback]; 978-1-64889-857-0 [PDF, E-Book]

Cover design by Vernon Press.

Cover image by pikisuperstar on Freepik.

Table of Contents

Abbreviations   v

Introduction   vii

Paniel Reyes Cárdenas
The University of Sheffield

Roberto Casales García
UPAEP University

Daniel R. Herbert
The University of Sheffield

Chapter 1   **The Modern Theoretical/Practical Reason Dualism and the Realist/Nominalist Medieval Controversy**   1

Paniel Reyes Cárdenas
The University of Sheffield

Chapter 2   **Distinct Perceptions and Belief**   17

Evelyn Vargas
Universidad Nacional de la Plata

Chapter 3   **Can Wild Boars See Green? A Critique of Higher and First-Order Theories Surrounding Leibniz's Concept of Apperception**   37

Leonardo Ruiz Gómez
Universidad Panamericana

Chapter 4   **Leibniz on *Conscientia* and Personal Identity**   57

Roberto Casales García
UPAEP University

Chapter 5   **A Critical Review of the Structure of Scientific Knowledge in George Berkeley: *An essay Towards a New Theory of Vision***   73

Laura Benítez Grobet
Instituto de Investigaciones Filosóficas, UNAM

Chapter 6   **Kant, Spinoza, and Practical Rationality**   83

Anna Tomaszewska
Jagiellonian University in Kraków

Chapter 7   **Apperception and Self-Knowledge in Kant**   105

Stéfano Straulino
Instituto Tecnológico Autónomo de México

Chapter 8   **Moral Conscience in Kant's Late Philosophy:
Is it Relevant for the Concept of Radical Evil?**   125

Jimena Portilla González
Universidad Panamericana

Chapter 9   **Kant, Peirce, and the Rationality of Natural
Science**   141

Daniel R. Herbert
The University of Sheffield

Chapter 10   **The Limits of Self-Legislation**   175

Tom O'Shea
University of Edinburgh

Index   193

Abbreviations

Works by Hume

Treatsie/THN = Hume, David. *A Treatise of Human Nature*. Oxford: Clarendon Press, 1975.

EHU = Hume, David. *An Enquiry Concerning Human Understanding*. Edited by Peter Millican. Oxford World's Classics. Oxford, New York: Oxford University Press, 2008.

Works by Locke

Essays = Locke, J. *Ensayos Sobre El Entendimiento Humano*. Translated by E. O'Gorman. México: Fondo de Cultura Económica, 2013.

Works by Leibniz

AG = Leibniz, Gottfried Wilhelm. *Philosophical Essays*. Edited and translated by R. Ariew and D. Garber. Indianapolis: Hacket, 1986.

A = Leibniz, Gottfried Wilhelm. *Sämtliche Schriften Und Briefe*. Edited by the Akademie der Wissenschaften. Darmstadt-Berlin: Akademie-Verlag, 1875-1890.

GP = Leibniz, Gottfried Wilhelm. *Die Philosophischen Schriften von Leibniz*. Edited by C. I. Gerhardt. 7 vols. Berlin: Hildesheim, 1960-1961.

M = Leibniz, Gottfried Wilhelm. "Monadologie" in Gottfried Wilhelm Leibniz, *Die Philosophischen Schriften von Leibniz*, ed. C. I. Gerhardt, vol. 6 (Berlin: Hildesheim, 1960-1961).

Couturat = Leibniz, Gottfried Wilhelm. *Opuscules et Fragmentes Inédits de Leibniz. Extraits Des Manuscrits de La Bibliothèque Royale de Hanovre*. Edited by L. Couturat. Hildesheim: Olms, 1991.

Grua = Leibniz, Gottfried Wilhelm. *Textes Inédits d'après Les Manuscrites de La Bibliothèque Proviciale de Hannovre*. Edited by Gastón Grua. Paris: Presses Universitaires de France, 1948.

Finster = Leibniz, Gottfried Wilhelm. *Der Briefwechsel Mit Antoine Arnauld*. Translated by R. Finster. Hamburg: Felix Meiner, 1997.

Robinet I = Leibniz, Gottfried Wilhelm. *Principes de La Nature et de La Grâce Fondés En Raison. Principes de La Philosophie Ou Monadologie*. Edited by André Robinet. París: Presses Universitaires de France, 1954.

Works by Immanuel Kant

BDG = Kant, Immanuel. "The Only Possible Argument in Support of a Demonstration of the Existence of God." In *Theoretical Philosophy*, 1755–1770. New York: Cambridge University Press, 1992.

GMS = Kant, Immanuel. "Groundwork of the Metaphysics of Morals." In *Practical Philosophy*. New York: Cambridge University Press, 1996.

KrV = Kant, Immanuel. *Critique of Pure Reason*. Translated by Paul Guyer and Allen W. Wood. Cambridge: Cambridge University Press, 1998.

KrP = Kant, Immanuel. *Critique of Practical Reason*. Translated by Lewis White Beck. Indianapolis: H. W. Sams, 1956.

KU = Kant, Immanuel. *Critique of the Power of Judgment*. Edited by Paul Guyer. Translated by Paul Guyer and Eric Matthews. Cambridge: Cambridge University Press, 2013.

MF = Kant, Immanuel. "Metaphysical Foundations of Natural Science (1786)." In *Theoretical Philosophy after 1781*, edited by Gary Hatfield, Henry Allison, Michael Friedman, and Peter Heath, 171–270. The Cambridge Edition of the Works of Immanuel Kant. Cambridge: Cambridge University Press, 2002. https://doi.org/10.1017/CBO9780511498015.004.

OP = Kant, Immanuel. Opus Postumum. New York: Cambridge University Press, 1993.

WDO = Kant, Immanuel. "What Does It Mean to Orient Oneself in Thinking?" In *Religion and Rational Theology*. New York: Cambridge University Press, 1996.

Works by Charles Sanders Peirce

EP 1 = Peirce, Charles S. "Grounds of Validity of the Laws of Logic: Further Consequences of Four Incapacities." In *The Essential Peirce*, edited by Nathan Houser and Christian J. W. Kloesel, 1:56-82. Indianapolis: Indiana University Press, 1992.

EP 2 = Peirce, Charles S. "Pragmatism and Abduction." In *The Essential Peirce*, edited by Peirce Edition Project, 2:226-240. Indianapolis: Indiana University Press, 1998

Introduction

Paniel Reyes Cárdenas

The University of Sheffield

Roberto Casales García

UPAEP University

Daniel R. Herbert

The University of Sheffield

There are perhaps few more characteristically 'modern' philosophical anxieties than those which concern the relation between facts and values. Although modernity is often presented in terms of confidence in the natural sciences, centuries of remarkable scientific discovery have accompanied the erosion of inherited moral assumptions and a growing unease about the status of normative standards. As such, the enormity of scientific progress notwithstanding, modernity seems troubled by doubts concerning the place of values in the great scheme of things.

It is customary, in accounts of the transition from mediaeval to modern philosophy, to remark upon a rejection of Aristotelianism and the embrace of a mechanistic understanding of nature. Whereas to Aristotle and his mediaeval followers, the natural world appeared to be populated by instances of various substance-kinds, each with its own *telos* or function determinative of its particular good, Descartes and his successors saw only units of matter subject to mechanical laws of motion. In the ancient and mediaeval worlds, it had therefore been widely assumed that values are inherent, or instantiated, within the natural world, such that the latter could serve as a guide to the former and the more one came to know about nature, the more one would come to know about value. With the dawn of modernity, however, and the resulting entrenchment of a mechanistic outlook towards nature, it could no longer be expected that an understanding of the natural world might be relevant to understanding value. Such a 'disenchantment' of nature has its legacy in philosophical concerns which remain with us today. If values are not inscribed in nature, then on what basis are evaluations made? Are values merely subjective projections upon an inherently valueless world? What becomes, in that case, of our concerns with such vital matters as the dignity of human beings, the best way to live and the right way to act? Of particular philosophical interest are questions concerning the role of reason in making sense of value. Does our alleged status as rational beings explain why we ought to regard some acts and states of affairs as better than others? Or is it because of some extra-rational facts about us that we are disposed to make the evaluations that we do?

The modern period in philosophy bears witness to an explosion of efforts to account for the possibility of value in a post-Aristotelian conception of nature. Although not very widely known as a contributor to ethical thought, Descartes's substance dualism sets the stage for modern debates concerning the relation between theoretical and practical reason by sharply distinguishing between a material domain vacant of value, and several minds or spiritual substances responsible for introducing values into our understanding of our experience. According to Descartes's dualistic picture, no state of the natural world has anything but mechanical properties and it is therefore necessary to look elsewhere, to the states of immaterial mental substances, if we are to understand how values enter the world. Spinoza's ethical concerns are explicit in the title of the work for which he has been most celebrated (as well as condemned) but are presented in the context of a mechanistic and deterministic outlook that presents value as relative to subjective interests. Amongst the great early-modern rationalist philosophers, Leibniz's long-neglected contributions to ethical philosophy are now the subject of much discussion. Despite his debts to Plato and Aristotle, however, Leibniz was no less the advocate of a mechanistic understanding of nature than any of his celebrated philosophical contemporaries and his ethical views must be understood within such a context.

Early modern empiricism, as represented in the works of Hobbes, Locke, Berkeley and Hume, is well-known for its contributions to ethical and political thought. His thoroughgoing mechanism notwithstanding, Hobbes thought it possible to develop a system of politics to which all reasonable agents could give their rational approval. Locke too was extremely critical of mediaeval scholastic philosophy and sought to replace it entirely with a philosophical outlook aligned with Newtonian physics. This acceptance of a "disenchanted" view of nature did not, however, prevent Locke from articulating a political philosophy based upon values of tolerance and individual dignity which has been amongst the most influential contributions any philosopher has made to the history of political thought. Berkeley's ethical and political views are less well-known, but are of a piece with his characteristically modern concern about the rise of materialist philosophy and the dangers which he detected such a philosophy to present for religion, morality and common sense. Of the great early modern empiricists, however, it is perhaps Hume who has made the most influential contribution to meta-ethics.

A late fruit in the development of the "practical" aspect of reason coalesced in the pervasive use of the concept of *praxis* after Kant. The term comes from Aristotle, representing one of the three basic activities that are proper to human beings, along with *poiesis* and *theoria*. Indeed, only human beings can exercise praxis because it is an activity that involves will and reason.[1] For Kant, however, praxis is the application of a theory to cases encountered in experience. This application has ethical content: Kant placed the practical above the theoretical and hence influenced the concept of *praxis* of all the German Idealists all the way down to Marx, where the concept became the engine of all Marx's thought and revolutionary activity. The issue emerging in such emphasis, however, seems to be the radicalisation of the separation of theory and practice, an issue attached to the Marxist interpretation of *praxis*. Hannah Arendt discusses *praxis* in the context of practical activity and theory in *The Life of the Mind* (1978). Arendt compared the *vita activa* to the *vita contemplativa* and made clear that the active life is the only way to be fully rational: reason needs to involve the two movements and hence discover that some activities end in themselves and that the lack of thinking can end up in evil. For Arendt, the dichotomy needs to be transcended.

The aim of the present collection is to examine this fertile period in the history of philosophy with respect to its significance for understandings of the relation between theoretical and practical reason, or, relatedly, facts and values. Our contributors have explored different important ways in which both the shortcomings and insights of the theoretical/practical distinction have shaped Western philosophy.

The book starts with a study by Paniel Reyes Cárdenas that explores the debate between realism and nominalism about universals, which took place towards the end of the greatest period of Scholastic Philosophy. It is not only important, but necessary for a full understanding of the distinction between theoretical and practical reasons to find the origins of the differing paths. Indeed, the suspicions of nominalist philosophers about the nature of reasoning itself had the consequence of a concept of reason that divides the objects of theoretical and practical reason: the theoretical world as a reflection of the items of experience and conceptual content, while practical reason will be a reflection of the world of will and action. This duality preludes the later famous fact/value dichotomy, but is derivative of a suspicion about the continuity of experiences both theoretical and practical as isolated sources of reason. This position is derivative of nominalism, and we could hence state that many modern philosophers are intellectual descendants of mediaevals such as

---

[1] Aristotle, "Poetics," in *The Complete Works of Aristotle*, ed. Jonathan Barnes, vol. 2 (United Kingdom: Princeton University Press, 1984), 1449b24.

William of Ockham, Jean Buridan and other nominalists. The realism that mediaeval scholastics defended avoided this division, and we can find a reconciliation with this tradition hinted in the thoughts of modern philosophers such as Leibniz, Hegel and Schelling for whom the "universals" are central to the unity of reason.

In "Distinct Perception and Belief," Evelyn Vargas examines through an organised presentation Leibniz's theory of perception to explain how to make sense of an experience as the perceiver's reasons for believing something about the state of the world. According to Vargas, early modern philosophers, following Kepler's model of the retinal image, are responsible for introducing the idea that perception and thought require some mental entities as immediate objects, having as a result that beliefs based on perception are uncertain and that there is metaphysical isolation of the mind. Far away from these sceptical consequences, Vargas holds that Leibniz had a theory of sense perception that can explain perceptual content, avoid the "veil of perception scepticism" and justify the reliability of senses. This chapter contributes with a relevant indication of the actuality of Leibniz's thought, that connects his ideas with those one Merleau-Ponty and the existentialists as an important precedent of the importance of the body as both perceiving and perceived.

Related to this topic, Leonardo Ruiz Gómez analyses some of the most relevant aspects of Leibniz's theory of apperception by making a comparison between first- and high-order theories. According to Ruiz, both approaches miss that apperception in Leibniz has a synthetic character since they seem to outline the lower levels of apperception unsatisfactorily. They miss an important sense of apperception that Ruiz regarded as "non-conscious sensation," a concept that should be distinguished from bare perception and also from any sort of conscious content. On a different approach, Roberto Casales takes Leibniz's distinction between perception, apperception, phenomenical or sensitive consciousness, and reflective *conscientia* to distinguish three different constitutive levels of identity implied in Leibniz's notion of personal identity. While the first level is intimately related to his notion of completeness and his principle of the identity of indiscernibles, according to Casales, Leibniz distinguishes this kind of individuation and simplicity from the kind of unity that can be found in his characterisation of natural machines. Living beings have a teleological structure by which every organ is related to each other, a nested structure that presupposes an organic-sensorial structure. This level, however, can also be distinguished from a third one, in which Leibniz articulates his conception of personal identity as related to the moral quality of rational beings.

In "A Critical Review of the Structure of Scientific Knowledge in George Berkeley: An Essay Towards a New Theory of Vision", Laura Benítez states that

Berkeley's theory of vision is relevant not only to articulate his epistemology but also to impulse the development of psychology. This empirical and psychological proposal also reveals that even when mathematics can be a useful instrument that, correctly applied, can contribute to the development of knowledge, according to Benítez, Berkeley recommends that we need to understand its limits at the level of acquisition of our sensible ideas. This chapter, then, shows how Berkeley's ideas on vision generated an ever-bigger gulf between the theoretical and the practical accounts of perception. The following contribution compares Spinoza and Kant's views about the distinction between theoretical and practical reason to understand in which sense, even when both philosophers defend the priority of the practical over the theoretical kind of rationality, they arrive at this conclusion from a very different way. Tomaszewska's contribution also shows the connections with contemporary debates, so her analysis is not only strong but timely, showing how the discussion works as a prelude to later accounts given in twentieth-century phenomenology. According to Anna Tomaszewska, while Spinoza takes the propensity of human consciousness to generate metaphysical illusions and misrepresent reality as a reason to defend the priority of practical reason, Kant places the practical over the theoretical reason trying to provide a coherent account of human action.

The following two contributions, by Stéfano Straulino and Jimena Portilla, also deal with Kant's philosophy's theoretical and practical aspects. In the first contribution, Straulino introduces us to the central problems that come from the relation between apperception and self-knowledge. According to Straulino's approach, by considering Kant's distinction between the pure and the empirical sense of consciousness, we can probe that self-consciousness does not occur unrestrictedly: we need to be related to something different from consciousness to be conscious of ourselves. Straulino's analysis is an excellent reflection on the "I think" in Kant. The discussion of perception and apperception with reference to human psychology offers an important contribution to the literature. It will also be of interest to students and scholars in other disciplines.

In Kant's philosophy, however, we can also see a practical approach to the problem of consciousness, precisely when we talk about moral conscience, considered, according to Portilla, as a relevant aspect for moral evaluation and, in consequence, for moral reasoning. As we can see in this chapter, Portilla relates not only moral conscience with the evaluation of our maxims but also with radical evil and self-deception, since moral conscience helps us prevent our moral disposition from mixing or using a completely immoral ground for our maxims. This is a very timely chapter. We need to learn how radical evil is grounded in the neutrality of consciousness, and therefore the importance of integrating reason is paramount.

In "Kant, Peirce, and the Rationality of Natural Science", Daniel Herbert analyses Peirce's criticisms of Kant's concept of synthetic reasoning and his lack of explanation of the possibility of synthetic *a posteriori* judgments. The first part of the chapter is a contribution in its own right offering new perspectives on Kant's analysis. However, the use of Peirce's critique in the second part locates this discussion in a wider constellation of thinkers, something that adds up to a glimpse of how it is possible to get out of the dichotomy of theory and practice. The difference regarding the need for a philosophical explanation of synthetic *a posteriori* judgments, according to Herbert, explains why Kant and Peirce are led to pursue significantly distinct inquiries with respect to the grounds of scientific knowledge. Whereas Kant takes it that a Transcendental Deduction is called for in order to satisfy the demand for an explanation of the a priori grounds of those synthetic a priori judgements without which natural science would be impossible, Peirce makes it his objective to explain the enabling conditions of the possibility of scientific knowledge as a long-running process of inquiry making use of synthetic inference.

Finally, in the last chapter of this book, Tom O'Shea questions the limits of self-legislation and some forms of constructivism that can be formulated from some modern approaches, like the Kantian and Humean conceptions of normativity. In order to do so, O'Shea outlines and critiques two neo-Hegelian forms of constructivism that present alternatives to the Kantian and Humean positions. The author takes the reader directly into the crux of the issue they wish to discuss. In doing so the author also provides an excellent historical framing and contextualisation of the problems involved in self-legislation.

The progression of the chapters allows us to appreciate that the theoretical and practical reason distinction was the seminal intuition to establish different theories of perception and reason that will underpin the theoretical. Practical reason, however, was to be developed through the efforts of making sense of how individuals can appropriate the autonomy and freedom that is supposed in the moral life. Our different contributions show how these parting ways finally have to meet up again, and this is how late modernity, particularly through German Idealism, exhibits a need to reintegrate the two aspects of reason that, interestingly, leads us back to the discussion that saw modernity emerge.

Then, the different contributions to this collection express distinctive aspects of the theoretical and practical reason distinction, showing some of its fundamental assumptions as well as considering how Western philosophy has been shaped by the articulation of reason in such a way. This understanding will help to figure out what are the needs for a more integrated conception of reason that helps articulate both its theoretical and practical dimensions.

Chapter 1

The Modern Theoretical/Practical Reason Dualism and the Realist/Nominalist Medieval Controversy

Paniel Reyes Cárdenas

The University of Sheffield

Abstract: This contribution explores the debate between realism and nominalism about universals that took place towards the end of the greatest period of Scholastic Philosophy. It is not only important, but necessary for a full understanding of the distinction between theoretical versus practical reason to find the origins of the differing paths. Indeed, the suspicions of nominalist philosophers about the nature of reasoning itself had the consequence of a concept of reason that divides the objects of theoretical and practical reason: the theoretical world as a reflection of the items of experience and conceptual content, while practical reason will be a reflection of the world of will and action. This duality preludes the later famous fact/value dichotomy, but is derivative of a suspicion about the continuity of experiences both theoretical and practical as isolated sources of reason. This position is derivative of nominalism, and we could hence state that many modern philosophers are intellectual descendants of mediaevals such as William of Ockham, Jean Buridan and other nominalists. The realism that mediaeval scholastics defended avoided this division, and we can find a reconciliation with this tradition hinted in the thoughts of modern philosophers such as Leibniz, Hegel and Schelling for whom the "universals" are central to the unity of reason.

Keywords: Ockham, realism of universals, nominalism, dichotomies of modernity, reason.

***

This chapter explores the most important and yet not acknowledged legacy of the late mediaeval philosophy that determined one of the core topics of modern philosophy: the theoretical and practical reason distinction. In that sense, the chapter is mainly historical in its approach, but in tracing those historical movements of ideas it is aimed to show the little explored and fundamental connection between late mediaeval philosophy and the spirit of modern philosophy, a substantial amount of philosophical discernment will be needed. I aim to revisit and see if the inherited dichotomy actually was a deep guiding principle of modernity. After showing evidence that the dichotomy was indeed inherited, I will also offer a reading whose purpose is to get a better picture of how Modern philosophy developed a way through and out of the received problem from late mediaeval scholasticism.

In addition, by fleshing out the problem of universals as the object of the discussion between the scholastic realists and the nominalists, and so explaining in a general way of how this problem connects with the distinction between nominalism and realism, we will proceed to understand the metaphysical origins of the typically modern distinction between theory and practice: the thesis is that the dualism of practical and theoretical reason presupposes a nominalist stance that separates the activities of reason in a world were facts and values cannot cohabitate harmoniously. Furthermore, even if there were facts and values, reason could not make a joint, unified and integrated sense of them. In order to proceed, I will explain how this distinction is already germinal and present in the founding thinkers of modernity, and the first and most important one is not a modern but a mediaeval philosopher: William of Ockham. We are aware that the theoretical/practical reason distinction was established by Immanuel Kant, as will be substantiated below, but the spirit of such distinction goes a long way back to the past and it is a key to understanding the whole modern project. Finally, one of the important conclusions we will aim to reach is how the spirit of this distinction is rooted in the late mediaeval controversy between nominalism and realism.

1.The controversy between realism and nominalism in late mediaeval philosophy

Scholastic mediaeval philosophy is a world of works and sources that hardly can be summarised in a few lines. However, one of the core controversies of mediaeval scholasticism, the controversy between realism and nominalism is relatively easy to understand in its core tenets. In the Latin West, the controversy goes back to the very beginning of the Middle Ages and was already present in the works of Boethius (d. 524) and early authors of the Carolingian period such as John Scotus Eriugena (815-877) who in spite of following the negative theology of Pseudo Dionysius, still will propose a theory of modes of being based on the universal idea of "nature". Thus, the early discussions normally will work out the problem upon a background of Neo-Platonism, in such contexts the problem of universal was the problem of how to make sense of Platonic forms and their relationship to the phenomenical reality[1]. The first negative approach to universals of early mediaeval Neo-Platonistic philosophy was strongly criticised in the eleventh century by Roscelin of Compiègne (1050-1125) (alleged creator of the utterance that describes universals as 'flatus vocis') and most consistently by Peter Abelard (1079-1142)[2].

However, the sophistication of the discussion did not come until we reached the age of mediaeval scholasticism, once the Aristotelian conceptual tools took hold in the technical discussions of the scholastic thinkers. Most specifically, the books that provided the jargon and techniques of discussions were those of Aristotle's *Metaphysics* along with the important commentaries of the Islamic philosophers Avicenna (Ibn Sina, 980-1037) and Averroes (Ibn Rushd, 1126-1198) and the Jewish philosophers Avicebron (Ibn Gabirol, 1021?-1070?) and Maimonides (1138-1204). With the Aristotelian distinction of modes of being, Scholastics were able to explain how a rational account of being can help explain the principles of individuation and universalisation by which the beings of existent realities can instantiate common properties and still retain their individual ways of being. The scholastics articulated the different modes of being that were understood in the Aristotelian tradition such as substance/accidents, form/matter, potency/act, essence/existence, and necessary/contingent. Thus, at the pinnacle of scholastic philosophy and theology, Thomas Aquinas (1225-1274) proposed a moderate realism in which the universals are accidents of an individual designated matter; Henry of Ghent (1217-1293) proposed that the individuals are determined by the universals that do not participate in their individuation (every determination is a kind of negation), and John Duns Scotus (1265?-1308) defended a more radical realism, as he explained that the common natures were individualised by the act of each being that is unique and he called 'haecceity'. All these versions of realism agree that universals are real, though, of course, not exactly in the same way.

Universals, then, are properties that can be discovered in every item of experience, thoughts, concepts and any being. Even the most abstract entity

---

[1] In the Christian East, the discussion always favoured a realist stance, as it is patent in the great patristic tradition that goes from Maximus the Confessor, Pseudo-Dionysius the Areopagite, the Cappadocian fathers until the time of John Damascene. Further discussion can be seen in Williams, I. P. "The Greek Christian Platonist Tradition from the Cappadocians to Maximus and Eriugena". And Lloyd, A. C. "The Later Neoplatonists", both in: Arthur Hilary Armstrong, *The Cambridge History of Later Greek and Early Medieval Philosophy* (Cambridge: Cambridge University Press, 2008).

[2] For a brilliant survey on the controversy in early mediaeval philosophy see Jorge Gracia, *Introduction to the Problem of Individuation in Early Middle Ages* (Washington: The Catholic University of America Press, 1984).

shares with the most concrete entity the similarity of having the unity of being conceived as one. Mediaeval philosophers acknowledged these realities in a variety of different ways. On the one hand, the authors who believed in the reality of universals are called realists; the ones who did not believe in the reality of universals are called nominalists, on the other hand. The realists accepted that the instantiation of universals in different things happen through principles of individualisation of properties into individuals; the nominalists denied that universals have a reality beyond their instantiations. The logical devices that distinguished the discussion are the actual origin of the term 'modernity'. Indeed, while the realists will defend a continuity with classical philosophy (sometimes called 'perennial'), the nominalists will proudly assert that their use was a *via moderna* that was a game-changer for the discussion. The nominalists will proudly appropriate the *via moderna* and its technical logical apparatus and label the previous discussion as proper of "the old ways", popularising their criticisms of what they called the *via antiqua*. The origin of modernity, therefore, needs to be identified in this controversy. Gillespie explains to us why the temporal dimension of the *via moderna* has no precedent in the history of thought, while in other times people were defined by their ethnicity, the cause for their loyalty, their faith, their country, etc., the moderns defined themselves in terms of a temporal juxtaposition of their own being in terms of time:

> The idea of modernity, as we understand it, is closely tied to the idea of antiquity. The distinction of 'ancient' and 'modern' derives from the tenth- century distinction of a *via antiqua* and a *via moderna.* Originally, this was not a historical but a philosophical distinction between two different positions on universals, connected to two different ways of reading Aristotle. The *via antiqua* was the older realist path that saw universals as ultimately real, while the via moderna was the newer nominalist path that saw individual things as real and universals as mere names. These logical distinctions provided the schema for a new understanding of time and being.[3]

2. The nominalists and their use of the *via moderna*

In what follows we will explore the origins of modern philosophy in the *via moderna* as it was developed by the main late mediaeval nominalists, with a particular emphasis on the Franciscan William of Ockham (1285-1347). Though William of Ockham can be considered the main influence and representative of

---

[3] Michael Allen Gillespie, *The Theological Origins of Modernity* (Chicago: The University of Chicago Press, 2008), 4.

nominalism he is not the only important representative of the *via moderna*, important late thinkers such as Jean Buridan (1301-1358), Jean Gherson (1363-1429), Nicholas of Autrecourt (1299-1369) and many more sided to the nominalist party. However, for the purposes of understanding where the discussion was directed and how it became the origin of modernity it will be enough to introduce Ockham's key overwhelming influence. The main thesis of the nominalists is a metaphysical thesis: the world is ultimately composed of individuals, and universals are not individuals, so therefore they are fictions which derive from individuals in a particular mind. In other words, the universe of a nominalist is not a continuous reality, but the set of all individual things that are present in the background we call 'reality'. The nominalists had a number of reasons to propose their fundamental thesis: on the one hand, the thesis appears to solve a logical problem of parsimony, on the other hand, the thesis also claims that the negation of universals is theologically motivated: God cannot share properties with the rest of the beings of the universe, He is completely and absolutely independent of the order of created reality.

However, to put her point across the nominalist needs to solve a problem that the realist does not have: knowledge presupposes our general and universal use of properties and different aspects of being. The *via moderna*, as it will be shown below, gave the nominalists a way of talking about our rational abilities by dealing with individuals and their properties as subordinated to them, properties will only be a way of talking about individuals. Is this, ultimately, a feasible strategy? In principle this parsimony will pay off: we can talk about this donkey and that man without referring to the "donkeyness" as a strange property that one has to know before knowing a given donkey: Further problems will emerge, however: the negation of commonality, community and continuity between and across individuals will steadily lead to an impossibility of accounting for the predicates that allow us to make rational sense of them: consider the example of humanity, if there is not objective humanity but only individual humans then what is the ultimate ground of distinguishing a human from a non-human? say, for instance and again, a donkey? It could be argued that one can ask a human individual and the human will be able to rationally account for his or her humanity, but this only works on a case-by-case basis. One can start to appreciate where nominalism is leading us: if rationality is or is not a capacity to recognise the different aspects of reality is not entirely clear. The nominalist is lead to conclude that there can be as many aspects of the world as individuals, and therefore little can be said beyond a descriptive inquiry. Reason then will lose its normative power (prescriptive value) and will scatter, sometimes theoretically, sometimes practically, depending on what we look at. In my opinion, such a strategy is not good enough even for its own accounting of the metaphysical structure of individuals, since the total rejection of universals lead them to the insecurities of the solipsistic modern doubt that will haunt the subject in its need to get a foundational certainty typical of the Cartesian rationalists as well as the empiricists. Individuals become self-contained entities without the bridging role of the universals, and ultimately will lead us to the Kantian things-in-themselves as a representation of the unbridgeable gap of a nominalistic world of individuals. We ought to return to the understanding of this situation after we have a clear view of what actually amounted to the nominalist late mediaeval view in its specifics.

2.1. Ockham's Nominalism

William of Ockham (1285-1347), a Franciscan friar from England, is the main representative of the influential late mediaeval nominalism that will become the basis and abiding influence of all nominalism in Modern thought. There are two distinct themes in Ockham's nominalism:

First, his rejection of universals and their different derived doctrines, such as Duns Scotus' formal distinction or Thomas Aquinas' moderate realism. Ockham is a harsh critic not only of the reality of universals but of all philosophical thought that assumes their reality to any extent. He produced sharp criticisms of the theory of universals, but he was ruthless all the same to criticise, for example, the reasoning that assumes them, such as Thomas Aquinas' ways to God or Bonaventure's exemplar ideas. He definitely championed an agenda of separating Theology from Philosophy as two separate and even opposed endeavours, it is possible to see that he will ultimately separate the will from reason, submitting the will to God and reason to logic. Ockham will not only separate theology and philosophy but metaphysics and ethics as independent endeavours.

Second, his programme of what can be called 'ontological reduction', *i.e.*, his eliminating many other kinds of putative entities, whether universal or not, and in particular his cutting the list of real ontological categories from Aristotle's list of ten to two (substance and quality).[4] Ockham insists that a universal substance of an individual is an impossible hypothesis:

> There is no universal outside the mind really existing in individual substances or in the essences of things…. The reason is that everything that is not many things is necessarily one thing in number and consequently a singular thing.[5]

---

[4] Paul Vincent Spade, trans., *Five Texts on the Mediaeval Problem of Universals* (Indianapolis: Hackett Publishing, 1994), 100.
[5] William of Ockham, *Opera Philosophica et Theologica*, ed. Gedeon Gál, vol. II (St. Bonaventure, N. Y.: The Franciscan Institute, 1967), 11-12.

Ockham rejects universals because he takes them as a numerical added substance to the individuality of a being, and hence he will argue that an absurd conclusion follows:

> ...it would follow that God would not be able to annihilate one individual substance without destroying the other individuals of the same kind. For, if he were to annihilate one individual, he would destroy the whole that is essentially that individual and, consequently, he would destroy the universal that is in it and in others of the same essence. Other things of the same essence would not remain, for they could not continue to exist without the universal that constitutes a part of them.[6]

Ockham's nominalism is usually considered as a consequence of Ockham's principle of parsimony famously known as 'Ockham's razor'. The principle can be formulated as: "Avoid the unnecessary multiplication of entities".

However, there is not much parsimony about the multiplication of individuals that emerges by accepting Ockham's metaphysical thesis: there will be infinite different properties, every one of them unique to each individual in its own way. Moreover, Ockham accepts that different qualities ensue the multiplication of real individuals. Even non-existent individuals (*ficta*) are real in Ockham's account. His nominalism is a metaphysical theory that only accepts individuals as real, no matter how many, there is a parsimony of universals but not a parsimony of individuals.

The above means that Ockham's nominalism might not be the only reason for his rejection of 'universals'. One can find a deeper reason for his rejection of universals on theological grounds. In *The Principles of Theology*, Ockham's disciples explain that the parsimony of universals is a consequence of his desire to create an image of Divine Omnipotence that is absolute.

Hence, Ockham's razor appears to work eliminating universals along the Theological principle at hand in two ways: On the one hand, for Ockham, the reasons that others give for postulating certain entities are not good reasons: for example, Ockham considers Aristotle's ten categories as unnecessary and so reduced them to two: quality and substance. On the other hand, Ockham thinks that accepting postulated entities leads to contradictions, e.g., his opinion that universals are incompatible with God's omnipotence and are further unnecessary in order to make sense of the world of experience realities.

---

[6] William of Ockham, *Opera Philosophica et Theologica*, ed. Gedeon Gál, vol. I (St. Bonaventure, N. Y.: The Franciscan Institute, 1967), 51.

In consequence, Ockham's ontological reduction is both a reduction of categories and a reduction of universals. As we noted above, there is, however, a multiplication of tropes (individual properties) on a case-by-case basis.

Ockham's project of ontological reduction, though, does not apply to the theological doctrine of the Trinity, or any other needed postulated universal that accounts for any revealed truth. A whole category of this applies to revelation for Ockham's writings, but what may appear to us as an inconsistency is only the result of Ockham's acceptance of the doctrine of the double-truth: what might be true in the context of theology and revelation might as well be false for reason, and what might be true for reason might be false in the context of the faith. The doctrine of double-truth is a conscious break with the scholastic tradition that harmonises faith and reason, and for the purposes of our study shows that Ockham's nominalism implies a progressive fragmentation of human reason. Ockham aimed to preserve the theological prerogatives of theological thought, but the real outcome of his inheritance to modern philosophy is the progressive radicalisation that will eventually produce on the one hand the fideism of Luther and on the other hand the rationalism of Descartes.

In rejecting categories, Ockham rejects any real entity to categories of action, passion and relation. He accepts substance and quality because these two can be reduced to individuals, each substance as an individual entity while each quality as an individual trope: a quality instantiated in a unique way for each of the individuals that have it. We can then realise that even Ockham's concessions to realism are limited to a conceptualism of those properties of quality and substance, they can only be steady concepts but we cannot know about the way they are instantiated: there is a veil between our concepts and how the individuals are in themselves, the mediation of our concepts is a "supposition", a way of ascribing concepts in a systematic way. Ockham said "Nothing outside the soul is a universal",[7] and hence his nominalism represents the origin of a modern conception of reason: a reason that cannot be universal and thus is fragmented into a limited account of individuals (perhaps as a description of their physical properties, and no more).

---

[7] Spade, *Five Texts on the Mediaeval Problem of Universals*, 112. See: Gyula Klima, "Ockham's Semantics and Ontology of the Categories," in *The Cambridge Companion to Ockham*, ed. Paul Vincent Spade (Cambridge: Cambridge University Press, 1992), 118–42.

3. Theoretical and practical reason and modern philosophy

3.1. The dualism of theory and practice

In what follows we will carry an examination of the modern connection to the metaphysical controversy between nominalism and realism. For authors such as Michael Allen Gillespie the correct understanding of modernity can actually only come from an identification of its origins, he tells us about the entire epochal question this:

> The epochal question that gave birth to the modern age arose out of a metaphysical/theological crisis within Christianity about the nature of God and thus the nature of being. This crisis was most evident as the nominalist revolution against scholasticism. This revolution in thought, however, was itself a reflection of a deeper transformation in the experience of existence as such. Scholastics in the High Middle Ages were ontologically realist, that is to say, they believed in the real existence of universals, or to put the matter another way, they experienced the world as the instantiation of the categories of divine reason.[8]

Gillespie goes even further ant thinks that it is the particularly theological emphasis of nominalism that actually determined the destiny of what modernity was going to become:

> Nominalism turned this world on its head. For the nominalists, all real being was individual or particular and universals were thus mere fictions. Words did not point to real universal entities but were merely signs useful for human understanding. Creation was radically particular and thus not teleological. As a result, God could not be understood by human reason but only by biblical revelation or mystical experience. Human beings thus had no natural or supernatural end or telos.[9]

In this analysis, we converge with Gillespie in thinking that the nominalist/realist controversy was foundational for modernity, but our own emphasis will be on understanding what image of reason was so powerfully influenced by the controversy.

The dawn of modernity is usually placed in Cartesian philosophy, but the paradigm shift was more or less conscious in the works of Francis Bacon (1561-1626). Francis Bacon defended a view of induction as a *Novum Organum* that

---

[8] Gillespie, *The Theological Origins of Modernity*, 29.
[9] Ibid.

was suitable to empower the weakened reason of the 'Vetus Organum' (let us remember that the *Organon* was the general name given as the instrumental compilation of Aristotle's logical works). Bacon thinks that only an inductive use of reason can help the cause of knowledge because he first and foremost presupposes that reality is made only of individuals, so the only knowledge that counts is what can be generalised from the observation of individuals. Bacon opposes himself to the Aristotelian tradition that searches for 'first principles' and thereof will set an important precedent for the empiricist tradition. Gillespie tells us about Bacon and Descartes:

> The idea of a modern age or, as it was later called, modernity, was part of the self-understanding that characterised European thought from the time of Bacon and Descartes.[10]

Another important philosophical figure between Bacon and Descartes was Thomas Hobbes (1588-1679), it has been argued that even some important ideas that appear in Bacon's *New Atlantis* belong to Hobbes, who served for some time as his secretary, but the fact that Hobbes was an Ockhamist of sorts is evident in his 1665 first part of his philosophical system called *De Corpore*, which was a philosophical and physical attempt to show definitely that the only substances that exist are bodies. Hobbes's nominalist solution to the problem of universals is very similar to Ockham's but adds an element of Calvinism, everything happens as a result of God's predestining will and what appears to be a universal reason or law is nothing but God's predestined will that operates according to mechanical causality.

The renaissance and the humanist tradition that followed it were not nominalistic in an explicit way, but their disenchantment of Scholasticism in general marked a tendency to emphasise that reason cannot work the same way for the practical human life as for the theoretical realm. They believed that there was a 'Promethean' promise in developing the reason that touched the human realities as opposed to the systematic rigidness of the mediaeval schools. The humanists indirectly preserved the Ockhamist theory of the two truths and separated faith from reason and reason from logic. With the humanists, the *via moderna* started to look like a project of autonomy and self-making that inevitably would lead humanity to unlimited progress.

Martin Luther (1483-1546) is placed in an important part of modernity, not precisely as an advocate for the idea of progress through reason, but as an enhancer of the belief that facts of the world and values of morality are not connected in reason. Luther formed his theological character as a nominalist,

---

[10] Gillespie, *The Theological Origins of Modernity*, 5.

he himself acknowledged his Ockhamists character received through the teaching of Gabriel Biel (1420-1495) and other prominent nominalists of his own time. Luther was adamant in expressing his dislike of Scholastic philosophy, though he was very consistent in preserving the theological worries of Ockham. With Luther, the practical/theoretical divide of reason is the natural consequence of reason being sinful and essentially incapable of knowing God's being: the image of God of Luther is very Ockhamist, the image of a being whose absolute will is totally inscrutable to reason. The apparent usefulness of reason is nothing but one of its deceptions as "Satan's prostitute".

Renée Descartes (1596-1650), however, is by far the most influential representative of the modern shift of thought: Descartes' universal doubt and shift into the self as the ultimate ground of reason is clearly the beginning of modern philosophy. Nonetheless, Descartes' conception of the theoretical and practical aspects of reason is not too evident in his major works. Descartes' nominalism is more theological than metaphysical, the *res cogitans* or 'thinking thing' is only connected to herself and to God, and the world of *res extensa* (material things) is only accessible to an occasional action of God (this is the Cartesianism of Nicholas Malebranche), but we might as well be deceived about all our rational reconstruction of the world, if not by the belief that God is good. The world of material bodies is geometrically constructed and mechanical in its behaviour, its material laws are a clockwork of predetermined harmony.

John Locke (1632-1704) was also very influenced by Ockhamist nominalism, his way of considering primary and secondary qualities as only a matter of ideas that in fact have nothing to do with the experience of individuals is also clear in endorsing the idea that values are only something that happens in the inner realm of our thinking about facts, but the facts of the outside world of nature are brute and they do not have other properties than the ones that are object of perception. Irish Bishop George Berkeley (1685-1753), by reducing being to perception also shared the core nominalistic reduction that every property is a matter of what can be observed in individuals. But no-one went further than Scottish Philosopher and Historian David Hume (1711-1776), who was a consistent nominalist in excluding everything that cannot be presented as an individual impression, including even the substance and quality that Ockham would have maintained for theological reasons. Hume left a real conundrum about the value of reason, one challenge that Kant will definitely accept in all seriousness.

The properly expressed distinction between theoretical and practical reason is actually owed to Immanuel Kant (1724-1804), Kant defined the two realms of pure reason as separated in the following way:

Our cognitive faculty as a whole has two domains, that of the concepts of nature and that of the concept of freedom; for it is a priori legislative through both. Philosophy is also divided accordingly into the theoretical and the practical. [...] Legislation through concepts of nature takes place through the understanding, and is theoretical. Legislation through the concept of freedom takes place through reason, and is merely practical.[11]

Though this distinction is certainly derivative of Kant's own philosophy, as it is very well demonstrated in other chapters of this collection, the spirit of the distinction was something that Kant had to deal with: he inherited both the rationalist trust in the value of reason as well as the radically limiting solipsist threat that the empiricism of David Hume had reached. Did Kant succeed in reconciling the theoretical and practical reason in one? The answer is in the negative, and his third critique presents itself as a humble recognition that maybe in the free play of the imagination and the faculties, there might be a way to reconcile facts and values under the unifying power of the admirable.

4. Realism, Idealism and the reintegration of theoretical and practical reason

In this final section of the chapter, we will study how the epochal question of the theoretical and practical reason divide in modernity was made conscious in the philosophical systems of German Idealism, the focus of this section will be on the reintegration of these spheres of reason in the thought of Georg Wilhelm Friedrich Hegel (1770-1831). Hegel aims to reconstruct the unity of the object not as an individual, but as a concrete universal, and from the reconstruction of the object as both participating of universals and having an identity, we will see that Hegel will show us that reason can get re-constituted to account both for facts and values that coexist in the unity of the object.

In my opinion, thus, Hegel understands the unfolding drama of all the stories summarised in this text. Indeed, Hegel defends a stance on Universals that actually permits a whole new reformulation of the problem of theoretical and practical reason. For Hegel, there is a need for a holistic structure of the object that cannot prescind of bearing on account the reality of universals. Furthermore, the Holistic structure of the object is rendered in Hegel's account of universals. Indeed, universals inform the object as well as the subject because they *are* the logical (rational) aspect of things. Hegel takes on the

---

[11] Immanuel Kant, *Critique of the Power of Judgment*, ed. Paul Guyer, trans. Paul Guyer and Eric Matthews (Cambridge: Cambridge University Press, 2013), 62. From here on, "KU" will be used to refer to the canonical edition. (KU, AA 5:174).

hypothesis that Universals are instantiated in different ways, as the mediaeval philosopher Duns Scotus, following Aristotle, understood: in the mind as universals and in the thing as instantiations of a common nature. Stern converges with my reading of Hegel on the unity of the object through universals when he says:

> Hegel is making the essentially Aristotelian point, that the species-universal is a predicate in the category of substance, which tells us *what* the subject is. As such, he holds, it is paradoxical to separate the subject from the predicate, or to think of them in a merely external relation; instead, the universal must be thought of as inseparable from the individual[12]

One can find the holistic project of Hegel in his three most important works on the topic: the *Phenomenology of Spirit*, the *Science of Logic* and the *Philosophy of Nature*. Hegel argues that idealism is capable of grasping the substance-universal that underlies the plurality given to us by the senses. Hegel's philosophy is an idealism that is not opposed to the realism of the scholastics, his idealism is a realism of universals. Therefore, Hegel's argument transcends the empiricist reduction along with the atomistic account of reality, whatever those atoms might be. The account developed by Hegel appears as a sequence across nature, logic and spirit:

> We can therefore summarise Hegel's position by saying that for him, to think rationally is to set aside the distinctions imposed on things by the understanding, and to see the various determinations of reality as dialectically interrelated.[13]

From the above naturally follows that the object appears to be properly grasped. Some questions arise, then: is it necessary to recognise a principle of individuation or several? If so, which one will that be? Stern speaks about the "concrete universal": Is that "concretion" of the universal the instantiation of the universal? These questions still seem to me thus still open. In my

---

[12] Robert Stern, *Hegel, Kant and The Structure of the Object* (London: Routledge, 1990), 64.

[13] Robert Stern, *Hegelian Metaphysics* (Oxford: Oxford University Press, 2009), 58. See Paniel Reyes Cárdenas, "Contemporary Hegelian Scholarship: On Robert Stern's Holistic Reading of Hegel," *Tópicos, Revista de Filosofía*, no. 50 (2016): 123–49, and Robert B. Pippin, *Hegel's Idealism: The Satisfactions of Self-Consciousness* (Cambridge: Cambridge University Press, 1989). A parallel study in Paul Redding, *Analytic Philosophy and the Return of Hegelian Thought* (Cambridge: Cambridge University Press, 2007).

interpretation, the point of Hegel's absolute knowledge is that the concretion and individual aspects of things are not dismissed, but embraced. Hegel only shifted the emphasis and priority of universality and thus also provided criteria for individuation and particularity. However, even though Hegel started the process of reconstruction of philosophy as a reconstruction of a better concept of reason, his system sometimes goes to the extreme of losing a balance between what the medievals called principles of individuation and principles of universalisation. Be as it may, it is important to realise that the conclusion we aim to get is that the distinction between practical and theoretical reason, if adopted, has to be considered as a provisional way of searching for the unity of reason. In another work, I presented[14] the efforts made by Charles Sanders Peirce (1839-1914) of introducing his own pragmatism as a scholastic realism of universals, a system that very much like the Hegelian also aims to find the unity of reason as a road of inquiry.

In the twentieth century, there is another important observation on the separation between theory and practice that follows from nominalism and it is due to Hannah Arendt. Richard Bernstein explains in Hannah Arendt: The Ambiguities of Theory and Practice that:

> Her interpretation of modern history is concerned with the terrible consequences that have resulted from the fusing of these different realms and from the false expectations and hopes that arise when it is believed that satisfaction of men's private needs and social necessities is sufficient to achieve freedom.[15]

Arendt's analysis shows, then, that the ambiguities of theory and practice led modernity to ascribe the unity of reason only to theory, and steadily conducted humanity to a notion of "practice" and "praxis" that will ultimately conduct to individualism: transformative and voluntary action will be a matter of preference, not of universal and common reasons. Indeed, without the unity of universal reason, we will not be able to discover that there are actions that are "ends in themselves" (a kind of universals) and, as Arendt rightly remarks, evil can enter where reason is gone.

It is not altogether clear that the realist side of the controversy did not have important problems to solve, and in fact, the rise of the nominalist position

---

[14] See Paniel Reyes Cárdenas, Scholastic Realism: A Key to Understanding Peirce's Philosophy, 2018.

[15] Richard Bernstein, "Hannah Arendt: The Ambiguities of Theory and Practice," in *Political Theory and Praxis: New Perspectives*, ed. Terence Bal (Minneapolis: The University of Minnesota Press, 1977), 157.

might have been so overwhelming at the end of scholasticism out of a generalised feeling of dissatisfaction about the realist alternatives. This chapter does not intend to unilaterally side with scholastic realism as though it was a completely vindicated and consistent view. However, when realism was the dominant view scholastic philosophy was able to sustain a cross-fertilising and holistic view of reason: metaphysics, ethics, theory of knowledge, aesthetics, all rational approaches to different human problems were connected and in contact. The nominalist *via moderna* tried to solve the problems of scholastic philosophy by, as it is commonly said, throwing the baby with the bathwater; it not only pointed out the issues of extreme realism and an abandonment of the individual, but went to the opposite extreme leaving the rational powers of human being weakened to a fragmentary illusion of unity.

Bibliography

Armstrong, Arthur Hilary. *The Cambridge History of Later Greek and Early Medieval Philosophy*. Cambridge: Cambridge University Press, 2008.

Bernstein, Richard. "Hannah Arendt: The Ambiguities of Theory and Practice." In *Political Theory and Praxis: New Perspectives*, edited by Terence Bal. Minneapolis: The University of Minnesota Press, 1977.

Gillespie, Michael Allen. *The Theological Origins of Modernity*. Chicago: The University of Chicago Press, 2008.

Gracia, Jorge. *Introduction to the Problem of Individuation in Early Middle Ages*. Washington: The Catholic University of America Press, 1984.

Kant, Immanuel. *Critique of the Power of Judgment*. Edited by Paul Guyer. Translated by Paul Guyer and Eric Matthews. Cambridge: Cambridge University Press, 2013.

Klima, Gyula. "Ockham's Semantics and Ontology of the Categories." In *The Cambridge Companion to Ockham*, edited by Paul Vincent Spade, 118–42. Cambridge: Cambridge University Press, 1992.

Ockham, William of. *Opera Philosophica et Theologica*. Edited by Gedeon Gál. 17 vols. St. Bonaventure, N. Y.: The Franciscan Institute, 1967-1988.

Pippin, Robert B. *Hegel's Idealism: The Satisfactions of Self-Consciousness*. Cambridge: Cambridge University Press, 1989.

Redding, Paul. *Analytic Philosophy and the Return of Hegelian Thought*. Cambridge: Cambridge University Press, 2007.

Reyes Cárdenas, Paniel. "Contemporary Hegelian Scholarship: On Robert Stern's Holistic Reading of Hegel." *Tópicos, Revista de Filosofía*, no. 50 (2016): 123–49.

———. *Scholastic Realism: A Key to Understanding Peirce's Philosophy*, 2018. https://www.peterlang.com/document/1113428.

Spade, Paul Vincent, trans. *Five Texts on the Mediaeval Problem of Universals*. Indianapolis: Hackett Publishing, 1994.

Spade, Paul Vincent. "Ockham's Nominalist Metaphysics." In *The Cambridge Companion to Ockham*, edited by Paul Vincent Spade. Cambridge Companions to Philosophy. Cambridge: Cambridge University Press, 1999. https://doi.org/10.1017/CCOL052158244X.

Stern, Robert. "Going Beyond the Kantian Philosophy: On Mcdowell's Hegelian Critique of Kant." *European Journal of Philosophy* 7, no. 2 (1999): 247–69. https://doi.org/10.1111/1468-0378.00085.

———. *Hegel, Kant and The Structure of the Object.* London: Routledge, 1990.

———. *Hegelian Metaphysics.* Oxford: Oxford University Press, 2009.

———. *Routledge Philosophy Guidebook to Hegel and the Phenomenology of Spirit.* London: Routledge, 2002.

Williams, I. P. "The Greek Christian Platonist Tradition from the Cappadocians to Maximus and Eriugena." In *Arthur Hilary Armstrong, The Cambridge History of Later Greek and Early Medieval Philosophy.* Cambridge: Cambridge University Press, 2

Chapter 2

Distinct Perceptions and Belief

Evelyn Vargas

Universidad Nacional de la Plata

Abstract: Despite this discouraging description of both the historical context and Leibniz's doctrines, I will hold that Leibniz had a theory of sense perception, and that the theory could account for perceptual content and justification in ways that he would not be committed to the 'veil of perception scepticism' and would sustain the senses' reliability. In the following sections, I will introduce his notion of sense perception as distinct perception in his mature writings and show how it sums up his reflections on the nature of sense perception throughout some of his earlier philosophical and scientific texts. In his later texts, two phenomenal features of distinct perception will account for both the perceptual content and its role in epistemic justification: its being enhanced perception, and the role of memory.

Keywords: Leibniz, Perception, sensation, belief-formation, consciousness.

***

1. Introduction

Perception is a central concept in Leibniz's philosophy and its role exceeds that of our ordinary understanding of the concept. In his mature thought, it is supposed to account for fundamental features of the notion of substance. Less clear is whether the doctrine can account for *sense* perception as a source of knowledge of the world. His ontology of ordinary physical objects as mere aggregates and not true substances, and his account of the apparent interaction between mind and external objects in terms of the hypothesis of pre-established harmony are assumed to make problematic the possibility of perceptual knowledge of particular objects. But in order to evaluate a theory of perception we have to analyse how well it can make sense of its role as a source of empirical knowledge. We need to understand the theory in terms of the information that perceptual experience conveys to us and how this information is presented. More precisely, the theory must explain how to make sense of an experience as the perceiver's reasons for believing something about the state of the world.

Furthermore, early modern philosophers are considered responsible for the introduction of a view according to which sensory ideas are the immediate objects of perception and thought, a conception that would have led to the metaphysical isolation of the mind. For them, contemporary epistemologists and philosophers of mind contend, that perception seems to require intermediaries, that is, some special kind of representations that constitute the object of perceptual awareness.[1] Some interpreters trace the origin of this conception to Kepler's model of the retinal image [2] since Kepler also thought that the retinal image is what we directly see. Philosophers of the early modern era would use his theory as a model for perception in general. From an epistemological point of view, the theory would involve two major assumptions, mainly, that whatever we are perceptually aware of beyond the receptive image is learned by association or inference (for example, our representations of three-dimensional objects are not given in perception since the retinal image is two-dimensional), and also that we cannot subjectively distinguish hallucinations from veridical perceptions. If we can only have immediate epistemic access to some kind of mental entities, our access to material objects and their properties becomes problematic. As a result, beliefs based on perception are uncertain and the epistemic credibility of the senses is put into question. The early modern concern on the senses would cover not only their ability to justify knowledge about the nature of the physical world but also their mind independence.

These sceptical consequences would be based on the way early modern philosophers conceived the contents of perceptual experiences. But received views on the causal processes that give rise to perception were also under scrutiny and so the new theories raised another source of concern on the epistemic role of perception in justifying our beliefs and knowledge of how things are in the external world. The acceptance of the mechanical theory would determine some constraints on what there is in the world and what is - metaphysically- dependent on the perceiver, that is, the distinction between primary and secondary qualities is established. Given these assumptions, if our perceptions may not represent the external world, it may be the case that perception can only justify introspective beliefs.

---

[1] For example, ideas and sense-data.
[2] Mohan Matthen, "Introduction," in *The Oxford Handbook of Philosophy of Perception* (Oxford: Oxford University Press, 2015), 2.

Despite this discouraging description of both the historical context and Leibniz's doctrines, I will hold that Leibniz had a theory of sense perception, and that the theory could account for perceptual content and justification in ways that he would not be committed to the 'veil of perception scepticism' and would sustain the senses' reliability. In the following sections, I will introduce his notion of sense perception as distinct perception in his mature writings and show how it sums up his reflections on the nature of sense perception throughout some of his earlier philosophical and scientific texts. In his later texts two phenomenal features of distinct perception will account for both the perceptual content and its role in epistemic justification: its being enhanced perception, and the role of memory.

2. Leibniz's Late Theory of Perception

2.1. Sense as Distinct Perception

For Leibniz, sense and perception are not equivalent. For our present purposes, we are not concerned with his doctrine of substances, but it is important to notice that Leibniz distinguishes different degrees of perception. Sense,[3] or our representation of the world through the senses, is a special kind of perception, that is, a perception that is qualified as "enhanced" or "notable".[4] Roughly, perceiving with the senses is simply noticing something affecting our sensory organs. More precisely, in his *Specime inventorum de admirandis naturae generalis arcanis* written probably 25 years before the *Monadology*, he defines perceptual experience of external objects as a higher degree of distinct perception to which he applies the term *sensus*:

> Atque hoc principium actionum, seu vis agendi primitiva, ex qua series statuum variorum consequitur, est substantiae forma. Patet etiam quid perceptio sit, quae omnibus formis competit, nempe expressio multorum in uno, quae longe differt ab expressione in speculo, vel in organo corporeo, quod vere unum non est. Quodsi perceptio sit distinctior, sensum facit.[5]

---

[3] He uses the French word *sentiment* and the Latin *sensus*.

[4] In the "Monadologie"' (in Gottfried Wilhelm Leibniz, *Die Philosophischen Schriften von Leibniz*, ed. C. I. Gerhardt, vol. 6 (Berlin: Hildesheim, 1960-1961)), those perceptions have … 'de distingué et pour ainsi dire de relevée'. From here on, "M". (M, §24).

[5] Gottfried Wilhelm Leibniz, *Sämtliche Schriften Und Briefe*, ed. the Akademie der Wissenschaften (Darmstadt-Berlin: Akademie-Verlag, 1875). From here on, "A". (A 6, 4, 324).

As the passage cited shows, perceptual representation pertains to any substantial form,[6] since substantial forms are the principles of the actions of substances, Perception in this more general sense is defined in terms of his concept of expression. Given that all substantial forms are endowed with expressions, the perceptual experience such as seeing a tree in front of a house must be a more specific kind of expression. In the first place, expression in general is a dyadic relation in which one of the terms, the expressed, can be known through the other or the expression. If this is the case, there must be 'a constant and regulated relation' between what can be said about each of those terms. Leibniz summarises the results of its original enunciation in *Quid sit idea* as follows:

> Repraesentare autem dicitur quod ita respondet, ut ex uno aliud cognosci possit, etsi similia non sint, dummodo certa quadam regula sive relatione omnia quae fiunt in uno referantur ad quaedam respondentia illis in alio.[7]

The related terms are not required to be similar, but a certain rule must be obtained so that *every* feature in one term can be referred to something in the other term of the relation.[8] For example, a map can express a geographical area as well as an equation can represent a geometrical figure.[9]

But what distinguishes perception in every substantial form from other forms of expression is that it consists of the representation of the manifold in one being.[10] For Leibniz, every substance represents the universe by its own internal actions. These intentional representations in substances are completely different from non-intentional representations such as maps and equations. A reflected image in a mirror maybe regarded as an expression but the mirror is not a true unity, since material bodies are not true substances; perceptual expression, on the other hand, turns external relations, those in the object, into internal relations in the perceiver, and therefore, the expressed object can be known in the perceptual representation because this

---

[6] A 6, 4, 1615.

[7] A 6, 4, 1615.

[8] In his otherwise insightful approach to Leibniz's theory of knowledge, McRae misses this point, due perhaps to a too narrow understanding of Peirce's conception of diagrams as icons, which he uses to differentiate Leibniz's concept of expression. See Robert McRae, *Leibniz: Perception, Apperception and Thought* (Toronto: Toronto University Press, 1976), 21.

[9] A 6, 4, 1371.

[10] A 6, 4, 1625.

representation or expression is not arbitrary but in accordance to a rule. When this representation is noticed or enhanced, it constitutes sense perception.[11]

The analogy with non-intentional representation suggests that perceptual representation is only a sign of the perceived object, with expressions being the intermediaries between the mind and the external object. Then, the relevant question is whether the expressions are the immediate objects of perception in the way required by veil-of-perception scepticism. But before considering this question, it is necessary to introduce another aspect of Leibniz's mature conception. Not only do perceptions, in general, pertain to any substantial forms but distinct perceptions pertain to both human beings and animals. [12]

His new physical theory will provide the notions and principles for a theory of perception by providing an account of the physical mechanism of sense stimulation within the framework of his Dynamics. Impressions in the sense organ are endowed with relief and distinction by the action of the organs.[13] According to Leibniz, the anatomical disposition of the sense organ makes the effect of the physical stimulus more efficient. For example, the humours in the eye concentrate the light in a particular area and so the physical stimuli "agissent avec plus de force".[14] Leibniz thought that similar mechanisms could be found for the other senses.[15] Now in his early writings on medicine, he explains that in every living organism, the anatomical structure of the organ is adapted to its function,[16] and then the sensorial organs must be adapted to their perceptual function. The perceptual process in the organs is accounted for in terms of the dynamics of force. The sensorial organs must be ready to act when the object (or, more precisely, the rays of light or the vibrations in the air) provokes a disbalance of forces that has to be compensated by the reaction of the organ[17]. When a physical stimulus affects the organ, its reaction can be

---

[11] In the following sections I will use "perception" in this more restricted meaning, that is, as sense perception.

[12] In "Principles of Nature and Grace"' (in Gottfried Wilhelm Leibniz, *Die Philosophischen Schriften von Leibniz*, ed. C. I. Gerhardt, vol. 6 (Berlin: Hildesheim, 1960-1961)). From here on, "P". (P, §4; M, §26).

[13] P, §4.

[14] P, §4; M, §25.

[15] M, §25.

[16] Enrico Passini, *Corpo e Funzioni Cognitive in Leibniz* (Milan: Franco Angeli, 1996), 212 & 218.

[17] The force is not created but restored or compensated; from a metaphysical point of view, the subject of the force is the substantial form. See Justin E. H. Smith, "The Body-Machine in Leibniz's Early Physiological and Medical Writings: A Selection of Texts with Commentary," *The Leibniz Review* 17 (July 1, 2007), https://doi.org/10.5840/leibniz2007 175, 163 & 165.

compared to taking off an impediment in a similar way that the arrow is ejected when the arch is released, or a fire is caused by a small spark. Also, causal connections can be interpreted by means of the relation of expression since the effect expresses its cause.[18] When causal patterns are understood as a particular instance of this relation, they do not have to be lineal but functional systems, where cause and effect correspond to the active and passive terms, according to their level of activity.[19] One can say that the external body acts on the sensorial organ, and that our body responds to this change by an increase in its level of activity.

All perceptual mechanism is subject to this dynamical framework (for example, they are regulated by the principle of the equipollence of cause and effect), but the particular mechanisms for each of the senses must be known empirically.[20] Nevertheless, it is important to remember that the perception represents the impression of the external body on the organ. According to this point of view, an enhanced or distinct perception is one that represents the reaction of the organ in the perceptual process. But by itself, the dynamics of perceptual processes cannot respond to our original questions concerning the epistemological status of perceptual experience. For example, the account could be read in terms of the assumptions that led to the veil of perception doctrine; on the other hand, if the perception represents the state of the perceptual organ, perceptual awareness represents the state of the organ at the moment it is affected by the external body and reacts. For a sceptical objector, to say that the effect –*i.e.*, the perception- expresses its cause –*i.e.*, the external object- is not justified.[21] Also, the view attributed to early modern philosophers in our introduction assumed that since the receptoral image lacks many of the properties that we attribute to the objects we seem to perceive, it is the role of the intellect or the imagination, to provide the complex objects such as three-dimensional things that we say that we perceive. If only the activation of the organ corresponds to what is given in perception, this sensory information has to be supplemented by our other cognitive capacities in order to represent the complex object. It seems that whether or not to ascribe this view to Leibniz will depend on how we understand the enhanced impression that is represented,

---

[18] In "Discourse on Metaphysics" (in Gottfried Wilhelm Leibniz, *Philosophical Essays*, ed. and trans. R. Ariew and D. Garber (Indianapolis: Hacket, 1986)). From here on, "DM". (DM, §16).

[19] According to this reading, Leibniz rejects Suarez's conception of causality as real influence but offers a functional interpretation. See DM, §15.

[20] He criticises Descartes for not doing so but forging naïve hypotheses instead (Passini, *Corpo e Funzioni Cognitive in Leibniz*, 212).

[21] By the simple application of the modes of Agripa, and not by putting into question the external world.

that is, whether this more notable impression is the reaction of the organ or the physical stimulus. A first approach suggests that what is expressed in the perception has to be its cause since the change in the organ responds to them. But this in turn can be understood as the multiple stimuli such as the rays of light or the vibrations of the ear reaching the ear, or as the ordinary things that surround us, such as apples or cats. A theory of perception has to explain this later on.

2.2. Consecutions

In the *Principles of Nature and Grace* and the *Monadology*, animal perception is called 'sentiment' in order to distinguish it from perceptions as the actions characterising the internal actions of monads more generally. As we have seen, sentience is a more distinct perception[22] or a perception that has 'du relief et du distingué.[23] But in the same texts, sentience is defined as a perception that is "accompagnée de mémoire".[24] Consequently, animal perception can be described by its degree of distinctness, but also by the role that memory plays. The connections between perceptions that are grounded in memory constitute consecutions.[25] More precisely, the sensible image provides connections between the perceptions, and the connection between perceptions that are grounded in memory is called a "consecution".[26] Leibniz also remarks that most human behaviour can be explained in terms of consecutions, and that consecutions resemble reason,[27] that is, consecutions are similar to the connections provided by reason.[28] The example of the abused dog that runs away when it sees its master holding a stick is described as a consecution since the sensible image evokes another perception, in which the sensible image of its master holding a stick is attached to the feeling of pain.[29] In a similar way, the connections that memory provides can account for acquired and involuntary behaviour in both humans and animals. However, it is not clear how consecutions contribute to having distinct perceptions in the relevant epistemic sense.

In this section, I presented the features that characterise sense perception according to Leibniz. Sense perception is a form of expression or the

---

[22] M, §19.
[23] P, §4.
[24] M, §19; P, §4.
[25] M, §26.
[26] P, §5; M, §26.
[27] M, §26.
[28] P, §5.
[29] M, §26.

representation of a sensible manifold in one representation according to some rule or pattern of relations. This accordance must be understood in terms of the aetiology of perception and, therefore, it grounds a non-arbitrary relation between the content or expression and the expressed or what happens in the organs as a result of a physical stimulus acting on it. The anatomy of the organ is designed to increase specific physical stimuli corresponding to each sense modality. The soul records the interaction between the external bodies and the sensorial receptor reacting to them. An enhanced perception is a more distinct expression and then a form of action.[30] Distinct perceptions are also accompanied by memory in constituting consecutions, which associate the sensory image with other mental states and behaviours. However, these features characterise sentience in both human and non-human creatures, and therefore it might be questioned how they can account for reason-based relations between experience and belief.

3. Perceptual Content and Belief

In recent debates concerning the philosophy of perception early modern philosophers are regarded as responsible for a misconception of perceptual content which made problematic the relation between mind and world. The origin of this view is attributed to an implicit identification between the receptoral image and perceptual content or what we have immediate access to in perceptual awareness. The perceptual given so understood cannot account for the rational connection of perception and belief since our cognitive access to external objects can only be indirect and therefore uncertain. A subject's reason for believing something about the state of the physical world must be some rational constraint on her thoughts but, if the view is correct, our experiences may not represent how things are; for example, our visual experience may be a hallucination. Moreover, even when we could ascertain a causal connection between the world and our representation, the 'space of reasons' pertains to a different order; being able to give reasons must appeal to propositional content and our conceptual abilities.[31]

As we have seen in the previous section, Leibniz's sense perception is defined in terms of its distinctness, that is, perceiving the physical things that surround us consists of enhanced perceptions representing the higher intensity of the stimulus coming from them and our bodily reaction to it in the sensory organ. This account of perception in humans and animals is in accordance with his wider physical theory in terms of dynamical systems, but it is not evident how

---

[30] A 6, 4, 1620.

[31] A well-known diagnosis of this modern "anxiety" in John McDowell, *Mind and World* (Cambridge: Harvard University Press, 1996).

the view can make sense of the rational connection between perception and belief in the sense required to sustain a robust theory of perception. In fact, Leibniz actually said that we can make sense of the common-sense view that we … "receive knowledge from the outside by way of the senses".[32] In the following sections, I will examine some texts in which Leibniz offers some further features of distinct perceptions that could help us understand how Leibniz conceived this epistemological issue.

3.1. Confused Cognition

A more promising characterisation of distinctness that involves propositional content is presented by Leibniz in well-known opuscules written around 1685. So before examining the question of how perceptual contents are connected to belief, according to Leibniz, I will introduce the definitions of "distinctness" that Leibniz offers in those texts in order to examine whether the ability to have distinct perceptions involves an *intellectual* capacity to discriminate their content.

On the one hand, Leibniz´s definition of distinctness in the *Meditations* seems to apply to concepts and cognitions:

> A distinct notion is like the notion an assayer has of gold, that is, a notion connected with marks and tests sufficient to distinguish a thing from all other similar bodies.[33]

Similarly, in the Discourse:

> But when I can explain the marks which I have, the knowledge is called distinct. And such is the knowledge of an assayer, who discerns the true from the false by means of certain tests or marks which make up the definition of gold.[34]

These practical manipulations can be used as a definition of the thing tested.[35] But we do not have distinct notions of sensible qualities since we can only recognise them in an experience, and not by enumerating the marks that distinguish them

---

[32] Gottfried Wilhelm Leibniz, *Philosophical Essays*, ed. and trans. R. Ariew and D. Garber (Indianapolis: Hacket, 1986). From here on, "AG". (AG, §59).

[33] AG, §24.

[34] AG, §56.

[35] An expert can recognise a genuine diamond by testing its hardness, for example, so, for her a diamond is that precious stone that passes the hardness test. However, her distinct notion is not an adequate knowledge of the nature of diamonds. See AG, §24.

from one another.[36] However, he also says that our confused cognition of sensible qualities involves some kind of recognition and discernment:

> Therefore, knowledge is clear when I have the means for recognising the thing represented[37]

And according to the DM:

> When I can recognise a thing from others without being able to say what its differences or properties consist in, the knowledge is confused. It is in this way that we know something clearly, ...[38]

Our cognition of sensible qualities is confused.[39] Leibniz insists that the recognition of properties and things in perceptual experience does not appeal to the actualisation of distinct notions since it does not involve the enunciation of their distinguishing notes:

> Clear knowledge again, is either confused or distinct. It is confused when I cannot enumerate one by one marks [nota] sufficient for differentiating a thing from others, even though the thing does indeed have such marks and requisites into which its notion can be resolved. And so we recognise colours, smells, tastes, and other particular objects of the senses clearly enough, and we distinguish them from one another, but only through the simple testimony of the senses, not by way of explicit marks.[40]

This means that the confused recognition of perceptual properties does not involve judgment since we cannot enumerate the elements which distinguish the object and are included in its definition. In other words, if judgments do not simply endorse the content of perceptual experience but concepts have to be actualised in judgment, the perception of confused qualities does not involve the use of concepts. Leibniz's account of our recognition of sensible qualities

---

[36] He explains that our perception of sensible qualities is composed of perceptions of uncountable "minute shapes and motions alone" (AG, §27). The resulting sensible quality is some new thing (ens) that we fashion for ourselves (Ibid.). And although we can know shapes and motions by the intellect, this analysis cannot exhaust our perceptual awareness of a sensible quality, or as he says, its "know-not-what."

[37] AG, §24.

[38] AG, §56.

[39] AG, §24.

[40] AG, §24.

does not imply making explicit the notions that constitute their definition, and therefore, knowledge of sensible qualities is confused. Sensible qualities cannot be known by concepts, and so our perceptual experience of these qualities is not conceptual in the sense explained above. Now our perceptual experience seems to be about ordinary individual objects such as persons or waterfalls. If the knowledge of particular objects such as persons and waterfalls implies or even consists in the recognition of the object by means of their sensory qualities it might be the case that no actualisation of concepts is required. Consequently, the distinct perception of objects whose properties are confused would be a form of confused knowledge. But then we would need to explain how this apparently non-conceptual recognition of objects is possible, and how a confused recognition can be a distinct perception. Since Leibniz thought that a distinct notion may be composed of notions that can only be known confusedly insofar as we can make explicit those notions, it is possible that perception may involve notions that are confusedly known.

3.2. Distinct Perception of Objects

A recently offered solution to the apparently inescapable oscillation between coherentism and the so-called 'myth of the Given' claims that the content of perception must be conceptual. On this much-debated approach, perception must be able to justify our beliefs about the world but no mental state that does not have conceptual content can be a reason for a belief. The content of perceptual states cannot be different in kind from that of cognitive states as beliefs; they have to be conceptually-constituted contents. Causal accounts of perceptual processes cannot explain the normative dimension of justification. If, on the other hand, only the features of perceptual states are conceived as the immediate objects of perception, our beliefs would be based on mere subjective occurrences and cannot provide any reasons, that are a rational constraint, to believe something about the world.

I have stated that it seems that for Leibniz perceptual states have *representational* content insofar as they are expressions. Leroy Loemker, for example, had ascribed a representationalist realism to Leibniz and ascribed a causal role to external objects. [41] But representational realism opens the way to veil-of-perception scepticism. In contrast to representationalism, the conceptualist approach to perception sustains that the objects presented in perceptual contents are actual spatio-temporal objects rather than some singular internal object. But what is received in experience is always an already

---

[41] He cites Jag. 4 (now in A 6, 3.464). See Leroy E. Loemker, "Leibniz's Doctrine of Ideas," *The Philosophical Review* 55, no. 3 (1946), https://doi.org/10.2307/2181666, 239.

conceptualized 'this such.' The possibility of having that content requires a receptiveness that is also already *actively* discriminating.

Leibnizian distinct notions can be a compound of confused notions; this degree of distinct knowledge is not adequate knowledge. This is the case with sensible qualities but it is not evident what Leibniz thought of our knowledge of, say, coloured things rather than colours. Distinct perceptions may constitute confused inadequate knowledge, but, if some recognition of the thing represented is involved in human perception, it can be qualified as distinct to some degree. Now if perceptual awareness is only a form of confused cognition, the recognition of perceptual objects is not propositional since the properties or 'marks' constituting the definition of the object are not made explicit, and it does not require the use of notions we have conceived. But then, we need to explain how this non-conceptual recognition of objects is possible.

In a note written in the late 1670s, he explained the distinction between confused and distinct *perceptions* by using an example. When we see a crowd, Leibniz wrote, we perceive each of the men in it but only confusedly; but when we see a particular face *and at the same time we think* that it belongs to the man in front of us we have a distinct perception:

> Distincte percipimus, cujus partes vel attributa percipimus tanquam ad ipsum pertinentia, verbi gratia cum homine oblato vultum ejus percipimus, simulque cogitamus vultum ad hunc hominem pertinere. Alioqui cum oculos in turbam conjicimus singulos homines percipimus, singulorumque nobis obversorum vultus, sed confuse.[42]

In the same way, Leibniz continued, when we hear the sound of a waterfall at a certain distance it is necessary that we hear the noise of every drop of water; this is only a confused perception because ... 'there is no reason to hear one drop rather than another'.[43] But the perception of each individual drop is the necessary condition of the confused perception.

> Et cum sonitum aquae labentis e longinquo audimus, multorum quidem fluctuum strepitum audimus, nam non est ratio cur unius potius quam alterius; et, si nullius, utique nihil audiremus; confusa tamen haec perceptio est.[44]

---

[42] A 6, 4, 58.
[43] Ibid.
[44] Ibid.

The case of the face that stands out in a crowd seems to illustrate that indirect representational content appears in *distinct* perceptions. According to the first example when we see a face we also see a man, which is not straightforwardly represented. Then we can ask whether the indirectly represented content is the result of a process of inference and 'distinct perception' would become another name for perceptual judgment. If this is the case, the perceiver needs the relevant concepts to specify the representational content. Consequently, the range of the beings who have perceptual experiences would be drastically diminished.

Distinct perception involves indirect content. Perhaps this is what he means when he says that in our cognition of perceptual objects, something is clearly but confusedly recognised. The following passage seems to suggest that distinct perception involves intellectual abilities such as considering or attributing properties or even the concept of objecthood:

> Distincta itaque perceptio fit, dum aliquid nostri simile rebus attribuimus, nos enim scimus esse subjectum variorum attributorum, itaque similiter objecta consideramus tanquam substantias quasdam sive res.[45]

A contemporary text adds that we think or imagine[46] a subject or thing to which those attributes belong (as when we use demonstratives such as 'I' or 'this.').[47] He describes the process as a quasi-personification, and not as the inference of the notion of any particular substance. Insofar as the process does not consist in the explicit attribution of the part or property to this subject in a proposition, it qualifies for confused knowledge.

Now the passage in DDP itself suggests an alternate reading to the problem of indirect content. Leibniz is appealing to a known fact of the phenomenology of perception. When we see an apple we actually don't see the occluded portions of the fruit and when we see a man's face we can say we see a man – under normal circumstances - even when you can't see his legs and arms since we are confined to the limits of our immediate perspective. For some philosophers of perception, it is the nature of the content of perception that we are aware of the *presence* of the parts we do not actually see.

---

[45] Ibid.

[46] Leibniz substituted *imaginamus* for *cogitamus.*

[47] Nos subjectum seu substantiam cogitamus dum decims: Ego, ille, hoc, in his aliquid commune cogitamus, id est subjectum in corporis ipsis quoque quasi per prosopopoieiam. (A 6, 4, 26).

In the next proposition Leibniz clarifies that distinct perception does not involve affirmative or negative judgments; the thought to which he refers in the example of the human face is actually a representation of the imagination:

> Et distincta perceptio est, quae fit cum aliquo judicio sine affirmatione et negatione. Cogitatio est distincta imaginatio.[48]

Furthermore, this kind of comments cannot be dismissed as merely 'early Leibniz', because we find similar remarks in his later works as well. For example, in his notes on Malebranche's *Recherche* he writes:

> Mihi videtur omnis sensus seu perceptio involvere quandam affirmationen eamque a volutate independentem.[49]

Not only does Leibniz oppose Malebranche's sharp demarcation between the intellect as a passive faculty and the will as an active faculty, but he also holds that something is affirmed in perception that is independent of the will. If the will is the faculty to which the act of judgement is assigned, then perception does not involve the actualization of judicative abilities. In fact, Leibniz does not define judgement as an act of the will,[50] but as an act of the intellect. In any case, judging involves knowing the grounds of the judgement, or, as he says in the NE, some knowledge of the cause.[51] He also offers a definition of perceptual judgement in a marginal note to his *Definitiones cogitationesque metaphysicae*:

> Judicium de sensionibus illud est, in quo de subjecto et causa earum aliquid affirmatur vel negatur.[52]

According to this definition, perceptual judgement not only says something about the subject of the perception but also about its cause. In a similar way, Leibniz explains in the *Discourse* how we can say that we know external reality

---

[48] A 6, 4, 58.

[49] Leibniz is opposing to Malebranche's claim that the intellect is a passive faculty and the will is an active faculty: *Intellectus porro est facultas passiva, voluntas activa* (A 6, 4, 1807).

[50] It is an act of the intellect (*Affectiones rationales sunt Intellectus et Voluntatis. Intellectus, sunt Actus et Habitus interni, et cogitationum significationes. A c t u s i n t e l l e c t u s, ut conscium esse, assentiri vel dissentiri, ratiocinari vel judicio uti; Meditari, machinari aliquid.* A 6, 4, 602.

[51] NE, IV, xiv. Although he does not ascribe the view to himself, the case of perceptual judgement, and his criticism of Descartes' conception make this attribution plausible (see for example GP 4, 361).

[52] A 6, 4, 1394.

through the senses: when the external thing contains or expresses the reasons that lead our soul to certain thoughts.[53] More importantly, he holds that this and other ordinary ways of speaking[54] ... "have nothing false in them, ...".[55] Now, if the perceptual judgement makes those reasons explicit, then the causes of the perception are also the reasons that ground the judgement. Distinct perceptions express the dynamical process of our sensory organs reacting to bodies acting on them, and then, they may be the reasons for the perceptual judgement.

Distinct perception or sense has indirect content; this indirect content is not an explicit judgement but a representation of the imagination. Leibniz also says that we refer to the perceived content as something else of which it is a part or property and in this sense, we can say that something is affirmed but without involving an explicit judgement that attributes the part to the whole. The example of the face in the crowd suggests that what is affirmed is the subject to which we relate the sensory image, for example, the man to which the face belongs. The man is only confusedly recognised, but his face stands out in the crowd for some reason (his moves, the colour of his hair). So perceptual awareness presents us with, say, coloured things rather than some mental sense data. However, in being a confused cognition or non-propositional representation, it is not evident how this distinct perception can give rise to the perceptual judgement in which we attribute the representation in our mind to its external cause.

3.3. Consecution and Belief

In another list of definitions intended for his General Science project dated approximately between 1680 and 1685, sense is defined as an act of imagination that is united to some endeavour (conatus) to prevent the perceiver from diminishing her power to act or to increase it, that is, sensing involves an endeavour to act for her well-being. He writes:

> Itaque sentire est imaginari cum conatu impediendi aliquam imminutionem, vel procurandi auctionem nostrae potentiae, ex inde orto, quod eadem imago conjuncta nunc est, vel olim fuit, cum tali imminutione vel augment.[56]

Leibniz explains that this union between the imagination and the endeavour to act takes place because the image is or has been united to this change in the

---

[53] DM, §27; AG, §59.
[54] This concession applies to the common sense idea that one thing acts on another as well (Ibid.)
[55] Ibid.
[56] A 6, 4, 395.

subject's power to act.[57] Since imagination is a mere act of thinking it is not necessarily related to an endeavour to act in a certain way.[58] So in order to associate the image with the endeavour to act some "quasi-rules" are formed due to the repeated occurrence of the thought in conjunction with the change of power.

> Et quidem sciendum est cumnostrae cogitationi aut phaenomeno adjuncta est aliqua nostrae perfectionis vel potentiaeauctio aut diminutio, [nos] habere conatum efficiendi, ut ea cogitatio duret aut desinat. Reversa ea cogitatione, habere eundem conatum, nisi ea conjuncta sit cum cogitatione efficiente conatum contrarium. Quod si haec saepe contingant, oriri ex tot experimentis quasi regulas quasdam conandi aut non conandi in oblatis eaeque vel pendentes ex nostro experimento, vel ex traditione aliorum qui experti sunt,vel etiam eorum qui prophetarum instar dicant quid simus experturi.[59]

By experiencing this effect together with the image, a propensity to imagine the same effect or to act in the same way is formed.[60] Interestingly, Leibniz defines perception as a type of sense, that is, as a distinct sense, or also, as a sense that is certain.[61] Despite this change in terminology, what is important to notice is that *some* of our sensory representations can be distinct. Leibniz also characterises the perceived object as an actual or existing being,[62] thus it might be the case that sense becomes perceiving or is distinct when its object is an existing being. What he actually says is that by relating the thought of an object A with the corresponding endeavour to act the statement 'A is' is conceived.

> Et quoties ob aliquod phaenomenon conamur ita agere, ac si inde nisi nos impediremus secuturum esset aliud phaenomenon, conjunctum cum adjumento aut nocumento nostro, statuimus id esse, ...[63]

Statements include beliefs and knowledge but only knowledge is regarded as certain. Leibniz also compares the relation between sense and distinct sense (*i.e.*, perceiving, in the terminology of this opuscule) to that between believing and knowing[64] perhaps because perception is comparable to knowledge since

---

[57] Ibid.
[58] Ibid.
[59] A 6, 4, 394.
[60] Ibid.
[61] A 6, 4, 392; A 6, 4, 396.
[62] A 6, 4, 392.
[63] A 6, 4, 394.
[64] A 6, 4, 394-395.

both, unlike belief, are certain.[65] But to state that 'A is' is classified as a belief. Since beliefs are not certain, believing in the existence of the object is not sufficient for perception or distinct sense.

But Leibniz also says that a sensory content A can be associated to an endeavour to act due to one or more propositions of the form 'A is B':

> Quin et revera, etiam si sentias A, tamen si statuas A esse B, solet aliquis conatus esse conjunctus, quia solet ipsum A per aliam propositionem vel plures propositiones cum eo conjungi, quod nunc revera sentimus.[66]

More precisely, to state that 'A is B' consists in imagining a phenomenon A such that if we sense A now, we will act as if another thing B existed too. So to believe that 'A is B' is to have the disposition to act according to B when A is given.

> Itaque si revera sentias A, et ideo sic agas, ad promovenda vel impedienda, quae cum sentires B, utique statuis A esse B.[67]

Now Leibniz says that to affirm that 'A is B' is tantamount to act in a way that conforms to B when A is given. Then, if the sense perception of A is distinct due to its relation to some true proposition affirming that 'A is B', the endeavour to act not only makes distinct perception possible, it constitutes its content. Furthermore, the perceptual representation does not provide a bare referent but a 'this such', an A that is also B. Note, however, that the perceptual belief 'A is B' is singular and the quasi-rules are merely empirical. Perceptual belief is a guide for action but the connection between A and B is only empirical and subject to criticism.[68] If beliefs are habits that become actualised in judgements,[69] consecution can thereof explain both the propositional content we make explicit in judgement and animal behaviour. This is the case since perceptual processes respond to the same pattern in both animals and beings endowed with intellectual capacities.

---

[65] Then perception or distinct sense becomes certain, or distinct knowledge. For this the propositional content of the belief has to be made explicit in a judgement.

[66] A 6, 4, 395.

[67] Ibid.

[68] For instance, in terms of the criteria presented in *De modo distinguiendi*.

[69] Beliefs are habits of the intellect (A 6, 4, 602-3).

4. Conclusions

A pervading received view on perception holds that early modern philosophers introduced a conception that misunderstood the nature of perception and implied the isolation of the mind. By conceiving perceptual awareness as constituted by some intermediary mental entity, our beliefs concerning empirical objects can no longer be rationally supported by our perceptions so every philosophical theory of perception must respond to this challenge. From an epistemological point of view, perception as the justification of perceptual belief becomes extremely problematic if you do not want to hold that the content of perception is somehow conceptual since belief requires propositional content, and therefore, explicit concepts. Whether or not the misconception that led to this predicament can be attributed to some early modern philosophers, it would be at least controversial to ascribe it to Leibniz. His theory of sense perception as distinct perception does not prevent the mind from being affected by external bodies through its own sensory organs. From the point of view of the actions and passions of substances, distinct perception or sense consists of enhanced perceptions expressing external things. From an epistemological point of view, distinct perceptions are only confused cognitions and consequently, our knowledge of sensory qualities cannot be resolved into other distinct notions to provide an adequate definition of them. However, perceptual awareness does not require some mental intermediary entity from which the complex objects of perception have to be inferred. In perceiving some part or property that stands out in our sensory image, we implicitly recognise some object or thing of which it is a part or property. Consecutions explain belief formation in terms of habits that can be actualised in judgements. Leibniz also says that external things contain the reasons for our perceptual representation. Since the perceptual judgement makes explicit the causes of the perception, it can be said that the perception is the reason that grounds the judgement, and at the same time, that the external object is what we are aware of in perception but only confusedly. For beings endowed with intellectual capacities, then, the perceptual image can be associated with propositional content by the same mechanisms that explain consecutions in animals. This propositional content can then be evaluated when made explicit in judgement.

Bibliography

Heck, Richard G. "Nonconceptual Content and the 'Space of Reasons.'" *The Philosophical Review* 109, no. 4 (2000): 483–523. https://doi.org/10.2307/269 3622.

Kulstad, Mark. *Leibniz on Apperception, Consciousness, and Reflection.* München: Philosophia, 1991.

Leibniz, Gottfried Wilhelm. *Philosophical Essays.* Edited and translated by R. Ariew and D. Garber. Indianapolis: Hacket, 1986. [= AG]

———. *Sämtliche Schriften Und Briefe*. Edited by the Akademie der Wissenschaften. Darmstadt-Berlin: Akademie-Verlag, 1875-1890. [= A].

———. *Die philosophischen Schriften von Leibniz*. Edited by C. I. Gerhardt. 7 vols. Berlin: Hildesheim, 1960-1961. [= GP]

Loemker, Leroy E. "Leibniz's Doctrine of Ideas." *The Philosophical Review* 55, no. 3 (1946): 229–49. https://doi.org/10.2307/2181666.

Matthen, Mohan. "Introduction." In *The Oxford Handbook of Philosophy of Perception*, 1–26. Oxford: Oxford University Press, 2015.

McDowell, John. *Mind and World*. Cambridge: Harvard University Press, 1996.

McRae, Robert. *Leibniz: Perception, Apperception and Thought*. Toronto: Toronto University Press, 1976.

Passini, Enrico. *Corpo e Funzioni Cognitive in Leibniz*. Milan: Franco Angeli, 1996.

Smith, Justin E. H. "The Body-Machine in Leibniz's Early Physiological and Medical Writings: A Selection of Texts with Commentary." *The Leibniz Review* 17 (July 1, 2007): 141–79. https://doi.org/10.5840/leibniz2007175.

Chapter 3

Can Wild Boars See Green? A Critique of Higher and First-Order Theories Surrounding Leibniz's Concept of Apperception

Leonardo Ruiz Gómez
Universidad Panamericana

Abstract: This chapter aims to review two different accounts of the relationship between perception and apperception, namely the higher-order thought theory and the first-order thought theory. It will show that these accounts are missing an essential point in Leibniz's theory of apperception that may lead to misunderstanding his gnoseology. This point centres on the synthetic character of apperception, an idea that Leibniz consistently recalls in his *New Essays*. This text thus demonstrates that apperception plays a crucial role in what we will call "nonconscious sensation," a spot of oversight in the aforementioned interpretations.

Keywords: apperception, Leibniz, self-consciousness, sensation, gnoseology.

***

The relationship between perception and apperception in the context of Leibnizian philosophy has become a central topic among scholars. Understanding this subject is tantamount to grasping Leibniz's entire metaphysics, or at least that of his later period. Indeed, since initiating his monadological metaphysics—around 1700, if we are to follow Garber's division[1]— substances' prime (and only) activity is perception. Therefore, the theory of knowledge that Leibniz worked on from the

---

[1] D. Garber, *Leibniz: Body, Substance, Monad* (New York: Oxford University Press, 2011).

early stages of his philosophy gained an even more central position after this monadological turn.

This gnoseological issue is paramount not only for metaphysics but also for ethics and practical philosophy. The ideas of apperception and attention to gnoseological grounding are strongly associated with self-consciousness and moral consciousness, as are the notions of sin and belief.[2]

Among the many issues discussed on this topic, the one that has perhaps received the most attention lately relates to the question of how any perception becomes conscious, and if this question is equivalent to asking how one specific perception can be apperceived. Consequently, a correct taxonomy of the notions of perception, apperception, and reflection is highly important.

This chapter aims to review two different accounts of the relationship between perception and apperception, namely the *higher-order thought theory* and the *first-order thought theory*. It will show that these accounts are missing an essential point in Leibniz's theory of apperception that may lead to misunderstanding his gnoseology. This point centres on the synthetic character of apperception, an idea that Leibniz consistently recalls in his *New Essays*. This chapter thus demonstrates that apperception plays a crucial role in what we will call "nonconscious sensation," a spot of oversight in the aforementioned interpretations.

1. Introduction

Leibniz's *New Essays* focuses on the key concept of *petite perceptions*. In the prologue to this book, Leibniz states that many of his fundamental metaphysical theses may be derived from the mere notion of these minute perceptions: universal expression of substances, the inclusion of past and future properties on the present state of individuals, the theory of pre-established harmony, the denial of indifference of equilibrium, the Law of Continuity, the Principle of Identity of Indiscernibles, the denial of atoms, among others.

The main feature of these small perceptions is that a clear majority of them are nonconscious:

> Besides, there are hundreds of indications leading us to conclude that at every moment there is in us an infinity of perceptions, unaccompanied

---

[2] As Leibniz explicitly states in Gottfried Wilhelm Leibniz, *New Essays on Human Understanding*, ed. P. Remnant and J. Bennett (Glasgow: Cambridge University Press, 1996), §16; and Gottfried Wilhelm Leibniz, *Sämtliche Schriften Und Briefe*, ed. the Akademie der Wissenschaften (Darmstadt-Berlin: Akademie-Verlag, 1875), 517. From here on, "NE" and "A", respectively. (NE, IV, ch. 20, §16; A VI, 5, 517).

by awareness or reflection (*sans apperception et sans reflexion*); that is, of alterations in the soul itself, of which we are unaware (*nous ne nous appercevons pas*) because these impressions are either too minute and too numerous, or else too unvarying, so that they are not sufficiently distinctive on their own (*qu'elles n'ont rien d'assez distinguant à part*). But when they are combined with others they do nevertheless have their effect and make themselves felt, at least confusedly, within the whole[...] Memory is needed for attention: when we are not alerted, so to speak, to pay heed to certain of our own present perceptions, we allow them to slip by unconsidered (*sans reflexion*) and even unnoticed (*sans les remarquer*). But if someone alerts us to them straight away, and makes us take note, for instance, of some noise which we have just heard, then we remember it and are aware of just having had some sense of it.[3]

This passage demonstrates Leibniz's attempt to separate small perceptions from apperception (*apperception*), reflection (*reflexion*), attention (*attention*), distinction (*distinguant)* and awareness (*les remarquer*). If small perceptions are regarded as nonconscious, then we may consider "nonconscious" in this context as the lack of the above-mentioned properties.

With this particular use of the term perception, Leibniz's critique is double: first, against Cartesianism, which believes a soul could not exist without thinking; and, second, against John Locke, who believes that the soul is meant to consciously perceive every piece of mental content. Once Locke proves this thinking-consciousness equation, he criticises the Cartesian thesis on the necessary continuous activity of the soul; since we are not continuously conscious, then we are not continuously thinking. Leibniz disagrees with Locke by saying that the soul is always active[4] but criticises Descartes's thesis that all mental activity should be regarded as conscious thinking.[5]

This alone permits the conclusion that the notion of perception that Leibniz employs in his *New Essays* differs from our everyday use of the term. Nevertheless, it is reasonably easy to establish the domain of *petites perceptions* negatively by not assigning them as by-products of reflection, consciousness,

---

[3] There is a relevant distinction between Leibniz and Descartes views on perception and consciousness: while Descartes affirms that every thought or perception is conscious (René Descartes, "Principia Philosophiae," in *Œuvres de Descartes*, ed. Charles Adam and Paul Tannery, vol. 8 (Paris, 1897), AT: VIII, 160), Leibniz states that there are some perceptions that are unconscious. This is the case for most of our minute perceptions. (NE, pref.; A VI, 5,53-54).

[4] NE, pref.; A VI, 5,53-54.

[5] NE, 113.

and awareness. On the other hand, it is quite difficult to define the kind of perception that is not under this domain, *i.e.*, the conscious perceptions.

Another problem is found in precisely outlining the relationship between all the properties grouped on the "apperception" side, namely, how reflection, consciousness, awareness, and apperception should interact. Leibniz's ambiguity in his later works contributes to confusion in this regard. In some passages, Leibniz seems to imply a clear identification between apperception, consciousness, and reflection. Consider, for instance, the following fragment from the *Principles of Nature and Grace*:

> So it is well to make a distinction between perception, which is the inner state of the monad representing external things, and *apperception, which is consciousness or the reflective knowledge of this inner state itself* and which is not given to all souls or to any soul all the time.[6]

Another troubling passage comes from the *Monadology*, where we again find an alleged identification between consciousness and apperception:

> 14. The passing state which enfolds and represents a multitude in unity or in the simple substance is merely what is called *perception*. This must be distinguished from *apperception or from consciousness*, as what follows will make clear.[7]

In his *New Essays*, on the contrary, Leibniz speaks of *apperception* in a wide variety of contexts, many of which are related to pretty simple acts of sensation like noticing the sound of a distant mill, perceiving the waves of the sea, or perceiving a secondary colour such as green. It is hard to reconcile the idea that apperception is the ground for such simple mental activity and, at the same time, that it is related to higher operations such as reflection or self-consciousness.

Moreover, in both the *Monadology* and the *Principle of Nature and Grace*, there are passages in which Leibniz explicitly states that animals are not capable of

---

[6] Gottfried Wilhelm Leibniz, *Philosophical Papers and Letters*, ed. L. E. Loemker (Dordrecht: Kluwer Academic Publishers, 1976), 600. From here on, "PPL". (PPL, 600). The canonical reference is to Gerhardt's edition (Gottfried Wilhelm Leibniz, *Die Philosophischen Schriften von Leibniz*, ed. C. I. Gerhardt, 7 vols. (Berlin: Hildesheim, 1960)). From here on, "GP".

[7] In the "Monadologie" (in Gottfried Wilhelm Leibniz, *Die Philosophischen Schriften von Leibniz*, ed. C. I. Gerhardt, vol. 6 (Berlin: Hildesheim, 1960), §14). From here on, "M". (M, §14; GP, VI, 608-609).

reflection. Thus, they seem to conflict with the fragments from the very same texts quoted above where Leibniz identifies reflection and apperception.

> 29. But it is the knowledge of necessary and eternal truths which distinguishes us from simple animals and gives us reason and the sciences, lifting us to the knowledge of ourselves and of God. It is this within us which we call the rational soul or spirit.

> 30. It is also by the knowledge of necessary truths and by their abstractions that we rise to reflective acts, which enable us to think of what is called I and to consider this or that to be in us; it is thus, as we think of ourselves, that we think of being, of substance, of the simple and the compound, of the immaterial, and of God himself, conceiving of that which is limited in us as being without limits in him.[8]

> Animals that never think of such propositions are called 'brutes'; but ones that recognise such necessary truths are rightly called rational animals, and their souls are called minds. These souls are capable of reflective acts —acts of attention to their own inner states— so that they can think about what we call 'myself', substance, soul, or mind: in a word, things and truths that are immaterial.[9]

Since Leibniz seems to exclude reflection from animal perception and considering his commitment to the identification between reflection and apperception, we might conclude that Leibniz negates any apperception in animals. In this case, he exclusively ascribes apperception, reflection and grasping necessary truths to humans, rational souls, or spirits (in contrast to beasts, bare monads or minds). This corresponds to the standard reading of Leibniz's account of apperception and reflection, which McRae defended in his influential book, *Leibniz: Perception, Apperception, and Thought.* McRae himself noted that this interpretation is problematic since Leibniz "makes apperception or consciousness as an essential to sensation while elsewhere denying that animals are capable of apperception or consciousness".[10]

---

[8] M, §29-30, GP VI, 611-612.

[9] In the "Principles of Nature and Grace" (in Gottfried Wilhelm Leibniz, *Die Philosophischen Schriften von Leibniz*, ed. C. I. Gerhardt, vol. 6 (Berlin: Hildesheim, 1960), §5). From here on, "PNG". (PNG, §5; GP VI, 601).

[10] R. F. McRae, *Leibniz: Perception, Apperception, and Thought* (Toronto: University of Toronto Press, 1976), 33.

Nevertheless, some scholars have challenged this view[11] because, in the first place, Leibniz never explicitly claims that apperception cannot be ascribed to animals. In the passages referred to above, Leibniz only negates that animals are capable of reflection. So, if we are not to deny apperception to animals (and we should not since apperception seems to be essential to the process of basic sensation), doubt arises on the equivalence of apperception, reflection, and consciousness. In the second place, Leibniz ascribes apperception to a particular animal, namely, a wild boar, in the famous passage below:

> That is why the beasts have no understanding, at least in this sense; although they have the faculty for *awareness* (*faculté de s'appercevoir*) of the more conspicuous and outstanding impressions – as when a wild boar is *aware* of someone who is shouting at it, and goes straight at that person, having previously had only a bare perception of him, a confused one like its perceptions of all the objects which stand before its eyes and reflect light-rays into the lenses.[12]

This text again demonstrates that apperception is linked to very primitive acts of sensation. Remnant and Bennet even translate "faculté de s'appercevoir" for "faculty of awareness" in a perhaps minimalistic reading of the term. In this example, Leibniz uses apperception to distinguish between a wild boar's perceptual panorama before and after it notices a person shouting. It is easy to see that "apperception" here cannot imply an elaborate mental operation, but rather implies a fairly unsophisticated redirection of the animal's attention.[13]

---

[11] Antoine Charbonneau, "Perception, aperception et conscience chez Leibniz," in *Ithaque*, vol. 15 (Ithaque, Société Philosophique Ithaque, 2014), 1–24, https://papyrus.bib.umontreal.ca/xmlui/handle/1866/13255; R. J. Gennaro, "Leibniz on Consciousness and Self-Consciousness," in *New Essays on the Rationalists*, ed. R. J. Gennaro and C. Huenemann (New York: Oxford University Press, 2003), 353–69; Mark Kulstad, "Leibniz, Animals, and Apperception," *Studia Leibnitiana* 13, no. 1 (1981): 25–60; Alison Simmons, "Changing the Cartesian Mind: Leibniz on Sensation, Representation and Consciousness," *The Philosophical Review* 110, no. 1 (2001): 31–75, https://doi.org/10.2307/2693597.

[12] NE, 173.

[13] Some scholars rightly point out that some ambiguity exists between the terms "*s'apercevoir*" and "*apercevoir*." Gennaro, "Leibniz on Consciousness and Self-Consciousness"; Mark Kulstad, *Leibniz on Apperception, Consciousness, and Reflection* (Munich: Philosophia, 1991), 21; Arnaud Pelletier, "Attention Et Aperception Selon Leibniz: Aspects Cognitifs Et Éthiques," *Les Études Philosophiques*, no. 1 (2017): 103–17. The issue is that the corresponding verb for *perception* is *apercevoir*. Accordingly, it is not clear if Leibniz is referring to *apperception* or *perception* when using the verb *apercevoir*. Commentators tend to read "*s'apercevoir*" as the action of *apperception*, and "*apercevoir*" as the action of *perception*.

In short, different theses in Leibniz's writings seem to imply contradictory statements: a) that reflection, consciousness, and apperception are equivalent, b) that only rational souls (spirits) are capable of reflection, c) thus (from *a* and *b*), only rational souls (spirits) are capable of apperception, d) that apperception is a primary feature of rather basic acts of sensation, e) that animals are capable of these sorts of basic sensations.

2. First-Order and Higher-Order Solutions

To reconcile these allegedly contradictory theses, most commentators have dismissed (a) and (c). They dismiss (c) as mentioned because Leibniz did not make an explicit statement in this direction; it is rather only a consequence of granting (a) and (b). Thus, if (c) is to be discarded from Leibniz's core theses, then either (a) or (b) should also be rejected. Most scholars choose to dismiss (a), *i.e.*, the identification between reflection, consciousness, and apperception. This strategy supposes, in the first place, reinterpreting the texts in which Leibniz seems to explicitly make this statement[14] and, in the second, establishing a subtler taxonomy of the senses in which Leibniz uses the term "*apperception*" and "*s'apercevoir.*"

In the first part of this strategy, Gennaro[15] gives the best account. It is worth highlighting again the fragment from the *Principle of Nature and Grace:*

> So it is well to make a distinction between perception, which is the inner state of the monad representing external things, and *apperception, which is consciousness or the reflective knowledge of this inner state itself* and which is not given to all souls or to any soul all the time.[16]

Gennaro states that the expression "l'Apperception qui est la Conscience, ou la connoissance reflexive de cet état interieur" should be read as equating *apperception* and *self-consciousness*, instead of *mere consciousness*. In this context, Leibniz is seen as talking about a specific and highly sophisticated kind of apperception reserved for rational souls. Thus, this particular kind of apperception should be defined as "consciousness (or a reflective knowledge) of this inner state" rather than the usual interpretation of this passage as "consciousness or (also) a reflective knowledge of this inner state."

---

[14] PNG, §12; M, §14.

[15] Gennaro, "Leibniz on Consciousness and Self-Consciousness."

[16] All passages from the Principles of Nature and Grace and *Monadology* are from Loemker's translation: Leibniz, *Philosophical Papers and Letters.*

The problematic text from the *Monadology* is as follows:

> 14. The passing state which enfolds and represents a multitude in unity or in the simple substance is merely what is called *perception*. This must be distinguished *from apperception or from consciousness*, as what follows will make clear.[17]

Gennaro's interpretation of this passage is as follows: "apperception or consciousness" should not be read as equating both terms. In this case, perceptions of simple substances must be distinguished from apperception *and also* from consciousness.

Once we grant this interpretation, it is evident that "apperception" should be regarded as an analogical term; a subtler division is thus required. Kulstad[18] and Gennaro[19] have proposed a taxonomy of the notion of "apperception" in order to make sense of its different uses in Leibniz's work.

Gennaro has proposed three different meanings for the word "apperception".[20] The first one is defined as "nonconscious meta-psychological thoughts." The idea behind this definition is that apperception is considered a *higher-order thought* (HOT).[21] In this sense, the consciousness of first-order thoughts is only possible through the action of nonconscious higher-order thought. These thoughts of a higher order can also become conscious by an even higher-order nonconscious thought. Gennaro avoids an objection of infinite regress by stating that, at the highest level, there is always a nonconscious thought.

This basic sense of apperception ("nonconscious metapsychological thoughts" or *appercepcion₁*) is distinguished from "introspection," which is also divided into "momentary focused introspection," on the one hand, and "deliberate introspection," on the other. Introspection involves conscious higher-order thoughts over an inner state. Thus, apperception could also mean

---

[17] M, §14; GP VI, 608-609.

[18] Kulstad, *Leibniz on Apperception, Consciousness, and Reflection.*

[19] Gennaro, "Leibniz on Consciousness and Self-Consciousness."

[20] Gennaro, "Leibniz on Consciousness and Self-Consciousness", 359.

[21] Before Gennaro, defenders of the presence of a higher order thought theory in Leibniz's epistemology include Simmons, "Changing the Cartesian Mind"; Kulstad, *Leibniz on Apperception, Consciousness, and Reflection*; and J. Jalabert, "La Psychologie de Leibniz: Ses Caractères Principaux," *Revue Philosophique de La France et de l'Étranger* 136, no. 10/12 (1946): 453–72.

both a deliberate, rational (often called reflection) sustained consciousness or a brief, accidental and non-deliberative consciousness.[22]

Gennaro's taxonomy seems pretty useful in outlining Leibniz's different uses of the notion of apperception by providing an underlying framework for interpreting problematic passages in the *Monadology* and the *Principles of Nature and Grace*. In what follows, we will not discuss the relevant features of this classification, which is based on Gennaro's previous and more general work.[23] Instead, the following sections aim to examine if this characterisation fully grasps the wide range of meanings that can be attributed to Leibnizian terms.

Discussion on this topic has focused on the notion of higher-order thoughts. Is it indispensable to postulate different orders between perceptions and apperceptions to explain the passage from the former to the latter? Is this proposal properly grounded in Leibniz's writings? Is it even possible to admit this gap between first and higher-order thoughts within the scope of Leibniz's Law of Continuity?

On the first question, some scholars are opposed to explaining apperception in terms of higher-order thoughts.[24] The main argument among these authors rests on the idea that clarity and distinction gradually outline the difference between perception and apperception, precisely because the Law of Continuity appears in the very origin of the notion of *petites perceptions*.

> I called this the Law of Continuity when I discussed it formerly in the *Nouvelles de la republique des lettres* [...]. It implies that any change from small to large, or vice versa, passes through something which is, in respect of degrees as well as of parts, in between; and that no motion ever springs immediately from a state of rest, or passes into one except through a lesser motion; just as one could never traverse a certain line or distance without first traversing a shorter one [...]. All of which

---

[22] Gennaro uses the terms apperception₁, apperception₂ and apperception₃ for each one of the senses mentioned above. Kulstad, *Leibniz on apperception, consciousness, and reflection* uses the terms "mere reflection" (which Gennaro equates to apperception₁) and "focused reflection" (which confusingly includes apperception₂ and apperception₃).

[23] Gennaro, *Consciousness and Self-Consciousness: A Defense of the Higher-Order Thought Theory of Consciousness*.

[24] Charbonneau, "Perception, aperception et conscience chez Leibniz"; Larry M. Jorgensen, "The Principle of Continuity and Leibniz's Theory of Consciousness," *Journal of the History of Philosophy* 47, no. 2 (2009): 223–48, https://doi.org/10.1353/hph.0.0112; McRae, *Leibniz: Perception, Apperception, and Thought*.

supports the judgment that noticeable perceptions arise by degrees from ones which are too minute to be noticed.[25]

By taking the Law of Continuity into account, it seems plausible that the difference between conscious and non-conscious, on the one hand, and perception and apperception, on the other hand, does not constitute a definitive gap. It would be strange for Leibniz to postulate the whole system of *petite perceptions* in consideration of the Law of Continuity, only to establish a straightforward exception to the very same law afterwards. In this sense, defenders of the first-order theory suppose that apperception is directly associated with distinct perceptions (in contrast with confused perceptions). There is plenty of textual evidence in this direction:

> I have shown above that we always have an infinity of minute perceptions without being aware of them (*sans nous en appercevoir*). We are never without perceptions, but necessarily we are often without awareness (*sans apperception*), namely when none of our perceptions stand out (*perception distingués*).[26]

One may object that Leibniz contradicts *a priori* his Law of Continuity by defending the superiority of spirits (rational souls) over animal souls and bare monads in the *Monadology* and the *Principles of Nature and Grace*. If this were the case, we could find a workaround by fitting the gradation of perceptions into the Law of Continuity. Nevertheless, Leibniz himself argues that the alleged gaps in nature only merely appear so in order to guarantee harmony and beauty in the world:

> In nature everything happens by degrees, and nothing by jumps; and this rule about change is one part of my law of continuity. But the beauty of nature, which insists upon perceptions which stand out from one another, asks for the appearance of jumps and for musical cadences (so to speak) amongst phenomena, and takes pleasure in mingling species. Thus, although in some other world there may be species intermediate between man and beast (depending upon what senses these words are taken in), and although in all likelihood there are rational animals, somewhere, which surpass us, nature has seen fit to keep these at a

---

[25] NE, 56.
[26] NE, 161-162.

distance from us so that there will be no challenge to our superiority on our own globe.[27]

This text supports the idea that apperception implies a higher degree of distinctness, but not a higher-order thought that differs from the original first-order perception. The sophistication of mental states rises and falls gradually from species to species and from moment to moment in an individual. Consider the example mentioned above of the wild boar: it perceives everything in its visual range; after the person shouts, a particular subset of perceptions (those corresponding to the figure of the man) gain some degree of distinction, and so the wild boar ultimately apperceives the person. There is no need for a second-order thought to explain the difference between the boar's mental state before and after hearing the person's voice.

Of course, defenders of the first-order theory must admit that highly sophisticated reflection should be regarded as a higher-order thought since Leibniz himself seems to describe it in these terms: "acts of reflection and of considering what is called 'I', 'substance', 'soul', 'spirit'".[28] However, this does not problematise their position since (as higher-order theory defenders also believe) reflection and apperception should be distinguished. The question is, then, whether apperception at the "lowest levels" should be regarded as a higher-order thought or not. I am particularly interested in the kind of consciousness that apperception renders to world-directed mental states (according to the higher-order theory), and even more so in the nature of these world-directed mental states.

3. Problems with the Higher-Order Thought Theory

The term "apperception" first appears in Leibniz's *New Essays* in the first text quoted herein. We find there the famous example of the mill that produces a subtle sound that only calls our attention after some sort of alert sets off our awareness. Immediately after this fragment, Leibniz proposes another example to "give a clearer idea of these minute perception"[29]: a person standing by the beach might hear the noise of the sea as a confused roar. Nevertheless, in order to listen to this roar as a whole, he must hear every single "part" of this sound, namely, the noise of every wave, of every drop, of every fish flapping on the surface. Otherwise, he would have no chance of hearing the sea at all:

> We must be affected slightly by the motion of this wave, and have some perception of each of these noises, however faint they may be; otherwise

---

[27] NE, 473.
[28] PNG §5; GP VI, 601.
[29] NE, 53-54.

there would be no perception of a hundred thousand waves, since a
hundred thousand nothings cannot make something.[30]

It is important to point out that Leibniz is not talking here about any sort of
conscious process. Minute perceptions are not accompanied by reflection, or
by consciousness. Moreover, perception goes beyond the gnoseological realm
and is instead a metaphysical concept. This is evident when considering the
definition offered in the *Monadology*: "The passing state which enfolds and
represents a multitude in unity or the simple substance is merely what is called
perception".[31] Only the word "represents" (*represente*) refers to gnoseological
activity; however, Leibniz famously ascribes perception to all monads,
including those that lack gnoseological faculties.

This gives us strong reason to believe that apperception has an essential
function with regard to the most basic levels of knowledge. In the example of
the sea, Leibniz ascribes to perception the capacity of being affected by little
elements in the waves; thus, listening to the sea as a whole should be assigned
to an activity other than perception. Leibniz does not say it explicitly, but it is
reasonable to believe that this activity corresponds to apperception.

Hence, apperception is the condition for sensibility. This is, of course, nothing
new since Leibniz himself describes "sensation" (*sentiment*) as "perception
accompanied by memory",[32] undoubtedly assuming that sensibility involves
higher capacities than mere perception.

Nevertheless, this raises a problem for the higher-order theories described in the
previous section. Indeed, one may ask about the nature of first-order (world-
directed) thoughts to which higher-order thoughts refer. As Gennaro points out:

> So we have two kinds of perception for Leibniz: nonconscious and
> conscious. If I am right thus far, a nonconscious perception is a world-
> directed state that is not apperceived, that is, not accompanied by a
> HOT. On the other hand, a conscious perception is apperceived and so
> is accompanied by a HOT.[33]

As far as I understand Gennaro's point, the lowest level in the gnoseological
taxonomy is non-conscious perception. So, if we are to comprehend this in a
Leibnizian sense, Gennaro is talking here about the kind of activity that all

---

[30] NE, 54.

[31] M, §14; GP VI, 608-609.

[32] PNG, §4, GP VI, 599.

[33] Gennaro, "Leibniz on Consciousness and Self-Consciousness", 359.

monads share.[34] He then says that the lowest form of consciousness (which he calls *apperception₁*) is "nonconscious meta-psychological thoughts" or "nonconscious apperceptions." These conscious states suppose a world-directed mental state and a nonconscious higher-order thought of that particular mental state. If a higher-order thought is nonconscious, then conscious attention is directed toward an external object rather than any mental state.

Let us try to fit this taxonomy into the example of the wild boar. The difference between the mental states of the boar before and after the person shouts may be portrayed by the distinction between Gennaro's view of *perception* and *apperception₁*. Moreover, no other option seems viable in his taxonomy since Gennaro admits, despite himself, that Leibniz does not ascribe apperception₂ or apperception₃ to animals.[35] Accordingly, we should conclude that the boar, before noticing the person, would be in a state of mere *perception*, while after hearing the shouting, would become conscious of the person's presence and reach a state of *apperception₁*.

This interpretation has *prima facie* some difficulties. In the first place, it is a stretch to equate the mental state of an unaware boar with the activity of any given bare monad (which, as already noted, also perceives): the former seems to be on a level of *non-conscious sensation*, while Leibniz precisely calls the latter *non-conscious perception*. We must admit that Leibniz's words may contradict this objection since he describes the boar's unaware state as "bare perception" (*perception nue*). Nevertheless, it is hard to believe, when considering other texts, that Leibniz could identify even the lowest levels of animals' sensation with bare monads' perception. Secondly, it is hard to admit that such a wide gap exists between the boar's two mental states, that is, to admit that a higher-level thought mediates between its visual panorama and focused observation of the person. Perhaps it would be more accurate to say that the animal moves from a state of *apperception₁* to that of *apperception₂* (focused introspection). However, on the one hand, as mentioned, such an approach does not seem to coincide with Leibniz's thought. On the other hand, it is hard to see how Gennaro would describe the boar's second mental state as

---

[34] To be fair to Gennaro's account, we should consider that he distances himself from Leibnizian metaphysics of simple substances. Therefore, he does not need to outline what "bare perceptions" would mean in the context of non-living things. Nevertheless, his paper tries to put forward an accurate interpretation of Leibniz's gnoseology; accordingly, we consider Leibniz's metaphysical writings permissible in order to scrutinise the accuracy of this interpretation.

[35] Gennaro, "Leibniz on Consciousness and Self-Consciousness", 364.

some sort of introspection since introspection is defined by reference to internal mental states, and this is clearly a world-directed mental state.

In short, it seems that a) Leibniz spots a slight difference between the boar's two states, b) this difference is described in terms of apperception, c) this difference is more subtle than Gennaro's distinction between *perception* and *apperception₁*.

4. Problems with the First-Order Thought Theory

One might think that these considerations support the first-order theory. Certainly, it seems more natural to explain the wild boar example as a gradual change of distinction, where both perception and apperception are first-order thoughts. This is also compatible with the fact that Leibniz equally ascribes perception to animals, humans, and monads from which phenomena result. Bare monads therein have, then, a completely confused perception, while animals have a higher level of distinction, plus the ability to focus their attention on particular phenomena in order to perceive them even more distinctly. This seems to make a solid case in favour of the first-order theory, precisely because it is adequately grounded in textual evidence. Indeed, the passage about the wild boar seems to be expressed in these terms:

> [...]and [the boar] goes straight at that person, having previously had only a bare perception (*perception nue*) of him, a confused one like its perceptions of all the objects which stand before its eyes and reflect light-rays into the lenses.[36]

By erasing a straightforward division between perception and apperception, the first-order theory explains the ambiguity in the terms Leibniz uses. The fact that he describes "bare perception" as a more or less sophisticated act of sensation no longer represents a problem under this view. The first-order theory also has the advantage of connecting Leibniz's later philosophy with terminology from his earlier works, where "apperception" was not used and his whole taxonomy was described in terms of "distinction," "adequation," and "clearness" among others. Thus, the conceptualisation of apperception is the logical conclusion of the gradation of the properties with which Leibniz worked for decades[37].

Nevertheless, it is time to bring back the example of the sea and the sound of the waves. We already established that the notion of minute perceptions entails

---

[36] NE, 173.

[37] An early scheme of Leibniz's gnoseological system is in *Meditationes de cognitione, veritate et ide*is (1684) (A VI, 4, 585). See also: *Discourse of Metaphysics* §§XXIV-XXV, (A VI, 4, 1567-1570).

a more sophisticated activity identified with apperception. Let us try to outline the transition from non-conscious to conscious mental states: Leibniz clearly states that we are unable to hear the infinite minute perceptions that constitute the roar of the sea (*"ne se fasse connoître que dans l'assemblage confus de tous les autres ensemble"*); we only hear the roar of the sea *as a whole*. Accordingly, the sound that enters consciousness is not a subset of non-conscious minute perceptions that, by means of apperception, become distinct and conscious. It is clear that Leibniz's thought does not align with this account since he explicitly states that "the parts" of this sound cannot be apperceived individually. Moreover, it is nonsensical to talk of proper elements of sound because phenomena are divided *ad infinitum*, and so there are no *minima sensibilia*.[38]

This entails a problem for the first-order theory. Indeed, as mentioned, this position supposes that consciousness is a subset of bare perceptions that somehow become distinct in the process: "The increase in activity reduces to an increase in perceptual distinctness, and *when a perception becomes distinct enough it will be conscious*".[39] But this is directly opposed to the conditions Leibniz established in the example of the wave. "A perception" is undefinable in this context. When we hear the roar of the sea, we do not hear a particular group of distinct perceptions; we hear, instead, a *synthetic-apperceptual whole*. In other words, a bijective function does not result from relating a set of non-conscious perceptions and a set of conscious perceptions.[40] Apperception has, thus, a synthetic character that the first-order theory fails to take into account.

5. Sensation as the Missing Apperception

Finally, it is worth pointing out another example that Leibniz frequently uses in his *New Essays*, which speaks to the synthetic character of apperception:

> It is obvious that green, for instance, comes from a mixture of blue and yellow; which makes it credible that the idea of green is composed of the ideas of those two colours, although the idea of green appears to us as simple as that of blue, or as that of warmth. So these ideas of blue and of warmth should also be regarded as simple only in appearance. I freely admit that we treat them as simple ideas, because we are at any rate not

---

[38] Leibniz to De Volder (GP II, 268).

[39] Jorgensen, "The Principle of Continuity and Leibniz's Theory of Consciousness", 242.

[40] I have presented a functional model to describe the relationship between perception and apperception in L. Ruiz-Gómez, "Expresión, Percepción y Apercepción. La Construcción Sintética de Los Fenómenos," in *La Modernidad En Perspectiva. A Trescientos Años Del Fallecimiento de Leibniz*, ed. R. Casales García and J. M. Castro Manzano (Granada: Comares, 2017), 15–29.

aware of any divisions within them (*parce qu'au moins nôtre apperception ne les divise pas*).[41]

Immediately after this text, in the third manuscript referred to in the *Akademie Edition* as L[3], Leibniz includes the following paragraph:

> Et l'on voit encor par là qu'il y a des perceptions dont on ne s'apperçoit point. Car les perceptions des idées simples en apparence sont composées des perceptions des parties dont ces idées sont composées; sans que l'esprit s'en apperçoive[,] car ces idées confuses luy paroissent simples.[42]

This example reveals the central problem that both theories share. On the one hand, any defence of the first-order theory must admit that the apperception of green would be, in this case, an increase in the distinction between blue and yellow since green is conscious, while blue and yellow are not. Of course, this is not the case since Leibniz, in the last sentence, explicitly states that the false simplicity of green is related to confusion. In this scenario, the process of distinction is inverse to the one described earlier: analysis of green achieves distinction in phenomena that are, in the first place, non-conscious (blue and yellow). Moreover, the first-order theory would have to explain how green could become, by a gradual increase of distinction, blue and yellow (*i.e.*, radically different colours) in this continuous process.

On the other hand, any defence of the higher-order theory entails explaining this gap between primary and secondary colours by invoking second-order thought. In this case, seeing something as green implies both a non-conscious perception of blue and yellow and a perception of green. One might think that this kind of apperception corresponds to Gennaro's *apperception₁*, however, the idea that Leibniz would describe the act of "seen colour green" as "nonconscious meta-psychological thought" does not seem plausible. Furthermore, returning to the wild boar, let us suppose that the person who shouts is wearing a green jacket. In this case, one may conclude that, by seeing the green jacket (that is, by having the jacket in its visual panorama), the wild boar represents it with *apperception₁*, even before noticing the person. Thus, explaining the mental state of the boar through awareness is problematic since this mental state is also world-directed, and not accurately represented by *apperception₂*.

In short, both perspectives on apperception —higher and first-order theories— seem to unsatisfactorily outline the lower levels of apperception. It

---

[41] NE, 120.

[42] NE, c. 2, §1; A VI, 5, 120. Not included in Remnant and Bennet's translation.

is clear at this point that the lowest mental state level that involves apperception is (at least) similar to *non-conscious sensation*. This concept involves the basic hearing of the wave, the simple vision of green, and the boar's visual representation before focusing its attention. This mental state cannot be equated with bare perception, or with any sort of introspection.

Indeed, the notion of "sensation" is part of Leibnizian vocabulary. As mentioned, he defines it in the *Principles of Nature and Grace* as "perception accompanied by memory" and uses the term often, though inconsistently, in his *New Essays*, perhaps based on the specific sense that Locke gives the term. The definition of sensation as perception accompanied by memory is also problematic since memory is understood both as the ability to store representations in the mind[43] and as the capacity to remember.[44] In this sense, it seems to fit well with a higher-order thought description, but it does not thoroughly represent the kind of activity described herein. Indeed, all the examples above imply some sort of synchronicity between apperception and the perception from which it arises. If memory is understood as the ability to remember, then this definition of "sensation" is useless for our purposes. Otherwise, if Leibniz thinks that the distinction between bare monads' perceptions and more sophisticated minds' sensations leaves a trace in the soul to which consciousness could later return, then we are headed toward a notion of sensation that better describes the kind of activity considered herein.

6. Conclusions

The complex terminology that Leibniz uses in his later works regarding perception, apperception, sensation, consciousness, and attention makes it difficult to advance a definitive interpretation of these terms. Herein, we have discussed the advantages and disadvantages of first-order and higher-order thought theories.

We have shown how both interpretations miss an important sense of apperception that could be regarded as "non-conscious sensation," which should be distinguished from all monads' bare perception and, at the same time, from any sort of conscious content. In some of Leibniz's texts, this could be equated with the notion of sensation, though this term is also ambiguous in Leibniz's later works.

Thus, considering this sense of apperception is essential because it completes the foundation on which a complete Leibnizian gnoseology can be built (with the notion of bare perception as the basis of his metaphysics). A

---

[43] NE, 76-77.
[44] NE, 140.

misunderstanding of this primary concept could lead to miscomprehending the entire Leibnizian system.

Precisely describing "sensation" in Leibniz's final theory of knowledge is of utmost importance. The idea of "memory" as the ability to store representations should lead to a clear distinction between non-conscious perception and non-conscious sensation that could be useful for reorganising the whole taxonomy of conscious and nonconscious mental states. However, properly representing the complexity of Leibniz's gnoseology by proposing a proper taxonomy of perceptions and apperception is the topic of a future work.

Bibliography

Charbonneau, Antoine. "Perception, aperception et conscience chez Leibniz." In *Ithaque*, 15:1–24. Société Philosophique Ithaque, 2014. https://papyrus.bib.umontreal.ca/xmlui/handle/1866/13255.

Descartes, René. "Principia Philosophiae." In *Œuvres de Descartes*, edited by Charles Adam and Paul Tannery, Vol. 8. Paris, 1897.

Garber, D. *Leibniz: Body, Substance, Monad.* New York: Oxford University Press, 2011.

Gennaro, R. J. *Consciousness and Self-Consciousness: A Defense of the Higher-Order Thought Theory of Consciousness.* John Benjamins Pub, 1996.

———. "Leibniz on Consciousness and Self-Consciousness." In *New Essays on the Rationalists*, edited by R. J. Gennaro and C. Huenemann, 353–69. New York: Oxford University Press, 2003.

Jalabert, J. "La Psychologie de Leibniz: Ses Caractères Principaux." *Revue Philosophique de La France et de l'Étranger* 136, no. 10/12 (1946): 453–72.

Jorgensen, Larry M. "The Principle of Continuity and Leibniz's Theory of Consciousness." *Journal of the History of Philosophy* 47, no. 2 (2009): 223–48. https://doi.org/10.1353/hph.0.0112.

Kulstad, Mark. "Leibniz, Animals, and Apperception." *Studia Leibnitiana* 13, no. 1 (1981): 25–60.

———. *Leibniz on Apperception, Consciousness, and Reflection.* Munich: Philosophia, 1991.

Leibniz, Gottfried Wilhelm. *Die Philosophischen Schriften von Leibniz.* Edited by C. I. Gerhardt. 7 vols. Berlin: Hildesheim, 1960.

———. *New Essays on Human Understanding.* Edited by P. Remnant and J. Bennett. Glasgow: Cambridge University Press, 1996.

———. *Philosophical Papers and Letters.* Edited by L. E. Loemker. Dordrecht: Kluwer Academic Publishers, 1976.

———. *Sämtliche Schriften Und Briefe.* Edited by the Akademie der Wissenschaften. Darmstadt-Berlin: Akademie-Verlag, 1875.

McRae, R. F. *Leibniz: Perception, Apperception, and Thought.* Toronto: University of Toronto Press, 1976.

Pelletier, Arnaud. "Attention Et Aperception Selon Leibniz: Aspects Cognitifs Et Éthiques." *Les Études Philosophiques*, no. 1 (2017): 103–17.

Ruiz-Gómez, L. "Expresión, Percepción y Apercepción. La Construcción Sintética de Los Fenómenos." In *La Modernidad En Perspectiva. A Trescientos Años Del Fallecimiento de Leibniz,* edited by R. Casales García and J. M. Castro Manzano, 15–29. Granada: Comares, 2017.

Simmons, Alison. "Changing the Cartesian Mind: Leibniz on Sensation, Representation and Consciousness." *The Philosophical Review* 110, no. 1 (2001): 31–75. https://doi.org/10.2307/2693597.

Chapter 4

Leibniz on *Conscientia* and Personal Identity

Roberto Casales García
UPAEP University

Abstract: In order to understand Leibniz's notion of personal identity, we need to distinguish between three constitutive levels of identity: the first level is related to an ontological identity of individual beings (considering that every real substance, according to Leibniz, is a real unity and, therefore, a single individual); a second level, which belongs to living beings; and a third level, which corresponds to a rational being. On the first level, we found Leibniz's characterization of his principle of the identity of indiscernibles, which applies to every individual. On the second level, we have an organic and teleological structure of living beings, a kind of identity that belongs to the living being. Living beings, according to Leibniz, have a nested structure in which every organ is related to each other: this structure is granted by its dominant monad. This monad can subordinate any other monads of its body by having clear and distinguished perceptions. There is, however, a third level of identity, related only to rational beings since only they possess a reflective kind of consciousness which is different from the kind of perception that we find in other animals. Personal identity, which corresponds to this third level, depends on the moral quality of the self.

Keywords: personal identity, individuality, apperception, consciousness, moral quality.

***

1. Introduction

One of the key points needed to understand the development of Leibniz's notion of "personal identity", in particular the practical dimension that it assumes in his latest work, lies in analysing the different *logical*, *metaphysical* and *epistemological* aspects that are *systematically* intertwined with this notion[1]. Leibniz's notions of "personal identity", if my reading of the Hanoverian is correct, presupposes at least three constitutive levels that, by being closely related, ground a more robust theory of identity that directly responds to Locke's objections to a substantive theory of identity. While Locke maintains that the unity of substance is not "what comprises all kinds of identity",[2] but the spatio-temporal determination of everything in existence,[3] Leibniz argues that the key to talk about identity and diversity lies in a "*principe interne de distinction*",[4] namely, the substantial unit of monads.

In this way, although both philosophers agree that personal identity has to do with the way in which the subject of action is aware of herself; for the philosopher of Hanover this *conscientia* rests on an ontological or real ground of identity. This makes the self a determined individual, since, as he maintains in his *Nouveaux essais sur l'entendement humain:* "suivant l'ordre des choses, l'identité apparente à la personne même, qui se sent la même, suppose l'identité réelle à chaque *passage prochain,* accompagné de reflexion ou de sentiment du moy: une perception intime et immediate ne pouvant tromper naturellement".[5] The quoted text also implies that neither the personal identity nor the psychological continuity of the individual depends entirely on memory, at least not in the same sense in which Locke understands it,[6] but as a *moyenne*

---

[1] By pointing out these aspects, I acknowledge my intellectual debt with Manuel Sánchez Rodríguez and Neftalí Villanueva Fernández, who have studied the development of these aspects through the analysis of Leibniz's correspondence with Arnauld. In the opinion of these authors, "the unity of my various states in space-time can only be assured if we suppose that there is "the same individual substance" (metaphysical ground), which offers an a priori reason to say that we can truly remain ourselves even when we experiment diverse states and attributes (gnoseological-transcendental ground), that is, that such states and attributes can be considered as predicates that inhere in the same subject (logical ground)" (2011, 16). By situating this first approach within the framework of Leibniz's philosophy of 1686, however, Sánchez and Villanueva left aside the practical characterisation that this notion assumes in his latest works, where Leibniz associates these with the oral quality of the agent.

[2] J. Locke, *Ensayos Sobre El Entendimiento Humano,* trans. E. O'Gorman (México: Fondo de Cultura Económica, 2013). From here on, "Essays". (Essays, II, XXVII, §7).

[3] *Essays*, II, XXVII, §1.

[4] Gottfried Wilhelm Leibniz, *New Essays on Human Understanding,* ed. Peter Remnant and Jonathan Bennett (Glasgow: Cambridge University Press, 1996). From here on "NE". The canonical reference is to Gerhardt's edition (Gottfried Wilhelm Leibniz, *Die Philosophischen Schriften von Leibniz,* ed. C. I. Gerhardt, 7 vols. (Berlin: Hildesheim, 1960)). Frome here on, "GP". (NE, II, 27, §1; GP, V, 213).

[5] NE, II, 27, §10; GP, V, 219.

[6] *Essays*, II, XXVII, §§16-19.

liaison de conscienciosité (*medium bond of consciousness*) that establishes the relation between the personal and the real or ontological identity.[7]

A detailed analysis of this *medium bond of consciousness* leads us to study the perceptual and appetitive nature of monads, insofar as this is indispensable for understanding their individual nature. By doing this analysis we face, therefore, Leibniz's taxonomy of monads, which begins with the distinction between those monads that only have simple perception and appetite (*i.e.*, those whose perceptual and appetitive nature lack clarity and distinction), and those that rise to the level of sensation (*i.e.*, souls).[8] This distinction allows me to formulate a second constitutive level of identity insofar as it lets us talk about the organic-functional unity of living beings. Souls, in fact, possess the ability to subordinate other monads, endowing the living being with an internal teleological structure by virtue of which each organ, despite having different functions, is articulated and integrated into a unity.[9]

Unlike simple monads, whose perceptions and appetites are in a state of perpetual stupefaction, souls possess the quality of elevating some of their perceptions to the degree of sensation, memory, and apperception. The last one, in particular, constitutes a type of phenomenical consciousness, which allows some animals to be aware of some of their most outstanding sensory

---

[7] NE, II, 27, §10; GP, V, 219. Part of the specialised literature on this subject finds serious difficulties when establishing the relationship between personal and real or ontological identity, either because they argue that the Hanoverian does not give convincing arguments in order to oppose a psychological continuity based on memory, as Scheffler argues (Samuel Scheffler, "Leibniz on Personal Identity and Moral Personality," *Studia Leibnitiana* 8, no. 2 (1976), 224-225), or because they point to an apparent inconsistency in identifying the spiritual substance with the person and sustaining, simultaneously, the possibility of altering the latter while preserving the same personal identity, as is stated by Wilson (Margaret Dauler Wilson, "Chapter 25. Leibniz: Self-Consciousness and Immortality in the Paris Notes and After," in *Ideas and Mechanism: Essays on Early Modern Philosophy* (Princeton University Press, 1999), 135-138). These difficulties, however, can be qualified if we consider the distinction between each of these constitutive levels of identity, conceiving the ontological or real identity as something that underlies personal identity, and not as something that is equivalent. A similar position is found in Vailati (Ezio Vailati, "Leibniz's Theory of Personal Identity in the New Essays," *Studia Leibnitiana* 17, no. 1 (1985), 43).

[8] In the "Monadologie" (in Gottfried Wilhelm Leibniz, *Die Philosophischen Schriften von Leibniz*, ed. C. I. Gerhardt, vol. 6 (Berlin: Hildesheim, 1960-1961), §14). From here on, "M". (M, §19; GP, VI, 610).

[9] R. Casales García, "Teleología En La Teoría de Las Máquinas Naturales de Leibniz," in *La Unidad Del Viviente Desde Un Enfoque Interdisciplinario Del Origen de La Vida a La Generación de Hábitos*, ed. H. Velázquez, L. Contreras, and F. Mendoza (México: Tirant Lo Blanch, 2018), 468-469.

impressions[10], as it happens in the case of the boar that Leibniz mentions in his *Nouveaux essais sur l'entendement humain.*[11]

If my interpretation of the Hanoverian is correct, the phenomenical consciousness possessed by souls is indispensable not only for understanding the relationship between the sensitive impressions that living beings receive through their sensitive organs and their corresponding mental representations but also to talk about a kind of organic-sensorial identity that goes beyond mere ontological identity. This second constitutive level of identity, however, is distinguished from personal identity, to the extent that the latter presupposes an agent that is capable not only of being aware of her own perceptions, but also of herself, *i.e.*, that the agent possesses reflective acts of consciousness that allows her to self-ascribe her action and, therefore, to conceive her as a moral agent.[12] With this in mind, this research seeks to analyse which elements of Leibniz's philosophical proposal conform or characterise each of these three constitutive levels of identity, in order to understand in which sense they are present in the relation between *conscientia* and personal identity.

2. Ontological Grounds of Identity

The ontological grounds of identity in Leibniz, lead us both to the individual nature of monads, *i.e.*, their substantial unity, as well as to certain elements of his logic and epistemology, such as the principle of the identity of indiscernibles and the theory of perception are. According to a first characterisation of monads, they seem to be "atoms of substance"[13] or "les unités reelles et absolument

---

[10] Unlike what many authors like McRae, Beleval, and Näert maintain, namely, that apperception is an exclusive act of spirits and that we can identify simple apperception with *conscientia*, in the present chapter, besides pointing out the difference between both kinds of consciousness, I shall defend that animals are able to apperceiving some of their most outstanding sensations, even when it is true that Leibniz denied them reflection and, consequently, a consciousness of themselves and of their actions. See Christian Barth, "Leibniz on Phenomenal Consciousness," *Vivarium* 52, no. 3–4 (2014), https://doi.org/10.1163/15685349-12341280, 346; and Mark Kulstad, "Leibniz, Animals, and Apperception," *Studia Leibnitiana* 13, no. 1 (1981), 33.

[11] See NE, II, 21, §5; GP, VI, 159.

[12] See: R. Casales García, *Justicia, Amor e Identidad En La Ontología Monadológica de Leibniz* (Granada: Comares, 2018).

[13] Although the philosopher of Hannover advanced several criticisms to Pierre Gassendi's atomism, it should be noted that, as Andreas Blank shows Andreas Blank, "Sennert and Leibniz on Animate Atoms," in *Machines of Nature and Corporeal Substances in Leibniz*, ed. Justin E. H. Smith and Ohad Nachtomy, The New Synthese Historical Library (Dordrecht: Springer Netherlands, 2011), https://doi.org/10.1007/978-94-007-0041-3_8, 116), atomism is not entirely alien to his metaphysics, as it can be noticed in his

destituées de parties, qui soyent les sources des actions, et les premiers principes absolus de la composition des choses, et comme les derniers elemens de l'analyse des choses substantielles".[14] Each monad, in Leibniz's words, constitutes a "substance véritablement une, unique, sujet primitif de la vie et action, tousjours doué de perception et appétition, toujours renfermant avec ce qu'il est la tendance à ce qu'il sera, pour représenter toute autre chose qui sera".[15] Monads, therefore, are complete dynamic entities whose identity is based on their individual nature.

What does it mean, however, that monads are simple substances that constitute the "veritables Atomes de la Nature"[16]? In which sense does Leibniz sustain that monads are complete entities, *i.e.*, beings whose being involves both their actual and past being and their tendency to what they will be? One of the key points for answering these questions lies in Leibniz's notion of completeness, a notion inherited from Suárez that has appeared in Leibniz since his works of youth. This notion appears, quite concretely, in his 1663 *Disputatio Metaphysica de Principio Individui*, where he not only rejects both Aquinas and Duns Scotus by denying that the principle of individuation is in the *materia signata* or the *haecceitas*, but also sustains that "omne individuum suâ totâ Entitate individuatur".[17] Hence, monads must possess "une notion si accomplice, qu'elle soit suffisante, à comprendre et à en faire deduire tous les predicats du sujet à qui cette notion est attribuée".[18]

When we talk about individuality in terms of completeness, *i.e.*, of its *notio complete*, we refer fundamentally to three things: i) a truth-logical completeness, that can be understood through Leibniz's theory of truth; ii) a dynamic completeness through which monads are conceived as principles of their actions and therefore, as spontaneous; and iii) an existential-expressive

---

correspondence with De Volder, specifically when he defines simple substances as "a/tomon au/toplhrou/n, *Atom per se completum seu se ipsum complens. Unde sequitur esse Atom vitale seu Atomum habens e/ntele/xeia. Atom idem est quod vere unum*" (*Letter to De Volder of June 6 of 1701*, GP, II, 224).

[14] *Système nouveau de la nature et de la communication des substances*, GP, IV, 482.

[15] In *Double infinité chez Pascal et monade* (in Gottfried Wilhelm Leibniz, *Textes Inédits d'après Les Manuscrites de La Bibliothèque Proviciale de Hannovre*, ed. Gastón Grua (Paris: Presses Universitaires de France, 1948), 554). From here on, "Grua".

[16] M, §3; GP, VI, 607.

[17] In *Disputatio*, (in Gottfried Wilhelm Leibniz, *Sämtliche Schriften Und Briefe*, ed. the Akademie der Wissenschaften (Darmstadt-Berlin: Akademie-Verlag, 1875), §4). From here on, "A". (A VI, 1, 11).

[18] *Discours de métaphysique*, §8, A VI, 4B, 1540. See also: *Letter to Arnauld from July 14, 1686* (in Gottfried Wilhelm Leibniz, *Der Briefwechsel Mit Antoine Arnauld*, trans. R. Finster (Hamburg: Felix Meiner, 1997), 112). From here on, "Finster".

completeness by virtue of which the individuality of each monad is assumed in relation to its expressive nature, *i.e.*, as a "miroir vivant perpetual de l'univers".[19] Given this first sense of completeness, it is said that monads are complete entities of an individual nature insofar as, in the words of Leibniz, …

> …toute prédication véritable a quelque fondement dans la nature des choses, et lors qu'une proposition n'est pas identique, c'est-à-dire lors que le prédicat n'est pas compris expressément dans le sujet, il faut qu'il y soit compris virtuellement, et c'est ce que les philosophes appellent *inesse*. Ainsi il faut que le terme du sujet enferme tousjours celuy du prédicat, en sorte que celuy qui entendroit parfaitement la notion du sujet, jugeroit aussi que le prédicat luy appartient.[20]

The complete notion of an individual substance, in this sense, "*seu talis, ut ex ea ratio [reddi] possit omnium praedicatorum ejusdem subjecti cui tribui potest haec notio, erit notio Substantiae individualis et contra*".[21] According to this truth-logical connotation of completeness, we can only say that the attribution of a predicate P to a subject S is true when the notion of P is included within the notion of S.[22] This implies that the complete entity, according to Manuel Sánchez and Neftalí Villanueva, "not only allows a thing to be what it is, but mainly that a thing be what *only* it can be, in such a way that, at least for created things, essence is indistinguishable from existence".[23]

Since all the predicates that can be attributed to a substance can be deduced from its notions, in the sense that each monad possesses a complete notion that identifies itself as this or that individual, it follows that the notion of each simple substance "contient tousjours des traces de ce qui luy est jamais arrivé et des marques de ce qui luy arrivera à tout jamais".[24] This specific consequence leads us to a second meaning of completeness, that which alludes both to the temporal continuity of substances and their dynamic nature. Temporal continuity, on the one hand, guarantees the subsistence of monads through time, where past, present, and future maintain certain unity or harmony. The subject of action, despite all modifications it experiments over

---

[19] M, §56; GP, VI, 616.

[20] *Discours de métaphysique*, §8, A VI, 4B, 1540.

[21] *Principium scientiae humanae*, A, VI, 4A, 672.

[22] *De natura veritatis, contingentiae et indifferentiae atque de libertate et praedeterminatione*, A VI, 4B, 1515.

[23] Manuel Sánchez Rodríguez and Alberto Neftalí Villanueva Fernández, "El fundamento lógico-metafísico de la identidad personal en la filosofía de Leibniz en torno a 1686: análisis, influencia y revisiones," *Thémata: Revista de filosofía*, no. 46 (2012): 240.

[24] *Remarques sur la lettre de M. Arnauld*, Finster, 84.

time, conserves its individuality at every single moment, since, as Leibniz stated in §22 of his *Monadologie*, "comme tout present état d'une substance simple est naturellement une suite de son état precedent, tellement que le present y est gros de l'avenir".[25]

This holistic understanding of the individual, on the other hand, not only considers the totality of past, present and future predicates that can be attributed to each simple substance, but it also takes into account its dynamic nature, *i.e.*, the entire series of modifications that arise within it. Since "naturellement une substance ne sauroit ester sans action",[26] as Leibniz maintains in his *Nouveaux essais sur l'entendement humain*, it follows that the *notio completa* of each individual "envelope tous ses phenomenes, en sorte que rien ne sçauroit arriver à une substance qui ne luy naisse de son propre fond".[27] According to Leibniz, every monad is a primitive unit of action that, in accordance with his *Principes de la nature et de la grâce fondés en raison*, ...

> ...ne sauroit être discernée d'une autre que par les qualités et actions internes, lesquelles ne peuvent être autre chose que ses *perceptions* (c'est-à-dire les représentations du composé, ou de ce qui est dehors dans le simple), et ses *appetitions* (c'est-à-dire ses tendences d'une perception à l'autre) qui sont les principes du changement. Car la simplicité de la substance n'empêche point la multiplicité des modifications, qui se doivent trouver ensemble dans cette même substance simple ; et elles doivent consister dans la variété des rapports aux choses qui sont au dehors. C'est comme dans un *centre* ou point, tout simple qu'il est, se trouvent une infinité d'angles formés par les lignes qui y concourent.[28]

By considering the latter we can clearly infer two conclusions: first, that "tout ce qui arrive à l'ame et à chaque substance, est une suite de sa notion, donc l'idée même ou essence de l'ame porte que toutes ses apparences ou perceptions luy doivent naistre (*sponte*) de sa propre nature;[29] and second, that monads are centres or metaphysical points whose individual nature involves both the complete series of their present, past and future perceptions, and the

---

[25] GP, VI, 610.

[26] NE, Preface; GP, V, 46.

[27] *Letter to Arnauld dated between November 28 and December 8, 1686*, Finster, 192.

[28] *Principes de la nature et de la grâce fondés en raison*, (in Gottfried Wilhelm Leibniz, *Principes de La Nature et de La Grâce Fondés En Raison*. Principes de La Philosophie Ou Monadologie, ed. André Robinet (París: Presses Universitaires de France, 1954), §2). From here on, "Robinet I". (Robinet I, 29).

[29] *Discours de métaphysique*, §XXXIII, A VI, 4B, 1582.

tendency or law of the series that guarantees their substantial unity.[30] While the former implies that "toutes les substances simples ou Monades creées, car ells une certaine perfection(e)/xousi to\ e)ntelej), il y a une suffisance (au)ta/rkeia) qui les rend aources de leur actions internes et pour ainsi dire des Automates incorporels";[31] the latter provides the basis to articulate his theory of perception with his *notio completa*, and both with his notion of personal identity.

Taking both characterisations into account we discover that Leibniz's notions of spontaneity and *notio completa* involve a third sense of completeness that makes an explicit reference to the expressive nature of monads and, consequently, to their compossible being. According to this third sense of completeness, Leibniz states that "toute substance est comme un monde entire et comme un miroir de Dieu ou bien de tout l'univers, qu'elle exprime chacune à sa façon, à peu pres comme une même ville est diversement representée selon les differentes situations de celuy qui la regarde".[32] In this way, rather than being isolated and unrelated entities, monads are relational beings whose individual notions presuppose their interconnection with the complete series of individuals that compound the world.[33]

Even when Leibniz states in his *Monadology* that "les Monades n'ont point de fenétres, par lesquelles quelque chose y puisse entrer ou sortir",[34] characterisation that defines exactly what he means with his notion of spontaneity, it is also true that this spontaneity or self-sufficiency can only be possible insofar as monads possess a relational or expressive nature.[35] This is a reason to affirm that each monad "is a thing in itself in order to be a being for another".[36]

---

[30] *Essais de Theodicée*, III, §291; GP VI, 289.

[31] M, §18; GP VI, 609-610.

[32] *Discours de métaphysique*, §9, A VI, 4B, 1542; see also: *Letter to Landgrave Ernst of February 1686*, Finster, 4.

[33] *Primae veritates*, (in Gottfried Wilhelm Leibniz, *Opuscules et Fragmentes Inédits de Leibniz. Extraits Des Manuscrits de La Bibliothèque Royale de Hanovre*, ed. L. Couturat (Hildesheim: Olms, 1991), 521). From here on, "Couturat".

[34] §7, GP, VI, 607-608.

[35] R. Casales García, "El Conflicto Entre La Espontaneidad y La Comunicación Entre Las Sustancias: Un Tema Clave Para Comprender El Paso de La Ontología Leibniziana a Su Filosofía Práctica," in *Libertad y Necesidad En Leibniz. Ensayos Sobre El Laberinto Leibniziano de La Libertad*, ed. R. Casales García and R. Solís (Puebla: UPAEP, 2015), 210.

[36] F. Duque, "La Fuga Del Universo," in *G. W. Leibniz. Analogía y Expresión*, ed. Q. Racionero and C. Roldán (Madrid: Editorial Complutense, 1995), 299.

3. Organic-sensorial Identity

While the ontological or real identity of monads consists in their individual nature, "quorum realitas sita est in percipientium secum ipsis (pro diversis temporibus) et cum caeteris percipientibus harmonia",[37] as can be seen in Leibniz's correspondence with De Volder, the second constitutive level of identity presupposes the organic-sensory structure of living beings. It is an organic-sensorial structure in the way that every living being has a constitutive unity that intertwines the totality of organs that compose the body in order to articulate them with the perceptual and appetitive nature of its dominant monad or soul, as we can see in the descriptions of sensation that Leibniz advances in *Monadologie* §25 and *Principes de la nature et de la grâce fondés en raison* §4:

> Aussi voyons nous que la Nature a donné des perceptions relevées aux animaux par les soins, qu'elle a pris de leur fournir des organes, qui ramassent plusieurs rayons de lumière ou plusieurs ondulations de l'air pour les faire avoir plus d'efficace par leur union. Il y a quelque chose d'approchant dans l'odeur, dans le goût et dans l'attouchement et peut-être dans quantité d'autres sens, qui nous sont inconnus. Et j'expliqueray tantost, comment ce qui passe dans l'Ame représenté ce qui se fait dans les organes.[38]

And:

> Chaque Monade, avec un corps particulier fait une substance vivante. Ainsi il n'y a pas seulement de la vie partout, jointe aux membres ou organes ; mais même il y en a une infinité de degrés dans les Monades, les unes dominat plus ou moins sur les autres : mais quand la Monade a des organes si ajustés, que par leur moyen il y a du relief et du distingué dans les impressions qu'ils reçoivent et par conséquent dans les perceptions qui les représentent (comme par exemple, lorsque par le moyen de la figure des humeurs des yeux, les rayons de la lumière sont concentrés et agissent avec plus de force) cela peut aller jusqu'au *sentiment*, c'est-à-dire jusqu'à une perception accompagnée de mémoire, à savoir, dont un certain écho demeure longtemps pour se faire entendre dans l'occasion ; et un tel vivant est appelé *animal*, comme sa Monade est appelée une *Ame*.[39]

---

[37] *Letter to De Volder of June 30, 1704*; GP, II, 270.

[38] M, §25; GP, VI, 611.

[39] *Principes de la nature et de la grâce fondés en raison*, §4, Robinet I, 33-35.

While the first passage describes sensation in terms of the relation between the most outstanding perceptions of a living being and the organic structure of its sensorial organs, through which it is possible to obtain sensible impressions of greater force and efficiency; the second passage emphasises two things: the relation of subordination that exists between the different kinds of monads that compose a living being, among which the soul is conceived as a central or dominant monad that guarantees the *vinculum substantiale*[40]; and the correlation between the force and distinction of the sensible impressions and their corresponding mental representations, whose force is susceptible of being stored in the memory in order to be reproduced occasionally. In both cases, we presuppose a pre-established harmony between body and soul, in such a way that the amount of force or intensity of my sensitive impressions corresponds to the amount of clarity and distinction of their corresponding mental representations.[41]

In order to heighten my perceptions to the grade of sensibility and memory, which is what distinguishes souls from simple monads, it is necessary that some of them not only possess something distinctive but also possess sufficient mental strength to get my attention caught and, consequently, be sensibly apperceived.[42] We must consider, however, that a greater degree of distinction in our perceptions, although enough for our perceptions to be heightened to the level of sensation,[43] is not a sufficient condition to have apperception, as Jorgensen argues in a first approach to the notion of apperception. Following Barth's approach to phenomenical consciousness, there are two more conditions that a sensation must fulfil in order to be apperceived: that the sensation has the necessary degree of distinction in order to generate a habitual disposition, something that is only possible through a certain type of reproductive memory; and that this disposition has to be able to get our attention caught.

Regarding memory, we can observe that Leibniz distinguishes three types of memory: a virtual or ontological memory that guarantees continuity in the flux of perceptions, insofar as every monad conserves the entire traces of its past perceptions; reminiscence, which is in charge of "reproducing" previous sensations[44] without the object being present again[45]; and remembrance or *souvenir*, by means of which the subject of action not only notices the existence

---

[40] *Letter to De Volder of June 20, 1703*; GP, II, 252.

[41] *Principes de la nature et de la grâce fondés en raison*, §3; Robinet I, 33.

[42] Christian Barth, "Leibniz on Phenomenal Consciousness," *Vivarium* 52, no. 3–4 (2014), https://doi.org/10.1163/15685349-12341280, 40. (NE, II, 21, §5; GP, VI, 159).

[43] *Specimen inventorum admirandis naturae generalis arcanis*, A, VI, 4B, 1625.

[44] NE, I, 1, §5; GP, V, 73.

[45] NE, II, 19, §1; GP, V, 147.

of the external objects of his sensations but also his own being.[46] Although the first type of memory establishes a relation with the first constitutive level of identity, making possible for rational beings to remember some of their past perceptions, as Leibniz stated in his correspondence with Arnauld,[47] it is clear that this ontological or virtual memory is not related with sensible apperception or phenomenical consciousness, since it is within every monad in general, without considering if their perceptions are totally confusing or if they can be heightened to the degree of sensation.

Something different happens with remembrance or *souvenir*, since this type of memory presupposes that the subject is capable of reflection. Reflection is a capacity that the Hanoverian reserves for the specific case of spirits. Provided that Leibniz recognises that some animals can be aware of some of their sensations, *i.e.*, that they have a phenomenical consciousness even when they are not capable of reflection, it follows that the type of memory that the Hanoverian primarily associates with sensation and its corresponding kind of apperception is reminiscence. Insofar as it allows the subject to reproduce or repeat a previous sensation "with its original intentional content, without the intentional object itself being present". In order to apperceive some of our sensations, consequently, it is necessary for sensation to have enough mental strength to produce "l'effect d'une longe *habitude*, ou de beaucoup de perceptions mediocres reiterées",[48] so that the soul can notice its content.

Given this habit, reminiscence is understood as a certain kind of reproductive memory that "fournit une espèce de *Consecution* aux Ames, qui imite la raison",[49] insofar as it allows the monad to establish a connection between the most outstanding apperceived phenomena, as can be noted in *Essais de Theodicée* §65.[50] Phenomenical consciousness, however, is only possible when the sensation is not only accompanied by memory but also with a certain kind of attention that, by being understood as a cognitive tendency,[51] allows the living being to notice the content of their perceptions. Attention, in this sense, is introduced as a third condition for sensible or phenomenical apperception, something that agrees with a characterisation that Leibniz makes of sensation

---

[46] *Discours de métaphysique*, §34, A, VI, 4B, 1584.
[47] *Letter to Arnauld of July 14, 1686*; Finster, 150.
[48] M, §27; GP, VI, 611.
[49] M, §26; GP, VI, 611.
[50] GP, VI, 87; see also: *Principes de la nature et de la grâce fondés en raison*, §5; Robinet I, 39.
[51] Barth, "Leibnizian Conscientia and its Cartesian Roots", 348.

in a brief work of 1710, according to which "sensio enim est perception, quae aliquid distincti involvit, et cum attentione et memoria conjuncta est".[52]

By considering the former characterisation of sensation, it follows that we can only talk about sensation and phenomenical apperception when the percipient not only has distinct perceptions and the capacity to reproduce them, *i.e.*, reminiscence, but also the capacity to pay attention to them, either voluntarily or involuntarily. In either case, in Leibniz's opinion, "nous avons tousjours des objects qui frappent nos yeux ou nos oreilles, et par consequent l'ame en est touchée aussi, sans que nous y prennions garde, parce que nostre attention est bandée à d'autres objects, jusqu'à ce que l'object devienne assés fort pour l'attirer à soy en redoublant son action ou par quelque autre raison".[53] In this way, the organic-sensorial identity of a living being involves both a teleological-organic structure, through which the living being is enabled to have sensitive impressions of a higher degree and a perceptual and appetitive nature that allows its soul to attend to its most outstanding sensations.

4. Personal Identity and *Conscientia*

The type of phenomenical consciousness or sensible apperception that we found through the analysis of the second constitutive level of identity, *i.e.*, the organic sensorial identity of a living being, however, reaches a greater degree of complexity in the case of spirits, whose reflexive and rational nature allows them not only to be aware of the content of their perceptions but also of themselves as percipients. Spirits, besides sensible apperception, possess *conscientia*, a concept that Leibniz understands as "reflexio in actionem, seu memoria actionis nostrae, ita ut cogitemus nostra esse" that "involvit hoc ipsam substantiam veram seu τὸ ego".[54] According to this definition, *conscientia* is the reflective act of memory that accompanies some of the inner acts of the spirits,[55] allowing them to recognise their own self and to ascribe the causality of their own actions, in the sense that only...

> ... l'ame intelligente connoissant ce qu'elle est, et pouvant dire ce MOY, qui dit beaucoup, ne demeure pas seulement et subsiste Metaphysiquement, bien plus les autres, mais elle demeure encor la même moralement et fait le même personnage. Car c'est le souvenir, ou

---

[52] *Materia in se sumta seu nuda...*; GP, VII, 330.

[53] NE, II, 1, §14; GP, V, 105.

[54] *Table de Définitions*; Couturat, 495.

[55] NE, GP, V, 220-221.

la connoissance de ce moy, qui la rend capable de chastiment et de recompense.[56]

While sensible apperception is a first-order act that accompanies some of our sensations, *conscientia* is a reflective act of second-order that accompanies only some of our apperceived sensations. For Leibniz, in fact, spirits do not have *conscientia* of all their actions, which is demonstrated in the following way: if spirits were conscious of all their acts, that would imply that for each reflection there is, in turn, another act of reflection, but that that would lead us to an infinite regress that blocks progression towards new thoughts.[57] Despite this latter observation, spirits "nos semper nostrae cogitationes ita conscios esse, ut si qui nos admoneat, aut ipsi nos admoneamus cogitationis nostrae praecedentis sciamus nos eam habuisse".[58] Whether reflection is motivated by an external cause, or by an internal cause,[59] the reflective acts of *conscientia* are essential to talk about our personal identity, insofar as they allow us to attend to what is inside of us.

As a reflective act of memory, *conscientia* consists on the attention that we give to what is in us, including innate ideas,[60] which means that "nous sommes innés, pour ainsi dire, à nous-mêmes" in the same way that "les idées et les verités nous sont inées, comme des inclinations, des dispositions, des habitudes ou des virtualités naturelles".[61] All of this implies that spirits not only attend to the specific content of some of their perceptual acts, as it happens in the phenomenical consciousness, but also that they are capable of self-ascribing the causality of those acts. If my approach is correct, it follows that the last statement allows us to infer two conclusions about spirits: first, that some of their inner actions, besides being spontaneous, are free and, therefore, intentional; and second, that spirits, as subjects of action, can be conceived as moral agents.[62] Through the notion of *conscientia*, in Leibniz words, "non seulement je me represente mon action, mais encor je pense que c'est moy ou qui la fais, ou qui l'ay faite".[63]

Since only rational substances have this type of reflexive acts of *conscientia*, it follows that only spirits can impute themselves the causality of their acts, a thesis that is required not only to conceive them as moral agents but also to

---

[56] *Discours de métaphysique*, §34; A, VI, 4B, 1584.
[57] Barth, "Leibnizian Conscientia and its Cartesian Roots", 223. See also: GP, VI, 600.
[58] *Reflexio*, A, VI, 4B, 1471.
[59] Barth, "Leibnizian Conscientia and its Cartesian Roots", 226-227.
[60] Kulstad, "Leibniz, Animals, and Apperception", 33-34.
[61] NE, GP, V, 45.
[62] Barth, "Leibnizian Conscientia and its Cartesian Roots", 229.
[63] *Carta a Burnett del 2 de agosto de 1704*; GP, III, 299. See also: M, §30; GP, VI, 612.

constitute, by virtue of that agency, their own personal identity. Unlike mere souls, whose causality is oriented according to their instincts and their empirical associations,[64] spirits are able to act according to their free will, *i.e.*, to determine their actions in accordance with their own reason, choosing what, after deliberation, appears to them as the greatest apparent good.[65] Hence, only spirits are able to conceive their own existence, in Salas's opinion, "as a series of emergent acts that respond to a decision of the agent".[66]

Bibliography

Barth, Christian. "Apperception in the New Essays Concerning Human Understanding. A Critique of the Reflective Account and a Sketch of an Alternative Proposal." In *Natur Und Subjekt: IX Internationaler Leibniz-Kongress Unter Der Schirmherrschaft Des Bundespräsidenten, Hannover, Vorträge*, edited by H. Breger, 1:37–43. Hannover: Gottfried-Wilhelm-Leibniz-Gesellschaft, 2011.

———. "Leibniz on Phenomenal Consciousness." *Vivarium* 52, no. 3–4 (2014): 333–57. https://doi.org/10.1163/15685349-12341280.

———. "Leibnizian Conscientia and its Cartesian Roots." *Studia Leibnitiana* 43, no. 2 (2011): 216–36. https://doi.org/10.25162/sl-2011-0015.

Beleval, Y. *Études Leibniziennes. De Leibniz à Hegel*. París: Editions Gallimard, 1976.

Blank, Andreas. "Sennert and Leibniz on Animate Atoms." In *Machines of Nature and Corporeal Substances in Leibniz*, edited by Justin E. H. Smith and Ohad Nachtomy, 115–30. The New Synthese Historical Library. Dordrecht: Springer Netherlands, 2011. https://doi.org/10.1007/978-94-007-0041-3_8.

Casales García, R. "El Conflicto Entre La Espontaneidad y La Comunicación Entre Las Sustancias: Un Tema Clave Para Comprender El Paso de La Ontología Leibniziana a Su Filosofía Práctica." In *Libertad y Necesidad En Leibniz. Ensayos Sobre El Laberinto Leibniziano de La Libertad*, edited by R. Casales García and R. Solís, 203–18. Puebla: UPAEP, 2015.

———. *Justicia, Amor e Identidad En La Ontología Monadológica de Leibniz*. Granada: Comares, 2018.

———. "Teleología En La Teoría de Las Máquinas Naturales de Leibniz." In *La Unidad Del Viviente Desde Un Enfoque Interdisciplinario Del Origen de La Vida a La Generación de Hábitos*, edited by H. Velázquez, L. Contreras, and F. Mendoza, 467–80. México: Tirant Lo Blanch, 2018.

Duque, F. "La Fuga Del Universo." In *G. W. Leibniz. Analogía y Expresión*, edited by Q. Racionero and C. Roldán, 289–305. Madrid: Editorial Complutense, 1995.

---

[64] NE, II, 33, §18; GP, V, 252.
[65] *De libertate a necessitate in eligendo*; A, VI, 4B, 1450.
[66] Jaime de Salas, "Introducción," in *Escritos de Filosofía Jurídica y Política*, by Gottfried Wilhelm Leibniz, ed. Jaime de Salas (Madrid: Biblioteca Nueva, 2009), 54.

Kulstad, Mark. "Leibniz, Animals, and Apperception." *Studia Leibnitiana* 13, no. 1 (1981): 25–60.

Leibniz, Gottfried Wilhelm. *Der Briefwechsel Mit Antoine Arnauld.* Translated by R. Finster. Hamburg: Felix Meiner, 1997. [= Finster]

———. *Die Philosophischen Schriften von Leibniz.* Edited by C. I. Gerhardt. 7 vols. Berlin: Hildesheim, 1960-1961. [= GP]

———. *New Essays on Human Understanding.* Edited by Peter Remnant and Jonathan Bennett. Glasgow: Cambridge University Press, 1996. [= NE]

———. *Opuscules et Fragmentes Inédits de Leibniz. Extraits Des Manuscrits de La Bibliothèque Royale de Hanovre.* Edited by L. Couturat. Hildesheim: Olms, 1991. [= Couturat]

———. *Principes de La Nature et de La Grâce Fondés En Raison. Principes de La Philosophie Ou Monadologie.* Edited by André Robinet. París: Presses Universitaires de France, 1954. [= Robinet I]

———. *Sämtliche Schriften Und Briefe.* Edited by the Akademie der Wissenschaften. Darmstadt-Berlin: Akademie-Verlag, 1875-1890. [= A]

———. *Textes Inédits d'après Les Manuscrites de La Bibliothèque Proviciale de Hannovre.* Edited by Gastón Grua. Paris: Presses Universitaires de France, 1948. [= Grua]

Locke, J. *Ensayos Sobre El Entendimiento Humano.* Translated by E. O'Gorman. México: Fondo de Cultura Económica, 2013. [= Essays]

McRae, R. F. *Leibniz: Perception, Apperception, and Thought.* Toronto: University of Toronto Press, 1976.

Naert, Emilienne. *Mémoire et Conscience de Soi Selon Leibniz.* París: Libraire Philosophique J. Vrin, 1961.

Salas, Jaime de. "Introducción." In *Escritos de Filosofía Jurídica y Política,* by Gottfried Wilhelm Leibniz, 8–60. edited by Jaime de Salas. Madrid: Biblioteca Nueva, 2009.

Sánchez Rodríguez, Manuel, and Alberto Neftalí Villanueva Fernández. "El fundamento lógico-metafísico de la identidad personal en la filosofía de Leibniz en torno a 1686: análisis, influencia y revisiones." *Thémata: Revista de filosofía,* no. 46 (2012): 237–45.

———. "La estupefacción de Arnauld: el fundamento lógico-metafísico de la identidad personal en la filosofía de Leibniz en torno a 1686." *Agora: Papeles de filosofía* 30, no. 1 (2011): 11–30.

Scheffler, Samuel. "Leibniz on Personal Identity and Moral Personality." *Studia Leibnitiana* 8, no. 2 (1976): 219–40.

Vailati, Ezio. "Leibniz's Theory of Personal Identity in the New Essays." *Studia Leibnitiana* 17, no. 1 (1985): 36–43.

Wilson, Margaret Dauler. "Chapter 25. Leibniz: Self-Consciousness and Immortality in the Paris Notes and After." In *Ideas and Mechanism: Essays on Early Modern Philosophy,* 373–87. Princeton University Press, 1999.

Chapter 5

A Critical Review of the Structure of
Scientific Knowledge in George Berkeley:
An essay Towards a New Theory of Vision

Laura Benítez Grobet

Instituto de Investigaciones Filosóficas, UNAM

Abstract: Berkeley's theory of vision is relevant not only to articulate his epistemology but also to stimulate the development of psychology. This empirical and psychological proposal also reveals that even when mathematics can be a useful instrument that, correctly applied, can contribute to the development of knowledge, according to Benítez, Berkeley recommends that we need to understand its limits at the level of acquisition of our sensible ideas. This chapter, then, shows how Berkeley's ideas on vision generated an ever-bigger gulf between the theoretical and the practical accounts of perception.

Keywords: Berkeley, perception, theory of vision, empiricism, psychology.

***

1. Introduction

Berkeley states in the *New Theory of Vision* that the geometrical-mathematical approach to optical theories presents very specific limitations, therefore he proposes a different point of view in order to explain fundamental optical problems. That point of view is, as we say today, a psychological one.

2. Berkeley empiricism in *The new Theory of Vision*

By analysing the optical theory of Berkeley we can come to the conclusion that for him the most important problems of science in his time and particularly of optical science are their foundations as well as their methods. From his perspective, the foundations of knowledge have to be empirical ones. This entails that we do not have previous ideas in the intellect, but only those that we acquire by experience and of course we cannot have in our mind theories or abstract ideas responsible for the operations of our spirit, independently of our consciousness of them.

We have also to be alert about the limits of mathematical knowledge, that many authors, in the time of Berkeley, considered the most solid foundation for science. For him, mathematics is only a hypothetical construct and not really necessarily true. So this is its limitation with respect to optical science.

Moreover, for Berkeley, optical science is contingent in two senses: not only because we acquire visual perceptions empirically, but because the constant relations between those perceptions are submitted to a great diversity of circumstances. We can hence come to the conclusion that those relations or connections are not necessary but contingent ones.

In order to understand those central ideas in Berkeley's proposal, we have to advance in the characterisation of empiricism as is presented in *New Theory of Vision*.

As we know one of the principal aims of this essay by Berkeley is to explain how we can perceive with the sense of vision, distance, the magnitude and the position of objects. Nevertheless, those ideas in particular are not objects of direct visual perception; so the experience that we have of them is mediated by our habitual connection with other ideas that give rise to our judgments about the magnitude, distance and position of objects.

Having this fundamental empiricism as a departing point, it is not strange that Berkeley severely criticises some mathematicians who considered that in the mind exists some kind of "natural geometry" (angles of convergence and divergence) that allows us to calculate the distance of objects. For these mathematicians, even when we might be limited by averted vision, the tacit calculus allows us to navigate successfully through distances.

For Berkeley, this is a false supposition because if we are not conscious of a mathematical instrument existing in our minds, we cannot use it at all. For Berkeley, it is clear that children and beasts can perceive an object near or far, not because of geometry and its demonstrations, but because of the habitude of connection between ideas that we observe, which always go together:

> What seems to have misled the writers of optics in this matter is that they imagine men judge of distance as they do of a conclusion in mathematics, betwixt which and the premises it is indeed absolutely requisite there be an apparent, necessary connection: but it is far otherwise in the sudden judgments men make of distance. We are not to think that brutes and children, or even grown reasonable men,

whenever they perceive an object to approach, or depart from them, do it by virtue of geometry and demonstration.[1]

It is interesting that Berkeley uses an argument very close to the argument that Locke used against innate ideas. This is the case, in my opinion, because both authors reject some theories that admit the existence of some concepts or structures in the mind functioning independently of experience and of human consciousness. Those proposals are contrary to the foundations of empiricism. Thus, it is important to underline that Berkeley explains the specific mechanism through which we construct the vision of distance, position and magnitude of objects, solely through experience, even in the case of averted vision. In the case of distance, he says:

> The eye, or (to speak truly) the mind, perceiving only the confusion itself, without ever considering the cause from which it proceeds, doth constantly annex the same degree of distance to the same degree of confusion. Whether that confusion be occasioned by converging or by diverging rays, it matters not.[2]

With respect to the position or situation of objects, Berkeley refers us to the Molyneux problem, in order to demonstrate that only through experience a blind person can acquire tactile ideas. And finally, when he receives the faculty of vision he is aware that there is some connection between those two different kinds of perceptions and that everybody uses the same words for the ideas that proceed from tangible perception as well for those that proceed from visual perception. That, therefore, explains that the blind man that comes to acquire vision puts those different kinds of ideas in connection following the same human prejudice.

> The objects to which he had hitherto been used to apply the terms *up* and *down, high* and *low,* were such only as affected or were some way perceived by his touch: but the proper objects of vision make a new set of ideas, perfectly distinct and different from the former, and which can in no sort make themselves perceived by touch. There, therefore, nothing at all that could induce him to think those terms applicable to them: nor would he ever think it till such time as he had observed their connexion with tangible objects, and the same prejudice began to

---

[1] George Berkeley, "An Essay Towards a New Theory of Vision," in *George Berkeley Works*, ed. M. R. Ayers (London: Every Man's Library, 1975), 12.
[2] Berkeley, "An Essay Towards a New Theory of Vision.", 16.

insinuate itself into his understanding, which from their infancy had grown up in the understandings of other men.[3]

With the same argument, Berkeley sustains that there is no necessary connection between the tangible magnitude and the visual one and that only experience and habits can put them together.

The strong empiricism in Berkeley is based upon two interesting principles: the principle of heterogeneity of sensible ideas and the principle that vision is not another thing but an analogous structure to verbal language.

In relation to the first principle (that of heterogeneity), Berkeley considers that tangible objects and visual ones are completely different and the experience that we have of each group of objects is so different, that we can perceive something as multiple through the sense vision and as a unity through the sense of touch. Of course, these senses are not the same as an object, though we give them the same object and name because of our presuppositions.

In relation to the second principle, Berkeley considers that the ideas of vision are some kind of language. He thinks that the words signify the same as the things which they refer to and that we do not perceive in the first instance things in their proper nature; likewise, the visual ideas are signs of the tangible ones and we do not perceive them in their proper nature. We then put them together and give them the same name.

But because of the fact that we give the same name to ideas so diverse as those of the senses of vision and touch, we cannot come to the conclusion that they have something in common or that they share the same nature, because they are not common ideas to the senses of vision and touch, not even ideas of vision or touch with common properties.

This is the reason why Berkeley not only criticises Locke's abstract ideas but other abstract concepts of physics such as "vacuum space" or "tridimensional space"; for some mathematicians can be perceived through the senses of vision and touch.

Finally, Berkeley considers that language is a product of human convention subject to ambiguity; but God has established the "visual language" as a sign of tangible ideas, so it is universal and does not admit ambiguity. However, even though the relation between a visual sign and a tangible object is not necessary, it does not admit ambiguity. So this relation ends up being very close in meaning and, in this respect, Berkeley sustains that the relation in the mind

---

[3] Ibid., 36-37.

between visual ideas and tangible ones is very quick and subtle. Of course, this shows some tension in the face of the principle of heterogeneity of our ideas.

3. Berkeley's instrumentalism in the *New Theory of Vision*

As stated above, Berkeley sustains a very strong controversy about the structure of optical science. He refers not only to the weakness of their physical foundations as mere conjectures but also that their mathematical principles are mere suppositions. Berkeley thus considers that optical science requires other foundations; because it is not possible to infer from the mere geometrical analysis that distance is an immediate percept of our vision *i.e.* that we can see it (the distance).

Hence, the geometrical approach to the science of optics is not capable of giving us a complete account of the distance of objects. For Berkeley, the lines and angles that we use in order to measure distances do not have a real existence because they are mere hypotheses constructed by mathematicians. In fact, those lines and angles are not even perceived by the sense of vision, so it is impossible for the mind to make judgments about the real distance of an object using those hypotheses.

In brief, mathematics is only an instrument and its utility is related to the use that we give it knowing its limits. Mathematicians accordingly have a false presupposition when they consider that the only causes that the mind takes into account for making judgments about distance are limited to their postulates of angles and lines. This is due to the fact that they do not know the true nature of vision.

It is clear that Berkeley's proposal on optics is very far from the physical and mathematical general theories of his time, when he considered them incomplete. Berkeley judges these theories as insufficient since those scientific men who formulate them have not taken into account some important facts of mental order (psychological ones) that he has discovered. For example, the subtle connection between heterogeneous ideas on the one hand, or the confusion or distinction in relation to distance perception on the other hand.

Berkeley deems that mathematicians ignore the real operations of the mind: they get lost considering that the mind simply applies some geometrical laws or abstract ideas in order to perceive the distance, the magnitude or the position of objects.

Then, for Berkeley, we have to remember that in the first place, it is necessary to separate the ideas coming from vision from tactile ideas. He tells us that we should aim not only to understand that distance, magnitude and position are primarily perceived by the sense of touch and only afterwards by the sense of vision; but he also wants us to be aware of the fact that our computation systems are nothing but conventions. Our systems are useful instruments when we use them in our judgments on apparent magnitudes and we take them as a real foundation the tangible extension.

Moreover, Berkeley considers that mathematical computation in optics is not enough, due to the fact that our judgments about the magnitude of objects depend on different circumstances that cannot be mathematically defined. This is a very important consideration because Berkeley is saying that the mathematical instrument does not cover all the aspects that take place in the visual phenomenon. Berkeley writes:

> But this in general may, I think, be observed concerning mathematical computation in optics: that it can never be very precise and exact, since the judgements we make of the magnitude of external things do often depend on several circumstances, which are not proportionable to, or capable of being defined by, lines and angles.[4]

With respect to the position of objects, Berkeley sustains that human beings do not change the position of objects that shape inversely in the bottom of our eye, using the physical or geometrical laws of optics, *i.e.*, they do not require any "a priori" hidden structure in the mind, but only of experience and the relations between the ideas that they receive.

In short, Berkeley not only considers that mathematics is an instrument and, that like any human construct, is founded in diverse hypotheses that are not necessarily truth, but he makes clear the limits of its application with respect to the laws of geometry and computational systems. For example, the relativity of the unities that we apply to the external objects shows that it is only a construct guided by experience that can be useful but does not ultimately reveal anything essential about those objects. He points out:

> But for a fuller illustration of this matter it ought to be considered that number (however some may reckon it amongst the primary qualities) is nothing fixed and settled, really existing in things themselves. It is entirely the creature of the mind, considering either an idea by itself, or any combination of ideas to which it gives one name, and so makes it pass for an unit.[5]

---

[4] Ibid., 72.

[5] George Berkeley, *An Essay towards a New Theory of Vision*, ed. David R. Wilkins (Dublin: Trinity College, 2002), 29.

In Berkeley's view, we can use the mathematical instrument but we must be aware of its limits with respect to optics and also of the limits of geometry concerning its own study object. This warning is the case since for some mathematicians the object of geometry is the visible extension, when in fact the computational system for making a measurement comes from tangible extension, as Berkeley sustains thus:

> ...visible extensions in themselves are little regarded [in geometry], and have no settled determinate greatness, and that men measure altogether, by the application of tangible extension to tangible extension. All which makes it evident that visible extension and figures are not the object of geometry.[6]

In addition, there are some mathematicians that consider that the exactness of geometrical science comes from abstract ideas that can be perceived by any of our senses, but for Berkeley: "... there is not an idea such as abstract extension...", and finally he says: "... I suppose, it is clear that neither abstract nor visible extension makes the object of geometry"[7]

4. *An Essay Towards a New Theory of Vision*

As stated above, the principle of heterogeneity lies at the basis of Berkeley's theory of vision and in his own words we have it formulated thus:

> It is nevertheless certain, the ideas intermitted by each sense are widely different and distinct from each other; but having been observed constantly to go together, they are spoken of as one and the same thing.[8]

Those diverse ideas are connected by natural mechanisms of association. Berkeley refers to them as "*the natural course of nature*" that allows us to establish by habit different relations between our ideas. Those relations are not necessary ones, since they depend on diverse circumstances, so they are contingent. In the middle of these multiple variations, only habitual experience guides our judgment about sensible perception. This constitutes the second principle of the new (psychological) theory of vision. Berkeley says:

> In these and the like instances the truth of the matter stands thus: having of a long time experienced certain ideas, perceivable by touch,

---

[6] Ibid., 41.
[7] Ibid., 43.
[8] Ibid., 13.

as distance, tangible figure, and solidity, to have been connected with certain ideas of sight, I do upon perceiving these ideas of sight forthwith conclude that tangible ideas are, by the wonted ordinary course of Nature like to follow.[9]

In this new theory, there are not only the principles that we have mentioned above, but also some kind of "*pars destruens*", since we have to avoid some errors, and more specifically avoid two prejudices:

  a) To think that the connection between ideas is given by necessary principles.

  b) To consider that the ideas introduced by different senses and associated with habit really refer to the same object.

Thus, this new theory of vision is a psychological one in the sense that it is founded on the description of mental operations. However, it is very interesting that Berkeley believed that we associate ideas in a way that is very close to verbal language:

No sooner do we hear the words of a familiar language pronounced in our ears, but the ideas corresponding thereto present themselves to our minds ... We even act in all respects as if we heard the very thoughts themselves.[10]

In likewise manner, our mind associates by habitude the objects of tactile sensation with those of our vision giving properties of the first kind of objects to the second kind. Such is the case for distance, magnitude and position. Then, due to this association, we believe that we perceive them just by vision, though these are strongly bound to tactile perception. Berkeley says:

It hath been shewn there are two sorts of objects apprehended by sight; each whereof hath its distinct magnitude, or extension. The one, properly tangible, *i.e.* to be perceived and measured by touch, and not immediately falling under the sense of seeing: the other, properly and immediately visible, by mediation of which the former is brought in view.[11]

---

[9] Ibid., 13.
[10] Ibid., 14.
[11] Ibid., 15.

Along with the principles of heterogeneity of perception and the principle of connection between ideas, it is important to further add the principle of minimal perception or *minimum sensibile*. In fact, each sense found its limits in a minimum and indivisible percept. In the case of sense vision, minimal visual perceptions are extended and ontologically indivisible coloured points. For Berkeley, our vision only reaches a specific number of visual points and even though he does not introduce himself in this discussion he was nonetheless very close to the problem of the visual field. The principle of minimal visual perception does not change in relation to the magnification given by the microscope, since this instrument does not actually increase our visual field; in fact, we always perceive the same quantity of minimum sensible, but this happens in a "new world", the world of the objects out of our ordinary vision.

Finally, in this new theory, Berkeley upholds a pragmatic idea about vision when he affirms that the mind thinks primarily in the tactile object, but it does not develop an immediate consciousness of it since human beings are provided by God with the faculty of vision, aimed to consider firstly either the damage or benefit that the objects can give to their bodies, as well as either the pleasure or pain to their minds. However, even those practical consequences depend firstly on the tangible qualities of an object, the sense of vision can guide human beings by preventing damage and estimating the obtaining of benefits. In this last regard, the sense of vision is very useful.

5. Conclusion

In the name of a new proposal for knowledge, Berkeley, known as the philosopher of ideas, addressed his theory to the man who values common sense. The common-sensical person considers that she sees what she looks without mediation. Berkeley demonstrates to this commonsensical person through a "minute" analysis of some operations of the mind that sensation is not so simple. Berkeley shows that through each one of our senses, we receive a specific kind of ideas and we hence have to make a special effort to unite them. This labour is both epistemic and psychological if we want to obtain precise knowledge about the structure and operations of our perception.

In like manner, Berkeley addressed his theory to the scientists of his time who considered that knowledge of visual phenomena could be completely explained through geometrical-mathematical hypotheses.

Summing up briefly, the new theory of vision is an empirical and psychological proposal that reveals the true role of mathematics as a useful instrument that can contribute to the development of knowledge if correctly applied. The proposal, though, has some limits in explaining the acquisition of our sensible ideas. In the specific case of visual perception, it is necessary to analyse the operations of the mind that give us a better explanation about our human faculties. This latter case is the reason why Berkeley gives a definitive impulse to the development of psychology and his epistemological-empirical foundations.

Bibliography

Berkeley, George. "An Essay Towards a New Theory of Vision." In *George Berkeley Works*, edited by M. R. Ayers. London: Every Man's Library, 1975.

———. *An Essay towards a New Theory of Vision*. Edited by David R. Wilkins. Dublin: Trinity College, 2002.

———. *The Works of George Berkeley*. Edited by A. A. Luce and T. E. Jessop. London: Thomas Nelson and Sons, 1948-1952.

Chapter 6

Kant, Spinoza, and Practical Rationality

Anna Tomaszewska

Jagiellonian University in Kraków

Abstract: Although Spinoza does not explicitly distinguish between practical and theoretical reason, I suggest that this distinction be read as one between cognition (knowledge) and action (morality) – and compare the views of Spinoza and Kant with regard to it. From the anthropological perspective, which justifies construing human cognition as intrinsically limited, one can defend the claim that both philosophers ultimately prioritise practical over theoretical rationality. However, the way of arriving at this conclusion significantly differs in the case of Spinoza and Kant. The kind of prioritising practice over theory that could be attributed to Spinoza would result from the recognition of the propensity of the human mind to generate metaphysical illusions and misrepresent reality. Kant's placing practical over theoretical reason would mark his endeavour to provide a coherent account of human action which would also safeguard the 'interests' of reason.

Keywords: Spinoza, Kant, cognition, practical reason, theoretical reason, metaphysics, freedom, finitude.

***

1. Two caveats

Writing about Kant and Spinoza, considered together, is a tricky enterprise which can be undertaken after clearing up both factual and terminological ambiguities. When talking about Spinoza in the context of Kant's philosophy, one may refer either to a real person, *i.e.*, the author of the *Ethics* and the *Theological-Political Treatise*, or to a philosophical idea, an intellectual construction, and a 'spectre' emerging from eighteenth-century refutations, polemical writings and misinterpretations which must have influenced Kant's way of thinking about Spinoza.[1] Kant might not have had first-hand access to Spinoza's writings.[2] However, in many places, he refers to Spinoza more or less directly. Not only is the name of Spinoza mentioned, for example, in the *Critique of the Power of Judgment*,[3] in an essay "What Does It Mean to Orient Oneself in Thinking?"[4] and in the *Opus postumum*,[5] but both the pre-Critical writings, such as *The Only Possible Argument in Support of a Demonstration of the Existence of God*,[6] and the *Critique of Pure Reason*,[7] are full of indirect references to Spinoza.

---

[1] According to Giuseppe De Flaviis, "one can indeed very often have an impression that one has to do more with a reinvention of Spinozism than with an analysis of the contents specific to this doctrine [...]. It seems to me that reinventing a Spinozism that would go beyond the letter of Spinoza is the overall intent of Kant" (Giuseppe De Flaviis, *Kant e Spinoza* (Firenze: Sansoni Editore, 1986), 15). David Bell emphasises that prior to the *Pantheismusstreit*, the reception of Spinoza in Germany had been shaped by numerous refutations which "fixed an appallingly inaccurate image of Spinoza in the minds of the majority of literate Germans for over a hundred years" (David Bell, *Spinoza in Germany from 1670 to the Age of Goethe* (University of London: Institute of Germanic Studies, 1984), 2).

[2] According to a report by Johann Georg Hamann, "Kant has confessed [...] that he had never thoroughly studied Spinozism." Quoted in: Friedrich Heman, "Kant und Spinoza," *Kant-Studien* 5, no. 1–3 (1901), https://doi.org/10.1515/kant-1901-0157, 276.

[3] Spinoza is mentioned as an example of a "righteous man," albeit an atheist. See Immanuel Kant, *Critique of the Power of Judgment* (New York: Cambridge University Press, 2000), 317. From here on "KU, AA". (KU, AA 5:452).

[4] The context of Kant's reference to Spinoza is provided by the debate between Jacobi and Mendelssohn. See Immanuel Kant, "What Does It Mean to Orient Oneself in Thinking?," in *Religion and Rational Theology* (New York: Cambridge University Press, 1996), 15–16, including the footnote. From here on "WDO, AA". (WDO, AA 8:144).

[5] Immanuel Kant, *Opus Postumum* (New York: Cambridge University Press, 1993), 213. From here on, "OP, AA". (OP, AA 22:54; 22:59; 21:15; 21:19; 21:51). This late unfinished work, or a collection of notes, is full of references to Spinoza, to whom Kant often attributes the view that we "intuit all things in God," a metaphor used by Nicolas Malebranche, rather than Spinoza.

[6] "...the world is not an accident of God, for there are to be found within the world conflict, deficiency, changeability, all of which are the opposites of the determinations to be found in a divinity; God is not the only substance which exists; all other substances only exist in dependence upon God..." (Immanuel Kant, "The Only Possible Argument in Support of a Demonstration of the Existence of God," in *Theoretical Philosophy, 1755–1770* (New York: Cambridge University Press, 1992), 134). From here on, "BDG, AA". (BDG, AA 2:90-1)). In this passage, Kant rejects Spinoza's monism and pantheism.

[7] It has been argued that the dogmatic opponent in the Antinomy chapter of the First Critique represents Spinoza. See Omri Boehm, *Kant's Critique of Spinoza* (New York: Oxford University Press, 2014), chs. 2 and 3.

In this paper, I refer to Spinoza the real philosopher, rather than to the 'spectre' emerging from the Enlightenment refutations and assimilated in a particular way by Kant. In that I do so, I follow the example of Yirmiyahu Yovel who considers Kant and Spinoza as philosophers of immanence, albeit construed in two different ways: critically and dogmatically, and tries to find connections between the ideas of both thinkers.[8] Such an attempt can help better understand both philosophers through each other's ideas. The idea I consider to be connecting Kant and Spinoza is that of finitude as a feature that marks the condition of the human being, determining her way of thinking in relation to herself and other entities. From this anthropological perspective, I suggest, that one can analyse the distinction between theoretical and practical rationality in both Kant and Spinoza.

However, before we proceed with the analysis, another caveat must be added, and that regarding the distinction between the theoretical and the practical. The distinction originates in Kant, though it could perhaps be traced back even to the Mediaeval doctrine of double truth: that of philosophy and that of revelation. For Kant, the human cognitive faculty, and in particular reason, sets up laws[9] or principles.[10] This legislation manifests itself in two distinct domains: the domain of nature and the domain of freedom. In the *Critique of the Power of Judgment* Kant says:

> Our cognitive faculty as a whole has two domains, that of the concepts of nature and that of the concept of freedom; for it is a priori legislative through both. Philosophy is also divided accordingly into the theoretical and the practical. [...] Legislation through concepts of nature takes place through the understanding, and is theoretical. Legislation through the concept of freedom takes place through reason, and is merely practical.[11]

Thus, it seems that the distinction between the theoretical and the practical cannot be applied directly to Spinoza. For he does not conceive of the human cognitive faculty as legislative for nature but rather as its part, thus as subordinated to the same kind of laws that bind all other beings. In the Preface to Part III of the *Ethics*, one can read:

---

[8] See Yirmiyahu Yovel, *Spinoza and Other Heretics. The Adventures of Immanence* (Princeton: Princeton University Press, 1989), ch. 1.
[9] See Immanuel Kant, *Critique of Pure Reason* (New York: Cambridge University Press, 1998), 621. From here on, "KrV, A/B". (KrV, A 701/B 729; A 819/B 847; A 840/B 868).
[10] KrV, A 11/B 24; B 359; A 405.
[11] KU, AA 5:174.

...the laws and rules of Nature according to which all things happen and change from one form to another are everywhere and always the same. So our approach to the understanding of the nature of things of every kind should likewise be one and the same; namely, through the universal laws and rules of Nature.[12]

But since nature for Kant is the totality of objects available to human *cognition*, which totality he identifies as "a sum of appearances,"[13] whereas freedom is a prerequisite of *action*, an event significant from the point of view of morality,[14] the distinction between theoretical and practical reason can be construed as a distinction between cognition and action, motivating perennial questions about the relation between knowledge and morality (or ethics). Is theoretical cognition a prerequisite to moral action? Does the progress of knowledge contribute to the development of morality, or should the two domains be considered independently? Can it be the case that the more we know, along with the advancement of science, the better we become morally, so that occasional iniquities, accompanied by the emotions of "hatred, anger, envy, etc.,"[15] that we face in our lives should be attributed to ignorance and deficits in education? Or is the advancement of science indifferent from the moral point of view, and the iniquities should be put down to irremediable propensities inherent in human nature? And is there a reason for which we should value ethics more than science?

2. The Cartesian ideal

The distinction between the theoretical and the practical in Spinoza and Kant has as its background Descartes' rationalist project of philosophy as a system – represented by the metaphor of a tree in the Preface to the *Principles of Philosophy* – whose parts are logically, or deductively, connected according to the requirements of the universal method derived from mathematics.[16] For

---

[12] Baruch Spinoza, "Ethics," in *Complete Works* (Indianapolis/Cambridge: Hackett Publishing Company, 2002), 278.

[13] KrV, A 114.

[14] See Henry E. Allison, "We Can Act Only under the Idea of Freedom," *Proceedings and Addresses of the American Philosophical Association* 71, no. 2 (1997): 39–50, https://doi.org/10.2307/3130940.

[15] Spinoza, "Ethics," 278.

[16] René Descartes, *Principles of Philosophy* (Dordrecht/Boston/London: Kluwer Academic Publishers, 1982), xxiv. Edwin Curley remarks that despite many differences between Descartes' and Spinoza's rendering of philosophy as a deductive system of knowledge, its "general notion" – i.e., the idea of a science that "begins with metaphysics and ends in moral philosophy, after having considered the nature of man" – is common to both of them and

Descartes, philosophy is "the study of Wisdom" and by the wisdom he understands "not only prudence in our affairs, but also a perfect knowledge of all the things which man can know for the conduct of his life, the preservation of his health, and the discovery of all the arts."[17] Ethics, which forms part of the system of knowledge, a branch in the tree of philosophy, builds on physics which in turn has metaphysics (knowledge of God and the immortality of the soul) as its roots. But, as long as the knowledge of physics remains incomplete, we cannot reach "the highest and most perfect Ethics"[18] crowning the tree. Facing uncertainty and ignorance, Descartes recommends the inquirer to adhere to a provisional moral code which consists of a few prescriptions warranted by pragmatic, rather than epistemic considerations.[19]

Descartes' establishing that, for want of sufficient cognition to make it to the "most perfect Ethics," we need to accept that our actions are guided by provisional prescriptions, invites the distinction between the theoretical and the practical. The distinction resembles the one made by Kant to the extent that it is premised on the supposition that action can be guided by rules or norms which do not have their underpinnings in theoretical cognition. But provisional morality, unlike Kant's ethics, does not offer absolute moral norms and its prescriptions will cease to be applicable once the ideal of the "perfect Ethics" has been achieved. The situation of the moral agent guided by Descartes' provisional moral code can be compared to that of a doctor who decides to apply a treatment without having certainty about the causes of a patient's disease, resorting to the information and resources currently available in medicine.

Spinoza's *Ethics*, a work which starts from God and proceeds to the human mind, the physical world, human emotions (*affectus*), and the ways of mastering them, can be read as an attempt to bring about Descartes' project of a unified system of knowledge. However, at closer inspection, the work reveals that it is impossible to complete the project: rather than actualised, the system is posited by the thinking subject who is placed within it as a "mode" of "substance" identified with "God or Nature." From this perspective, the ideal of the "perfect Ethics" remains unattainable, as it demands too much from the subject, *i.e.*, that hers approximates the divine cognition. The prescriptions formulated in Part V of the *Ethics* should thus be taken as a remedy to a condition in which human beings find themselves inevitably and permanently,

---

"determines the structure of the works they wrote." Curley calls this general notion "the ideal of the unity of science" (Edwin Curley, *Behind the Geometrical Method. A Reading of Spinoza's Ethics* (Princeton: Princeton University Press, 1988), 5-6).

[17] Descartes, *Principles of Philosophy*, xvii.

[18] Ibid., xxiv.

[19] See ibid., xxv.

and which Spinoza calls "bondage."[20] The remedy presents itself as a kind of cognitive therapy whereby the human being learns to contain emotions, a result of the subject's cognitive limitations.[21]

By distinguishing practical from theoretical reason, Kant departs from the Cartesian project of a unified science of which ethics forms a part – not exclusively because, on his tenets, it is impossible to succeed in completing this project, but primarily because he thinks that to have knowledge in the sense of Descartes and the rationalists would be detrimental to morality. In the second-edition Preface, Kant pronounces the famous words which can serve as the motto of the First Critique: "I had to deny knowledge in order to make room for faith."[22] Elsewhere, he makes the following enunciation concerning knowledge: "Apart from opinion and faith (*Glauben*), the third level of holding true (*Fürwahrhalten*) is knowledge. Would it not be better if we had it? No; because then all morality would fall away."[23]

On the face of it, it might seem that Kant rejects knowledge and embraces a fideist or a sceptical position since he claims that the denial of knowledge is a prerequisite to morality and faith. Indeed, Kant's statements imply that morality and faith should not be based on *any* kind of knowledge: neither originating from experience, nor from pure reason. Thus, Kant precludes both science and metaphysics as possible foundations of morality. However, this does not mean that he opts for fideism or scepticism. This is because he conceives of morality – "the domain of the concept of freedom"[24] – as independent of theoretical cognition and governed by its own kind of laws. That the normativity intrinsic to nature essentially differs from the normativity which pertains to the domain of freedom allows considering the two domains as mutually independent. Yet, since the normativity of the two domains ultimately has its source in reason, Kant can defy the accusations of fideism or scepticism. To the extent that reason is legislative in the domain of freedom, Kant can safeguard rationality within the practical. Kant's position, though,

---

[20] In the Preface to Part IV of the *Ethics*, Spinoza explains this term as "man's lack of power to control and check the emotions," as a result of which man "is not his own master but is subject to fortune" (Spinoza, "Ethics," 320).

[21] The latter can be done in a number of ways, e.g., by acquiring knowledge of the cause of the emotions; detaching the emotions from the thought about their external cause whose sufficient cognition we do not have; or directing them to things we understand rather than those we do not. See ibid., 372–3.

[22] KrV, B xxx.

[23] Immanuel Kant, "Danziger Rationaltheologie nach Baumbach," in *Gesammelte Schriften*, Band 28 (Berlin: Akademie der Wissenschaften zu Göttingen, 1972), 1292 (the fragment translated by author).

[24] See KU AA, 5:174 quoted above.

building on the dualism of nature and freedom, challenges the Cartesian ideal of the unity of science, the ideal of rationality guided by universal methodological standards.

3. The limits of knowledge

As we have seen above, according to Kant, if we had all possible knowledge, we could not be moral. This claim is puzzling because it seems to suggest, *prima facie*, that omniscience precludes morality – a picture that contradicts the traditional theistic conception of God as both omniscient and good. But such considerations are premature since Kant does not advocate a theological doctrine that would radically subvert theism: having denied the possibility of our knowledge of the objects of metaphysics, he cannot legitimately state what God is like. Rather, the claim about our knowledge ruling out morality should be read against the background of the anthropological assumptions underlying Kant's critical philosophy.

On these assumptions, human cognition is considered to be intrinsically limited. The limitations are determined by the structure of human cognitive capacities. Our cognitive setup enables us to acquire knowledge of things *as* spatial and temporal only, thus as "appearances," even though we can *think* of objects outside the spatio-temporal framework. Kant calls the doctrine which defends this claim transcendental idealism.[25] Ignoring the fact that our cognition is intrinsically constrained results in a "transcendental illusion," that is, in assigning to objects "in themselves" properties that they have only in virtue of being related to our minds.[26] The mechanism that generates the transcendental illusion also underlies what Kant calls "enthusiasm." This is a mental distortion, occurring for example in religious or political fanatics, which consists in the fact that "that which is in man is represented as something which is outside him, and the product of his thought [*Gedankenwerk*] represented as a thing in itself (substance)."[27] The consequence of ignoring our cognitive limitations – adopting a dogmatic instead of a critical attitude[28] – is

---

[25] "I understand by the transcendental idealism of all appearances the doctrine that they are all together to be regarded as mere representations and not as things in themselves, and accordingly that space and time are only sensible forms of our intuition, but not determinations given for themselves or conditions of objects as things in themselves. To this idealism is opposed transcendental realism, which regards space and time as something given in themselves (independent of our sensibility)" (KrV, A 369).

[26] KrV, A 297/B 354.

[27] OP, AA 21:26.

[28] In a note titled "On philosophical enthusiasm," Kant says that "Spinozism is the true conclusion of dogmatic metaphysics" and "if one will not tread the path of critique, then one must let enthusiasm run its course" (Immanuel Kant, *Notes and Fragments* (New

thus the illicit belief that all possible things must be subordinated to the structures of the human mind. Rejecting dogmatism, Kant abandons therefore a kind of anthropocentrism.[29] Dogmatism, a position on which all objects, and not just the 'appearances', would, as it were, match human cognitive capacities, is for Kant detrimental to morality because it leaves no space for a source of moral obligation that would lie outside the kind of cognition that is available to human beings and that presents its objects as causally determined elements of a unitary spatio-temporal framework.

Let us now turn to Spinoza. In his account, human cognitive limitations follow from the ontological status of the human being as a mode of substance, rather than the substance itself, which in Part I of the *Ethics* he argues to be identical with God or Nature (*Deus sive Natura*). For something to be a mode of substance means for it to be ontologically and epistemologically dependent on "something else,"[30] *i.e.,* not to be able to exist independently and be cognised without reference to an external thing. Spinoza explains human cognitive limitations in terms of the fact that we entertain "inadequate ideas," that is,

---

York: Cambridge University Press, 2005), 327–8. From here on, "HN, AA". (HN, AA 18:436)). So, for Kant, both dogmatism and enthusiasm result from not endorsing the critical stance. "Spinozism," which he mentions in the note, refers to the intellectual construct mentioned in Section 1, rather than to the doctrine of the real Spinoza.

[29] According to Stephen Palmquist, Kant rejects anthropocentrism in favour of a theocentric perspective. Palmquist writes: "His seminal doctrine of the *primacy* of practical reason represents the culmination of this line of thinking: an anthropocentric System would give primacy to theoretical reason, treating human knowledge as its central feature; Kant denies such knowledge only in the sense of rejecting its *centrality*, because his System puts the theocentric faith of practical reason in its place" (Stephen Palmquist, *Kant's Critical Religion. Volume Two of Kant's System of Perspectives* (Ashgate: Aldershot, 2000), 12). I do not *fully* agree with Palmquist, though. For one may call a philosophical position theocentric if it stipulates that the existence of God provides the foundation for a particular domain relevant for human cognition or action. Thus, for example, Descartes' philosophy is theocentric, because it stipulates that the existence of God should guarantee the certainty of rational cognition. For Kant, however, the existence of God is not foundational for any domain of human cognition or action. Morality does not rest on the claim concerning the divine existence and religion is a consequence of morality, not in reverse. That said, I think that Palmquist is right when he reads Kant's practical philosophy as demanding rejection of a variety of the anthropocentric stance. In his practical philosophy, Kant "makes room for faith," so the denial of anthropocentrism does not directly imply a theocentric view, but rather enables a range of alternatives to anthropocentrism.

[30] Definition 5 in Part I of the *Ethics* reads: "By mode I mean the affections of substance, that is, that which is in something else and is conceived through something else" (Spinoza, "Ethics," 217).

"fragmentary and confused,"[31] rather than "clear and distinct," hence true ideas.[32] In the *Treatise on the Emendation of the Intellect*, he avers:

> [I]f it is in the nature of a thinking being [...] to form true or adequate thoughts, it is certain that inadequate ideas arise in us from this, that we are part of some thinking being, some of whose thoughts constitute our mind in their entirety, and some only in part.[33]

According to the *Ethics*, the thinking being of which we are a mode is a substance considered from the point of view of the attribute of thought. In other words, insofar as we think, we are a part of a being for which thought is an essential feature. Thought articulates itself in ideas which should be considered in relation to other ideas, *i.e.* modes of the attribute of thought. Each attribute can be conceived only "in itself and through itself, so that its conception does not involve the conception of any other thing,"[34] which however is not the case with regard to the modes of the attributes. To conceive or explain a particular idea, which is a mode of the attribute of thought, we need other ideas. But, in the case of dependent beings like us, the series of ideas we can relate to one another constitutes a fragment of a greater being which eludes our grasp, a being that we presume to be a part of an infinite being or the infinite being itself.[35] The ideas that we are not able to relate to other ideas will remain unexplained, thus they will not be true or adequate for us, but rather "confused and mutilated, effects separated from their real causes," as

---

[31] Ibid., 279.

[32] Baruch Spinoza, "Treatise on the Emendation of the Intellect," in *Complete Works* (Indianapolis/Cambridge: Hackett Publishing Company, 2002), 18.

[33] Ibid., 20.

[34] Baruch Spinoza, "The Letters," in *Complete Works* (Indianapolis/Cambridge: Hackett Publishing Company, 2002), 762.

[35] Whether he conceives of it as God or Nature, Spinoza attributes infinity to the unique substance of which human beings are "modes." In the *Treatise on the Emendation...*, speaking of Nature, he writes: "For this entity is unique and infinite; that is, it is total being, beyond which there is no being" (Spinoza, "Treatise on the Emendation of the Intellect," 21). In Chapter II of the *Short Treatise on God, Man, and His Well-Being*, Spinoza characterises God in this way: "we say that he is a being of whom all or infinite attributes are predicated, of which attributes every one is infinitely perfect in its kind" (Baruch Spinoza, "Short Treatise on God, Man, and His Well-Being," in *Complete Works* (Indianapolis/Cambridge: Hackett Publishing Company, 2002), 40). Also in the *Ethics* infinity is taken to be the essential property of God; Definition 6 in Part I reads: "By God I mean an absolutely infinite being, that is, substance consisting of infinite attributes, each of which expresses eternal and infinite essence" (Spinoza, "Ethics," 217).

Gilles Deleuze has put it.[36] In Deleuze's words: thought "surpasses the consciousness that we have of it,"[37] hence many things that can otherwise be thought of or explained have to remain outside our grasp.

Furthermore, Proposition 7 of Part II of the *Ethics* establishes Spinoza's doctrine of the parallelism of the attributes: "The order and connection of ideas is the same as the order and connection of things."[38] This means that ideas – the modes of thought – must somehow correspond to things, which are the modes of extension. However, the modes of thought cannot enter relations with the modes of extension, or the modes of any other attribute, since each attribute can be conceived only "in and through itself." Thus, we cannot explain an occurrence within the attribute of thought by referring to an occurrence within the attribute of extension. Accordingly, for those ideas that "surpass our consciousness," there are also things whose connections with other things are inaccessible to us. Now, the mind, which Spinoza identifies with a congeries of ideas, is "a representation of the body [...] in the thinking thing."[39] As one can read in Proposition 13 of Part II of the *Ethics*: "The object of the idea constituting the human mind is the body – *i.e.*, a definite mode of extension actually existing, and nothing else."[40] If we call relations between things causal relations, it follows that the mind – "the very idea or knowledge of the human body"[41] – cannot represent adequately some of the causal relations pertaining to the mode of extension that provides its object, and to this mode of extension and other modes that affect it. In other words, our bodies, composed of complex causal series, form part of causal series that go beyond the scope of our minds, hence beyond our cognition, a fact which negatively affects the possibility of self-knowledge.

Following Deleuze, one can observe that according to Spinoza not only do we entertain non-conscious thoughts, but there are events going on in our bodies that escape our conscious grasp. But can the term "consciousness" be used legitimately in Spinoza's theory of the mind? What would consciousness amount to on this account? How could its existence be explained? What would it originate from? Spinoza's conception of the mind does not entitle one to talk about consciousness as the distinctive feature of the mind. Rather, it would be more appropriate to claim that every mode of physical reality has its own mind

---

[36] Gilles Deleuze, *Spinoza: Practical Philosophy* (San Francisco: City Lights Books, 1988), 19.

[37] Ibid., 18.

[38] Spinoza, "Ethics," 247.

[39] Spinoza, "Short Treatise on God, Man, and His Well-Being," 94.

[40] Spinoza, "Ethics," 251.

[41] Ibid., 258.

because the mind is an idea of a particular object that corresponds to it. But since ideas are modes of substance considered from the point of view of the attribute of thought, they do not explain themselves, every idea or a set of ideas needs to be related to another idea or a set of ideas to be explained. To have a mind means therefore no more than to be intelligible, to form part of a series that does not need any 'consciousness' or 'subjectivity' to proceed. Accordingly, Spinoza's theory of mind and knowledge – in exact opposition to the theory of Descartes – is not a theory of the knowing subject, but rather a theory of the intelligibility of the object of knowledge.

The last claim might have a bit of Kantian flavour, although it stops halfway through to the idea of transcendental philosophy as a theory of the object of cognition regarded in its relation to the cognising subject.[42] Attempting to construct a theory from which subjectivity would be entirely eliminated – a theory from the viewpoint of eternity, "*sub specie aeternitatis*"[43] – Spinoza, paradoxically, extends subjectivity, or mental properties, onto things one would be far from ready to attribute mental properties to. For on his conception of the mind, one must ascribe such properties to tables and chairs insofar as these objects constitute an intelligible reality. Such a conception clearly flies in the face of the ordinary way of understanding what subjectivity or mental properties consist of, and radically changes the meanings of "mind" and "subjectivity."

4. Spinoza and the illusion of freedom

Denying the necessary connection between consciousness and knowledge, by extending knowledge on everything that is (*i.e.,* substance and its modes) and reconceiving the mental in terms of the intelligible, Spinoza does not only invite the doctrine of panpsychism;[44] he also severs the relation between knowledge and action. The "order of ideas" (knowledge) and the "order of things" (actions understood as occurrences in physical reality), which represent the modes of thought and of extension, respectively, are to be regarded as mutually independent: the objects belonging to either "order" – ideas and physical things – follow from, and thus can be explained only by other objects of the same kind. Thus, 'knowledge' cannot affect 'action'. This seems to imply that, in Spinoza's account, there can be no connections between theory and practice.

---

[42] "I call all cognition transcendental that is occupied not so much with objects but rather with our mode of cognition of objects insofar as this is to be possible a priori. A system of such concepts would be called transcendental philosophy" (KrV, A 12).

[43] Spinoza, "Ethics," 374.

[44] As Michael Della Rocca notes, "mentality, for Spinoza, extends everywhere. Such a view is known as panpsychism." M. Della Rocca, *Spinoza* (New York: Routledge, 2008), 110.

On the other hand, since Spinoza claims that there is an identity between the "order of ideas" and the "order of things," the two cannot constitute separate domains but must rather be conceived as coextensive. Thus, unlike Kant, Spinoza would not distinguish the domain of nature and the domain of freedom. Indeed, his concept of freedom – spelt out in Definition 7 of Part I of the *Ethics* as follows: "That thing is said to be free [*liber*] which exists solely from the necessity of its own nature, and is determined to action by itself alone"[45] – seems to suggest that he recognises no discrepancy between the concept of freedom and the concept of natural necessity.

Accordingly, on the account proposed by Spinoza, to the extent that an action is determined by properties inherent to the agent, it is free. In other words, to be free means to have causal power: to be the source of a series of causes and effects. But then, since everything that is, *i.e.*, that belongs to Nature, is part of an infinite causal series, all beings must enjoy at least a degree of freedom as far as they can operate as causes in relation to other beings. On such a view, the concept of freedom loses its common meaning: for not only can it be predicated on the same objects that are subordinated to the deterministic "laws and rules of Nature," but it can also be attributed to any part of reality, non-conscious objects like tables and chairs included, provided that they can also be claimed to have causal power. This renders the concept of freedom at best inflated and at worst absurd.

Yet, there are also passages which signal that Spinoza associates freedom with the activity of thinking. As Stuart Hampshire has argued, on Spinoza's tenets, the mind is capable of emancipating itself from scientific determinism, since intellectual activity, apparently available to the minority of people, makes it possible for us to detach ourselves, as it were, from the external causes of our actions (or the occurrences in our bodies and the physical world): "the detachment from causes in the common order of nature [...] lasts while self-critical thinking lasts."[46] To illustrate the point, in the *Short Treatise on God, Man and His Well-Being*, Spinoza defines freedom as:

> ...a firm reality which our understanding acquires through direct union with God, so that it can bring forth ideas in itself, and effects outside itself, in complete harmony with its nature; without, however, its effects

---

[45] Spinoza, "Ethics," 217.
[46] Stuart Hampshire, "Spinoza's Theory of Human Freedom," *The Monist* 55, no. 4 (1971), 566.

being subjected to any external causes, so as to be capable of being changed or transformed by them.[47]

Moreover, in the *Theological-Political Treatise*, Spinoza presents freedom as an inseparable feature of thought, stating: "no man [...] can give up his freedom to judge and think as he pleases, and everyone is by absolute natural right the master of his own thoughts."[48]

Thus, we can distinguish two alternative conceptions of freedom in Spinoza, both of which lead to paradoxical results. On the first of these conceptions, freedom would refer to causal power, which means that all existing things could be conceived as possessing a degree of freedom. Such a conception runs counter to common intuitions, on which being free is inseparable from being aware of one's freedom. On the second conception, freedom would be a property of thought, but because Spinoza denies any connections (both ontological and logical) between modes of different attributes, it would be a property that would have no causal efficacy. This property would amount to the fact that 'ideas', the modes of substance considered from the point of view of the attribute of thought, do not enter causal relations with 'things', the modes of substance considered from the point of view of the attribute of extension, hence ideas cannot result from the mind being affected by 'external' objects. Consequently, whether we are free has no genuine bearing on our actions.

Since the concept of freedom seems to have no specific meaning, *i.e.*, it does not seem to designate any real property of objects, freedom should be regarded as an illusion of an erring mind, as Spinoza suggests in a Scholium to Proposition 35, Part II of the *Ethics*:

> Men are deceived of thinking themselves free, a belief that consists only in this, that they are conscious of their actions and ignorant of the causes by which they are determined. Therefore, the idea of their freedom is simply the ignorance of the cause of their actions. As to their saying that human actions depend on the will, these are mere words without any corresponding idea.[49]

This is a third account of the concept of freedom in Spinoza. I shall call it critical. In this proposal, the idea of freedom originates from an illicit transition, carried out by the mind, from the lack of the idea of a cause of action to the

---

[47] Spinoza, "Short Treatise on God, Man, and His Well-Being," 101.
[48] Baruch Spinoza, "Theological-Political Treatise," in *Complete Works* (Indianapolis/ Cambridge: Hackett Publishing Company, 2002), 567.
[49] Spinoza, "Ethics," 264.

belief that there is no such cause. But a mind that makes inferences from its own contents to the features of reality outside the mind can be conceived of as a mind that has not recognised its own limitations, hence a mind that has not engaged in critical thinking. The reason why an uncritical mind does not recognise its limitations would be that the mind takes the ideas it entertains for the ideas that represent reality adequately, thus, that are true.[50] Such a mind could be called uncritical because it would fail to recognise the fact that it can comprehend only a fragment of reality – of a network of causal-explanatory relations. In other words, an uncritical mind would not be able to realise the difference between itself and the rest of reality – a characteristic that could be found in Kant's account of "transcendental illusion."

In the above-quoted passage, Spinoza explains the illusion of freedom in that he refers to the capacity of consciousness to *mis*represent reality. But it is rather unclear how this capacity itself could be explained. According to Axiom 2 of Part II of the *Ethics*, "man thinks."[51] If the claim were understood in the Cartesian vein – *i.e.*, as equating thinking, *cogitatio*, with any mode of consciousness – then this would suggest that for Spinoza consciousness ("thinking") is the essential feature of human beings, a claim he would endorse without justification but rather as a foundational assumption of his philosophy. Unlike Descartes, though, Spinoza does not start from this assumption, and he does not ground it in first-person experience. Does he suggest then that it is self-evident that "man thinks"?

According to Leszek Kołakowski, Spinoza's account of consciousness yields paradoxes. For as a feature that "makes us uniquely human," our consciousness proves to be "metaphysically quite groundless." While it confirms our "specificity," it is also the source of erroneous beliefs we hold concerning it: "it is this very capacity of self-observation that deludes us into thinking, with pathetic arrogance, that it is we who are the creative force behind our physical movements, which in fact are all purely mechanical."[52] One could take Kołakowski's observation further and conclude that due to this capacity, together with our ontological status as finite beings, modes of substance, *i.e.* God or Nature, it is ineluctable for us to generate false beliefs and metaphysical illusions, such as the illusion of freedom.

I have suggested that, according to Spinoza, we can think that we are free as long as we have not engaged in what could be called critical thinking. But how

---

[50] For an account of an adequate idea, see Definition 4 of Part II of the *Ethics* (Spinoza, "Ethics," 244).

[51] Ibid.

[52] Leszek Kołakowski, "The Two Eyes of Spinoza," in *The Two Eyes of Spinoza and Other Essays on Philosophers* (South Bend: St. Augustine's Press, 2004), 6.

can we ever engage in critical thinking if freedom is an illusion and our thought is governed by rules intrinsic to it that exactly correspond to causal relations governing the occurrences in the physical world? Is critical thinking, as it were, a natural consequence of what could be called the development of thought? Or does it require an independent trigger motivating, as it were, a sudden change in one's consciousness enabling one to see the illusionary nature of (at least some of) the ideas one entertains? But what would account for the trigger itself? Unless one assumes that thought is genuinely free and can break away from the series of determinations, such phenomena as critical thinking do not really seem to be explainable. But apparently, to claim that our thinking is free is not an option for Spinoza.

5. Kant's defence of freedom

In contradistinction to Spinoza, the role Kant assigns to critical thinking does not conduce to uncovering the ungroundedness of our concepts and beliefs, including the ideas of metaphysics (*i.e.* God, freedom, and the immortality of the soul),[53] but to showing how these concepts and ideas can be accommodated despite their inadequacy from the viewpoint of cognition. These ideas spring from "the nature of reason itself";[54] hence, dismissing them would be equivalent to undermining our rationality. Indeed, there is a common point between Spinoza's and Kant's accounts of the origin of metaphysical illusions, which consists of an attempt to regard the ideas of metaphysics as the results of our epistemic practices. But whereas Spinoza attributes such ideas to the distortions in these practices – for example, we arrive at the idea of freedom because we stop searching for the causes of our actions – Kant derives metaphysical illusions from reason's misconstruing its role in relation to cognition.

On Kant's account, an idea that has its source in reason cannot provide us with an object of cognition but proves to be regulative for our epistemic practices in that it prescribes an end to them.[55] Thus, Kant's critique consists in determining the tasks of reason and specifying possible constraints within

---

[53] KrV, B xxx; B 7.

[54] "By the idea of a necessary concept of reason, I understand one to which no congruent object can be given in the senses. Thus the pure concepts of reason [...] are transcendental ideas. They are concepts of pure reason; for they consider all experiential cognition as determined through an absolute totality of conditions. They are not arbitrarily invented, but given as problems by the nature of reason itself, and hence they relate necessarily to the entire use of the understanding. Finally, they are transcendent concepts, and exceed the bounds of experience, in which no object adequate to the transcendental idea can ever occur" (KrV, B 384).

[55] KrV, A 644/B 672.

which reason can contribute to cognition. As such, the critique focuses primarily on the capacities of human reason, rather than on its putative objects. The critique of reason, therefore, does not aim at undermining reason's authority, but at protecting it by investigating the goals and competencies of reason: it forms thus "a science of the mere estimation of pure reason, of its sources and boundaries."[56] In the Introduction to the *Critique of Pure Reason*, Kant characterises this "science" as follows:

> Such a thing would not be a doctrine, but must be called only a critique
> of pure reason, and its utility would really be only negative, serving not
> for the amplification but only for the purification of our reason, and for
> keeping it free of errors, by which a great deal is already won.[57]

By carrying out its negative task, the critique of reason is supposed to uproot "materialism, fatalism, atheism, [...] freethinking unbelief, [...] enthusiasm and superstition [...], and finally also [...] idealism and skepticism,"[58] and prepare the ground "for the advancement of metaphysics as a well-grounded science."[59]

Against this background, Kant's defence of freedom comes in two stages corresponding to the distinction between theoretical and practical reason. Firstly, he shows that, if the distinction between 'appearances' and 'things in themselves' is endorsed, the "causality through freedom"[60] may be regarded as compatible with the determinism of nature; for depending on the adopted perspective, one and the same occurrence can be described by reference to two different sets of laws: what we *cognise* as causally determined, thus as an 'appearance', can be *thought of* as independent from causal determinations when considered as a 'thing in itself'.[61] Thus, Kant contends that "freedom and nature, each in its full significance, would both be found in the same actions, simultaneously and without any contradiction, according to whether one compares them with their intelligible or their sensible cause."[62]

However, the fact that we can think of ourselves as free provided that we abstract from the empirical determinations of our actions, does not prove that we are genuinely free: for, as in the case of Spinoza, the awareness of freedom

---

[56] KrV, A 11/B 25.

[57] Ibid.

[58] KrV, B xxxiv.

[59] KrV, B xxxv-vi.

[60] KrV, A 539/B 567.

[61] See Henry E. Allison, *Kant's Transcendental Idealism: An Interpretation and Defense* (New Haven and London: Yale University Press, 2004).

[62] KrV, A 541/B 569.

might be illusory. Here comes the second stage in Kant's defence of freedom – that is an argument for the objective reality of freedom. This argument can be outlined in the following way: Action requires that the will of the agent be determined by a law. As there are two kinds of causality distinguished by Kant: the causality of nature and the causality "through freedom," so the will (in its choice of a maxim – a "subjective principle of volition"[63]) can be determined in a twofold manner: either by the laws pertaining to an object of the will (*i.e.* a desired good), or by a law intrinsic to the will itself, *i.e.* the moral law. Only in the latter case does the will manifest autonomy; otherwise its determination must be heteronomous.[64] Kant grounds the law intrinsic to the will and binding for it in its choice of maxims in "a fact of reason," which is "consciousness of this fundamental law" that "one cannot reason [...] out from antecedent data of reason" and that "is not based on any intuition, either pure or empirical."[65] Although the "fact of reason" does not derive from the "consciousness of freedom,"[66] Kant maintains that "this fact is inseparably connected with, and indeed identical with, the consciousness of freedom of the will."[67] Thus, only if we are free can we act morally, and *vice versa*. The relation between morality and freedom should not be taken as the inference from one property to another, but rather as what one could call a relation of mutual conditioning, a bit of analogy with the relation between the act of thinking and the existence of the thinking subject in Descartes' *Cogito*.

The practical indispensability of freedom – the fact that it cannot be omitted in a coherent account of moral action – endows its idea with objective reality, albeit "in a practical respect": freedom and morality are reciprocal concepts[68] so that dismissing one of them would imply dismissing the other. Therefore, theoretical reason cannot argue freedom away, given that there are compelling reasons not to do so. Let us sum up with a passage from the *Groundwork of the Metaphysics of Morals*:

> [E]very being that cannot act otherwise than under the idea of freedom is just because of that *really free* in a practical respect, that is, all laws that

---

[63] Immanuel Kant, "Groundwork of the Metaphysics of Morals," in *Practical Philosophy* (New York: Cambridge University Press, 1996), 56. From here on, "GMS, AA" (GMS, AA 4:402).

[64] See GMS, AA 4:433.

[65] Immanuel Kant, *Critique of Practical Reason* (New York: Cambridge University Press, 2015), 164. From here on, "KpV, AA" (KpV, AA 5:31).

[66] Ibid.

[67] KpV, AA 5:42.

[68] See Henry E. Allison, "Morality and Freedom: Kant's Reciprocity Thesis," *The Philosophical Review* 95, no. 3 (1986).

are inseparably bound up with freedom hold for him just as if his will had been validly pronounced free also in itself and in theoretical philosophy.[69]

6. The primacy of practical reason

According to Jonathan Israel, "for the Radical Enlightenment," a tendency in the history of thought that has Spinoza as one of its fathers (though certainly not the sole one),[70] "there is only one source of truth – science and scientifically based scholarship in the humanities…"[71] In this proposal, the distinction between practical and theoretical reason does not seem to be warranted; rather, theoretical rationality has the upper hand, subsuming within itself all other areas of human activity. But it seems to me that such a picture of Spinoza's philosophy is not the only acceptable one. I would like to suggest that in Spinoza there is also a space for prioritising the practical over the theoretical, though the way that leads to this conclusion significantly differs from the way that can be followed in the case of Kant.

We have seen that Spinoza can be attributed to the view on which critical thinking – the source of which cannot entirely be explained, a somewhat puzzling aspect of Spinoza's rationalist doctrine – makes it possible to recognise that the finite human mind generates inadequate ideas. Our consciousness gives rise to a whole host of illusions. Among the illusions, there is the above-discussed illusion of freedom, but we could also add the illusion of final causality,[72] the imperfection of Nature,[73] good and evil,[74] or providence.[75] In this picture, not only our moral beliefs but also beliefs concerning Nature, the beliefs we acquire in the course of scientific investigations, are can involve inadequate ideas, since they are products of a finite mind operating *sub specie durationis*, hence limited by time and relying on imagination, rather than on reason alone.[76]

---

[69] GMS, AA 4:448. The italics are by author.

[70] See Jonathan I. Israel, "Spinoza and Spinozism in the Western Enlightenment: The Latest Turns in the Controversy," *Araucaria. Revista Iberoamericana de Filosofía, Política, Humanidades y Relaciones Internacionales* 20 (2018).

[71] Jonathan I. Israel, "Spinoza and Early Modern Theology," in *The Oxford Handbook of Early Modern Theology, 1600-1800*, ed. U. Lehner, R. A. Muller, and A. G. Roeber (New York: Oxford University Press, 2016), 579. For more on the Radical Enlightenment and the primacy of the practical, see ch. 4 in: Anna Tomaszewska, *Kant's Rational Religion and the Radical Enlightenment: From Spinoza to Contemporary Debates* (New York: Bloomsbury, 2022), 67–88.

[72] Spinoza, "Ethics," 321.

[73] Ibid.

[74] Ibid., 326.

[75] Spinoza, "Theological-Political Treatise," 444.

[76] See Spinoza, "Ethics," 269.

Briefly: from the viewpoint of the finite subject, our attempts at the acquisition of knowledge – the domain of 'theoretical reason' – are by and large limited.

Arguably, Spinoza's philosophy can offer two kinds of remedy in this situation: first, one can try to understand one's condition by engaging in critical thinking and, second, one can abandon one's pursuit for complete, absolute knowledge – for truth contained in adequate ideas – for the sake of living or acting in accordance with Nature. This anti-theoretical turn does not have to imply a non-rational attitude because Nature is the very embodiment of rationality for Spinoza. From the finite perspective particularly for human beings,[77] theory should give way to practice, and the activity of forging concepts and conceptions should be replaced by the activity that has genuinely ethical purport: the actualisation of one's power (*conatus*)[78] in a community of individuals striving for the same goal, to which practising "justice and charity, or love towards one's neighbour,"[79] can vastly contribute. It could even be suggested that, in Spinoza's view, practice, the pursuit of an ethical life more than the search for knowledge, would enable us to approximate the absolute: for we exercise our share of rationality in that we live and act in accordance with Nature.

For Kant, on the other hand, the primacy of practical reason derives from the fact that it is only from the practical perspective that the vital interests of reason can be safeguarded. The objective reality of the ideas of metaphysics can be established in practice, that is, insofar as we are able to act morally, not insofar as reason's cognitive demands are satisfied. Only for practical reasons, therefore, is it possible to transcend the limitations inherent in our cognition. Yet, does the reality of an idea from the merely practical perspective amount to anything more than the idea constituting a necessary condition of the coherence of a particular way of thinking, or a conceptual scheme? Does Kant's claim that we "cannot act otherwise than under the idea of freedom" mean anything over and above the claim that the idea of freedom forms part of a coherent account of action? Indeed, one cannot think of oneself as responsible for an action if one does not presuppose that one has been free in undertaking it.[80] But why should we appreciate a particular way of thinking about our agency? And moreover, why should we value thinking of ourselves as responsible agents? Why should we care about preserving a conceptual scheme, given that we are not able to achieve certainty about whether the scheme reflects the way things really are?

---

[77] See Nancy Levene, "Spinoza the Radical," in *Reassessing the Radical Enlightenment*, ed. S. Ducheyne (London: Routledge, 2017), 114.
[78] Spinoza, "Ethics," 283.
[79] Spinoza, "Theological-Political Treatise," 518.
[80] Cf. Allison, "We Can Act Only under the Idea of Freedom."

A Kantian reply to these concerns might be given along the following lines: Why we value thinking about our agency in the way Kant recommends – and why we thereby care about preserving the ideas of metaphysics – is because we are rational. Attributing moral agency to oneself while at the same time denying the reality of freedom means that the structure of action shall be construed on analogy with the structure of an occurrence, an event that happens as part of a network of causes and effects. In this picture, attributing agency to oneself would be equally legitimate as attributing agency to chairs and tables, as well as pieces of rocks falling as a result of the force of gravity. Since for the modern, post-Cartesian mind, it is absurd to talk about the agency of chairs and rocks – for comparison, recall the picture of "enchanted" Nature as a language by means of which God communicates with us[81] – the concept should be dropped or brought back to a conceptual scheme which is not fraught with paradoxes or contradictions.

As we have seen with Spinoza, philosophical thinking leads to paradoxes since our mind has the power to generate metaphysical illusions. We can accept these paradoxes and resign from the pursuit of absolute knowledge, submitting ourselves to the unbending rules of Nature. But we can also try to remove the paradoxes and contradictions from our thinking by placing concepts in their proper contexts. We can remove the paradoxes and contradictions in that we clarify our thoughts by reflecting on the structure of thought alone, not on the way things are. Kant recommends this option.[82]

Bibliography

Allison, Henry E. "Morality and Freedom: Kant's Reciprocity Thesis." *The Philosophical Review* 95, no. 3 (1986): 393–425. https://doi.org/10.2307/2185 466.

Allison, Henry E. "We Can Act Only under the Idea of Freedom." *Proceedings and Addresses of the American Philosophical Association* 71, no. 2 (1997): 39–50. https://doi.org/10.2307/3130940.

Allison, Henry E. *Kant's Transcendental Idealism: An Interpretation and Defense*. New Haven and London: Yale University Press, 2004.

Bell, David. *Spinoza in Germany from 1670 to the Age of Goethe*. University of London: Institute of Germanic Studies, 1984.

---

[81] See Charles Taylor, *The Language Animal: The Full Shape of the Human Linguistic Capacity* (Cambridge, MA: The Belknap Press of Harvard University Press, 2016), esp. 3–50.

[82] The work on this chapter has been supported by National Science Centre in Poland, funding the project *Between Secularization and Reform. Religious Rationalism in the Late Seventeenth Century and in the Enlightenment* (grant no. 2018/31/B/HS1/02050) at the Institute of Philosophy of the Jagiellonian University in Kraków in the years 2019–2024.

Boehm, Omri. *Kant's Critique of Spinoza.* New York: Oxford University Press, 2014.

Curley, Edwin. *Behind the Geometrical Method. A Reading of Spinoza's Ethics.* Princeton: Princeton University Press, 1988.

De Flaviis, Giuseppe. *Kant e Spinoza.* Firenze: Sansoni Editore, 1986.

Deleuze, Gilles. *Spinoza: Practical Philosophy.* San Francisco: City Lights Books, 1988.

Della Rocca, Michael. *Spinoza.* New York: Routledge, 2008.

Descartes, René. *Principles of Philosophy.* Dordrecht/Boston/London: Kluwer Academic Publishers, 1982.

Hampshire, Stuart. "Spinoza's Theory of Human Freedom." *The Monist* 55, no. 4 (1971): 554–566.

Heman, Friedrich. "Kant und Spinoza." *Kant-Studien* 5, no. 1–3 (1901): 273–339. https://doi.org/10.1515/kant-1901-0157.

Israel, Jonathan I. "Spinoza and Early Modern Theology." In *The Oxford Handbook of Early Modern Theology, 1600-1800*, edited by U. Lehner, R. A. Muller, and A. G. Roeber. New York: Oxford University Press, 2016, pp. 577–593.

Israel, Jonathan I. "Spinoza and Spinozism in the Western Enlightenment: The Latest Turns in the Controversy," *Araucaria. Revista Iberoamericana de Filosofía, Política, Humanidades y Relaciones Internacionales* 20 (2018): 41–57.

Kant, Immanuel. *Critique of Practical Reason.* New York: Cambridge University Press, 2015.

———. *Critique of Pure Reason.* New York: Cambridge University Press, 1998.

———. *Critique of the Power of Judgment.* New York: Cambridge University Press, 2000.

———. "Danziger Rationaltheologie nach Baumbach." In *Gesammelte Schriften*, Band 28. Berlin: Akademie der Wissenschaften zu Göttingen, 1972.

———. "Groundwork of the Metaphysics of Morals." In *Practical Philosophy*. New York: Cambridge University Press, 1996, pp. 37–108.

———. *Notes and Fragments.* New York: Cambridge University Press, 2005.

———. *Opus Postumum.* New York: Cambridge University Press, 1993.

———. "The Only Possible Argument in Support of a Demonstration of the Existence of God." In *Theoretical Philosophy, 1755–1770.* New York: Cambridge University Press, 1992, pp. 107–201.

———. "What Does It Mean to Orient Oneself in Thinking?" In *Religion and Rational Theology.* New York: Cambridge University Press, 1996, pp. 1–18.

Kołakowski, Leszek. "The Two Eyes of Spinoza." In *The Two Eyes of Spinoza and Other Essays on Philosophers.* South Bend: St. Augustine's Press, 2004, pp. 1–15.

Levene, Nancy. "Spinoza the Radical." In *Reassessing the Radical Enlightenment,* edited by S. Ducheyne. London: Routledge, 2017, pp. 107–126.

Palmquist, Stephen. *Kant's Critical Religion. Volume Two of Kant's System of Perspectives.* Ashgate: Aldershot, 2000.

Spinoza, Baruch. "Ethics." In *Complete Works*. Indianapolis/Cambridge: Hackett Publishing Company, 2002, pp. 213–382.

———. "Short Treatise on God, Man, and His Well-Being." In *Complete Works*. Indianapolis/Cambridge: Hackett Publishing Company, 2002, pp. 31–107.

———. "The Letters." In *Complete Works*. Indianapolis/Cambridge: Hackett Publishing Company, 2002, pp. 755–959.

———. "Theological-Political Treatise." In *Complete Works*. Indianapolis /Cambridge: Hackett Publishing Company, 2002, pp. 383–583.

———. "Treatise on the Emendation of the Intellect." In *Complete Works*. Indianapolis/Cambridge: Hackett Publishing Company, 2002, pp. 1–30.

Taylor, Charles. *The Language Animal: The Full Shape of the Human Linguistic Capacity*. Cambridge, MA: The Belknap Press of Harvard University Press, 2016.

Tomaszewska, Anna. *Kant's Rational Religion and the Radical Enlightenment: From Spinoza to Contemporary Debates*. New York: Bloomsbury, 2022.

Yovel, Yirmiyahu. *Spinoza and Other Heretics. The Adventures of Immanence*. Princeton: Princeton University Press, 1989.

Chapter 7

Apperception and Self-Knowledge in Kant

Stéfano Straulino

Instituto Tecnológico Autónomo de México

Abstract: The aim of this work is to analyse these two senses of consciousness and show that, for Kant, self-consciousness does not occur unrestrictedly: a relation with something other than consciousness is needed for it to become conscious of itself. I carry out these objectives throughout six sections. In the first one, I lay out the Kantian principle of pure apperception. In the second one, I present the limits of pure perception through Kant's critique of rational psychology. Then, in the third section, I set the basis to understand the relation that Kant establishes between the I think and the I exist. In the fourth one, I show that pure apperception, despite being pure, is not possible without the opportunity of perception. Next, in the fifth one, I introduce the notion of empirical apperception, establish its relation with pure apperception, and elucidate its meaning. Finally, in the last section, I explain the way in which empirical self-consciousness is determined, in relation to the knowledge of objects of the external sense.

Keywords: apperception, self-consciousness, rational psychology, perception, Kant.

***

1. Introduction

In several places of his work, Kant distinguishes between two senses of self-consciousness: a pure one and an empirical one. This distinction is recorded in various formulations that Kant uses to refer to both types of self-consciousness. He calls the first one transcendental, pure or original apperception, synthetic unity of consciousness, transcendental unity of consciousness, transcendental subject = x, I think. Although these formulations capture different nuances, they all refer to what Kant calls properly "pure apperception". On the other hand, Kant refers to the second sense of self-consciousness as a subjective unity of consciousness, an empirically determined consciousness of my own existence, and inner experience. These notions, whose various formulations should not be ignored either, refer to what Kant calls "empirical apperception". According to the first sense of self-consciousness, we are aware of ourselves as subjects. According to the second sense, we are aware of ourselves as objects, that is, we know ourselves.

The aim of this work is to analyse these two senses of consciousness and show that, for Kant, self-consciousness does not occur unrestrictedly: a relation with something other than consciousness is needed for it to become conscious of itself. I carry out these objectives throughout six sections. In the first one, I lay out the Kantian principle of pure apperception. In the second one, I present the limits of pure perception through Kant's critique of rational psychology. Then, in the third section, I set the basis to understand the relation that Kant establishes between the *I think* and the *I exist*. In the fourth one, I show that pure apperception, despite being pure, is not possible without the opportunity of perception. Next, in the fifth one, I introduce the notion of empirical apperception, establish its relation with pure apperception, and elucidate its meaning. Finally, in the last section, I explain the way in which empirical self-consciousness is determined, in relation to the knowledge of objects of the external sense.

2. Transcendental apperception as the synthetic unity of consciousness

Kant's most famous treatment of transcendental apperception is undertaken in the second edition of the *Critique of Pure Reason*, in paragraphs §16 to §18 of the Transcendental Deduction. Kant begins his argument by stating:

> The *I think* must *be able* to accompany all my representations; for otherwise something would be represented in me that could not be thought at all, which is as much as to say that the representation would either be impossible or else at least would be nothing for me. That representation that can be given prior to all thinking is called *intuition*. Thus all manifold of intuition has a necessary relation to the *I think* in the same subject in which this manifold is to be encountered.[1]

I intend to highlight two aspects of the way in which Kant approaches the theme of pure apperception in this passage and in the ones that follow it. First, it is necessary to point out that when Kant says that "the *I think* must be able to accompany all my representations", he is not saying that by having a representation, I must be immediately aware of my thought as a thought. When

---

[1] Immanuel Kant, *Critique of Pure Reason*, trans. Paul Guyer and Allen W. Wood (Cambridge: Cambridge University Press, 1998). From here on, "KrV". (KrV B131-132).

I think something, it is not necessary that I should, at the same time, think that I am thinking that representation. Rather, what is established here is that a representation is not mine unless I can ascribe it to myself, *i.e.*, I can say that I think it, that I am aware of it.[2] In other words: if I cannot say that I think a representation, then it cannot be the case that such representation is mine or means something to me.

Second, I want to highlight that this principle is also what allows me to gather a manifold in a single consciousness. "[T]he manifold of representations that are given in a certain intuition would not all together be my representations if they did not all together belong to a self-consciousness [...] because otherwise they would not throughout belong to me".[3] That is, all representations must belong to the same and only consciousness. Therefore, Kant also calls this principle "transcendental unity of consciousness". All my representations are in fact mine because they belong to the same consciousness:

> The thought that these representations given in intuition all together belong to me means, accordingly, the same as that I unite them in a self-consciousness, or at least can unite them therein [...] only because I can comprehend their manifold in a consciousness do I call them all together my representations.[4]

Thus, the *I think* is the consciousness of unity that makes synthesis possible. This self-consciousness occurs in relation to the consciousness of a plurality, and in it, it becomes clear that the consciousness of particular representations is not possible without the consciousness of the unity that allows them to be linked.[5] If the understanding is to execute its acts of synthesis on a manifold, that manifold must be gathered in the same consciousness. This is what Kant means in §15 when he explains that the possibility of a combination in general needs a previous unity.[6]

---

[2] Béatrice Longuenesse, "Kant's 'I Think' versus Descartes 'I Am a Thing That Thinks'", in *Kant and the Early Moderns*, ed. Béatrice Longuenesse and Daniel Garber (Princeton: Princeton University Press, 2008), 15.

[3] KrV B132.

[4] KrV B134.

[5] Pedro Stepanenko, *Unidad de La Conciencia y Objetividad. Ensayos Sobre Autoconciencia, Subjetividad y Escepticismo En Kant* (UNAM: Instituto de investigaciones filosóficas, 2008), 39.

[6] KrV B131.

In this sense, it is possible to understand Kant's treatment of the synthetic unity of consciousness as a response to a Humean problem.[7] Kant would have agreed with Hume's stance,[8] according to which the possibility of being aware of our representations does not imply the perception of the self that has these representations:

> The consciousness of oneself in accordance with the determinations of our state in internal perception is merely empirical, forever variable; it can provide no standing or abiding self in this stream of inner appearances, and is customarily called inner sense or empirical apperception. That which should necessarily be represented as numerically identical cannot be thought of as such through empirical data.[9]

Since representations are given to us in the inner sense as a rhapsodic succession, the mere empirical consciousness of these cannot account for an identical self. Without the transcendental apperception as a synthetic unity of consciousness, "I would have as multicoloured, diverse a self as I have representations of which I am conscious".[10]

If the only possible consciousness were the empirical one, the self would not be more than a rhapsodic flow of representations. But then, the very possibility of connecting these with each other could not be explained; it would not be possible to link different representations in a unitary experience. Hence, the *I think* as an identical consciousness that accompanies all my representations is a condition of the possibility of the combination of these representations. Not only is the synthetic unity of consciousness necessary to be able to say that a representation is mine, but it is also a condition to which all intuitions must be subjected in order to be an object: without this synthesis, the manifold would not be united in a consciousness.[11]

These two remarks (that the *I think* indicates both that a representation is mine and that I am aware of it, and that it allows the unity of all my representations in a consciousness) allow us to establish plainly that the focus of Kant's treatment of the transcendental apperception is not placed on the I that thinks itself, but on the necessary unity in which all my representations

---

[7] Patricia Kitcher, "Kant on Self-Identity," *The Philosophical Review* 91, no. 1 (1982): 41–72, https://doi.org/10.2307/2184668.

[8] David Hume, *A Treatise of Human Nature* (Oxford: Clarendon Press, 1975), 1.4.6, 3-4. From here on, "Treatise".

[9] KrV A107.

[10] KrV B134.

[11] KrV B138.

must be placed. It is necessary to be clear, then, that this self-consciousness is not a perception of the self, but rather it is the consciousness of the unity of all my representations in a single consciousness. Certainly, in the *I think* I am aware of myself as a subject and as an existence.[12] But that consciousness is not the axis on which the elucidation of the transcendental apperception revolves. Kant is not interested in showing that the awareness I have of a representation can show the certainty of my existence. He is interested in showing that all my representations are placed under the unity of a single act.[13] In other words: apperception, as explained by Kant, is not an act whose object is the self. Rather, the *I think* becomes apparent as long as I have representations and I become aware of a pre-categorial unity among these representations: the unity that makes them belong to the same consciousness.

3. Rational psychology

Although the paragraphs related to transcendental apperception are not posed as a response to rational psychology, in the sketch we have just outlined we can already find that Kant approaches this topic differently than the rational psychologist would. For Kant, the *I think* is the condition of possibility of the unity of all thoughts. Consequently, no judgment can be made about this "I", since as a unity that finds all combinations, it is already implied in any judgment. The rational psychologist, on the other hand, tries to establish the knowledge of the self-starting precisely on the *I think*.

As it is well known, in the chapter on Paralogisms included in the Transcendental Dialectic, Kant aims to show the illusory nature of rational psychology's knowledge of the soul. Rational psychology, or rational doctrine of the soul, is the study of the soul as a thinking self, independently of all experience. Thus, rational psychology would be the science built on the single proposition "I think".[14] It cannot contain any object of perception, no empirical predicate, without immediately becoming empirical psychology.

Kant links the conclusions of rational psychology, that is, the supposed properties of the soul, with the four titles of the table of categories. Thus, rational psychology attributes substantiality, simplicity, personality and separate existence to the soul.[15] Attributing these characteristics to the soul is the same as saying that we have knowledge of the soul. This, from Kant's point of view, is impossible. Knowledge can only occur insofar as understanding and

---

[12] KrV B418-422, B422 note.
[13] Longuenesse, "Kant's 'I Think' versus Descartes 'I Am a Thing That Thinks'", 16.
[14] KrV A342-A343 / B400-401.
[15] KrV A403-404.

sensibility work together. There is only knowledge in the proper sense if the understanding exercises an act of synthesis on a manifold given by the sensibility. Knowledge of the self would imply the consciousness of an intuition of myself as determined with respect to a function of thinking (which, incidentally, is possible if that intuition of myself is given to my inner sense). But this is impossible for the *I think*, since there is no intuition of it.[16] For this reason, the conclusions of rational psychology cannot be valid and are due to some error in the argumentation.

This error in argumentation is what Kant calls a "transcendental paralogism." A paralogism is an incorrect syllogism from the point of view of the form. In the case of transcendental paralogisms, which are the ones that concern us here, this error occurs when the middle term is used with two different meanings in both premises. Kant calls this a *sophisma figurae dictionis*, that which we could call a fallacy of amphibology. The transcendental aspect of paralogism consists in the amphibology occurring because the middle term is used in a transcendental sense in one premise and in an empirical sense in the other.[17] In this ambiguity lies the inevitability of the illusion of paralogism outside of critical philosophy. The confusion of rational psychology lies, then, in trying to apply categories that only have significance on the empirical level to a purely intellectual representation. It treats the transcendental self as if it were the noumenal self.[18]

In any case, the starting point of rational psychology is not questioned by Kant: the consciousness of the *I think* is undoubted. But it is inevitable to make a mistake if one tries to know something about this self. For example: the category of substance cannot be applied to it since the condition for this application is something permanent in the phenomenon,[19] but the unity of consciousness does not offer any intuition to which the category of substance may be applied.[20] Thus, rational psychology slips from the fact that the "I" of the *I think* is necessarily a subject (in a logical sense) and not a predicate, to the thought that it is a substance. It also slips from the fact that the I is not a multiplicity in a logical sense, to the idea that it is a simple substance. It passes from the fact that the I is one and the same in each thought, to the idea of personal identity through time. Finally, it passes from the fact that I can

---

[16] KrV B406-407.

[17] KrV A341 / B399, A402, B411.

[18] Alejandra Baher, "La relación entre autoconciencia pura y existencia en la segunda edición de la Crítica de la razón pura," *Revista de Estudios Kantianos* 3, no. 2 (October 30, 2018), https://doi.org/10.7203/REK.3.2.12776, 209.

[19] KrV A183 / B226.

[20] KrV B421-422.

distinguish my existence as a thinker from the things I think, to the existence of a thinking substance independent of what it thinks.[21]

Therefore, rational psychology aims to take the I as an object of possible knowledge. "Yet this I is no more an intuition than it is a concept of any object; rather, it is the mere form of consciousness, which accompanies both sorts of representations".[22] It is the representation of an I from which nothing can be said, a "transcendental subject of thoughts = x".[23] Thus, whatever the transcendental subject is in itself, we are only authorised to say that we know it as an "x" that executes certain functions. But the nature of "x" cannot be established from these functions, nor it can even be assured that there is a nature behind these functions.[24] Then, this self-consciousness is empty of any content whatsoever. There is nothing to think in it other than that all the possible representations that can be thought of as its own agree in the predicate of being a representation of the self and harmonising with the conditions of such unity.[25]

4. The existence of the thinking self

Contrary to the expectations of rational psychology, transcendental apperception cannot be the foundation or the object of any knowledge since it offers no intuition. Yet, Kant states that the "I think" is an empirical proposition and contains within itself the proposition "I exist".[26] I do not intend here to fully elucidate the sense of existence that Kant attributes to the *I think*.[27] What I intend to do next is to lay the basis for a correct understanding of the empirical character of the proposition "I think". And then, from that point on, to show that pure apperception, despite being pure, is not possible without the opportunity of perception.

Whenever Kant says that the *I think* includes the I exist, he clarifies that this existence is indeterminate. Since the determination of existence as a category relates to an object of which one has a concept, and since the *I think* as

---

[21] KrV B407-409; Longuenesse, "Kant's 'I Think' versus Descartes 'I Am a Thing That Thinks'", 22-25.

[22] KrV A382.

[23] KrV A346 / B404.

[24] Frederick C. Beiser, *German Idealism: The Struggle Against Subjectivism, 1781-1801* (Cambridge: Harvard University Press, 2002), 161.

[25] Baher, "La relación entre autoconciencia pura y existencia en la segunda edición de la Crítica de la razón pura", 209; Dieter Henrich, *The Unity of Reason. Essays on Kant's Philosophy.* (Cambridge: Harvard University Press, 1994), 29.

[26] KrV B422 note, see B418-422, B429-430.

[27] For a detailed account on this matter, see Baher, "La relación entre autoconciencia pura y existencia en la segunda edición de la Crítica de la razón pura", 208-223.

consciousness of the unity of representations cannot offer such an object, the existence of the *I think* is always indeterminate. To establish how my existence is to be determined, I need an intuition of myself given to me in the inner sense.[28] But if the latter were given to me, then I would know myself as a phenomenon and we would no longer be talking about pure apperception.[29]

However, according to Kant, the awareness of my own existence (as it occurs in transcendental apperception) already contains an indeterminate intuition that gives me notice of my own existence.[30] For that reason, Kant says that the *I think* is an empirical proposition and encloses an existence.[31] What needs to be elucidated is how it is possible to be aware of the existence of the *I think* if it is an intellectual representation and, even more, how an intellectual representation can give rise to an empirical proposition. Following Baher,[32] we can find the key to this question in the footnote to KrV B422:

> [The I think] expresses an indeterminate empirical intuition, *i.e.*, a perception (hence it proves that sensation, which consequently belongs to sensibility, grounds this existential proposition), but it precedes the experience that is to determine the object of perception through the category in regard to time; and here existence is not yet a category, which is not related to an indeterminately given object, but rather to an object of which one has a concept, and about which one wants to know whether or not it is posited outside this concept. An indeterminate perception here signifies only something real, which was given, and indeed only to thinking in general, thus not as appearance, and also not as a thing in itself (a noumenon), but rather as something that in fact exists and is indicated as an existing thing in the proposition "I think".[33]

If the proposition "I think" expresses that something in fact exists (*etwas, was in der That existirt*), then that "something real" which is given to thinking in general must be the activity of the understanding (the thinking in the *I think*), and it is given insofar as it affects the inner sense. That is to say, Kant alludes here to self-affection, although this can only occur with the opportunity of a

---

[28] Krv B157, B420, B422, B429-430.
[29] KrV B155-156.
[30] KrV B422 note, A343/B401.
[31] KrV B418, 420.
[32] Baher, "La relación entre autoconciencia pura y existencia en la segunda edición de la Crítica de la razón pura", 213-218.
[33] KrV B422-423 fn.

perception on which the synthesising activity of the understanding is executed.[34] Follow Kant:

> For it is to be noted that if I have called the proposition "I think" an empirical proposition, I would not say by this that the I in this proposition is an empirical representation; for it is rather purely intellectual, because it belongs to thinking in general. Only without any empirical representation, which provides the material for thinking, the act I think would not take place, and the empirical is only the condition of the application, or use, of the pure intellectual faculty.[35]

Although this corroborates the fact that some empirical representation must serve as an opportunity for the action of the understanding of the inner sense, there are still questions to be answered: in what sense does the proposition "I think" is empirical? Does the need for an empirical representation as the opportunity for thinking makes the proposition "I think" empirical? I do not believe this to be the case, because the empirical representation on which the act of understanding is executed is not itself the content of the proposition "I think". It is empirical because something affects the inner sense, but in this case, what affects it is the act of understanding (although this act certainly cannot be performed if it is not over the matter that is offered by perception). Now, although the inner sense is affected by the act of the understanding, no manifold is offered in this self-affection that can be in turn linked by the understanding. Then, it is not possible to exercise an act of synthesis. Therefore, Kant says that the existence denoted in the "I think, I exist" is not yet a category. Thus, it should be noted that although in the statement "I think, I exist" the self appears as the logical subject, there is not a true reference to the self: the agent of the act expressed in that proposition is not given, only the act is given. That is, with the "I" I do not mean the synthetic unity of consciousness, but the specific exercise of an act. The *I think* is not about the unity of consciousness in a purely formal sense, but about the concrete exercise of an act. It is that act, executed on an empirical representation, that gives the empirical character to the proposition "I think". Precisely, the proposition "I think" is empirical if I formulate it while I think and I refer to that same act of thinking. But it would not be an empirical proposition when it is only mentioned, without referring to the very act of thinking in which it is thought. For example, when I say, "I think that...", that "I think" is empirical because its formulation already

---

[34] Baher, "La relación entre autoconciencia pura y existencia en la segunda edición de la Crítica de la razón pura", 216-217.
[35] KrV 423 fn.

contains the execution of that same act of thinking. Therefore, in this case, it already contains the proposition "I exist". But when I say for example "He thinks that...", the proposition "he thinks" does not necessarily include the execution of that act of thinking and thus, is not included in it and is not an empirical proposition (against rational psychology, that identifies thinking with existing, and would make all thinking beings necessary beings[36]).

In short: an indeterminate empirical sensation of our own existence is given in the transcendental apperception, insofar as the understanding affects our inner sense. This sensation is not, however, of the self that thinks (which is impossible), but of the act of synthesis, while addressing an empirical representation. It is in this sense that the *I think* includes the I exist. But this does not mean that I know my existence (that is, this existence cannot be taken categorially) since, although I have notice of an act, I have no intuition of the self that exercises the act. Therefore, that existence is indeterminate: I cannot know anything about the "I" that I mention in the *I exist*. I do not know what exists, nor how it exists.[37]

5. Perception and apperception

In the passage of the second edition of the *Critique* in which the principle of the synthetic unity of apperception is introduced, Kant points out that transcendental apperception is original, which means that it cannot be derived from some other consciousness. That is, this consciousness cannot be accompanied, in turn, by any other.[38] This does not mean, however, that this act can be carried out unrestrictedly, without any condition. I intend to point out, on the contrary, that all we have said so far about apperception as a synthetic unity of consciousness, rational psychology and the existence contained in the proposition "I think" is enough to clearly establish the necessary intervention of perception in the act of pure apperception. Being transcendental apperception the consciousness that produces the representation of the *I think* that must be able to accompany all representation, it itself is not possible without other representations to accompany.

This is clear, for example, in the very principle of the synthetic unity of apperception. This is, according to Kant, "itself identical, thus an analytical proposition, yet it declares as necessary a synthesis of the manifold given in an intuition, without which that thoroughgoing identity of self-consciousness

---

[36] KrV B422 fn.
[37] See KrV B420, B422.
[38] KrV B132.

could not be thought".[39] But our understanding is of such a nature that, although it puts the connection, it does not put that which is connected: "An understanding, in which through self-consciousness all of the manifolds would at the same time be given, would intuit; ours can only think and must seek the intuition in the senses".[40] Thus, the synthetic unity of consciousness cannot be thought of unless it accompanies our representations and, in the first place, our perceptions. The unity that is thought under the *I think* that can accompany all my representations is not perceived by itself, but, precisely, insofar as I can call *mine* multiple representations.

So, this *I think* that gives unity to my representations and enables me to say they are mine, is, in a way, more a "mine" than an "I". Taken independently of my representations, it is nothing. The *I think* can only be stated insofar as it is making a synthesis, and it can only make a synthesis if the manifold that it synthesises is given. In this way, he can only say "I" if he can say "mine", but it can never be acknowledged as an "I" independently of such representations. Without a manifold to unify, at best we could speak of a potential self without the possibility of displaying its synthesising action and, therefore, it could not be found as existing in the act of thinking.[41] Perhaps we should even say that the synthetic unity of apperception, considered independently of all perception, cannot be taken even as an *I think* (much less as an I exist). I can logically think of a synthetic unity of consciousness that synthesises nothing, as a merely formal condition of all thinking. But then I cannot say that such I or that such unity exists.[42] Moreover, this means that I could not even say "I". It could not say, or think, anything. Without a manifold to be synthesised, the self could not affirm itself as a self.

This is precisely what the Kantian arguments against rational psychology make clear. Since rational psychology seeks to establish knowledge of the self independently of any reference to experience, its object of knowledge is some sort of nothingness. It lays for its foundation a representation devoid of any content:

> I, of which one cannot even say that it is a concept, but a mere consciousness that accompanies every concept. Through this I, or He, or It (the thing), which thinks, nothing further is represented than a transcendental subject of thoughts = x, which is recognised only

---

[39] KrV B135.

[40] KrV B135.

[41] Claudia Jáuregui and Alejandro Vigo, "Algunas Consideraciones Sobre La 'Refutación Del Idealismo,'" *Revista de Filosofía* II (1987), 33.

[42] Baher, "La relación entre autoconciencia pura y existencia en la segunda edición de la Crítica de la razón pura", 221.

through the thoughts that are its predicates, and about which, in abstraction, we can never have even the least concept [...].[43]

Even the immediate awareness of one's existence (which rational psychology admits regardless of whether external things are given or not[44]) requires the relation between consciousness and something other than itself. Certainly, what consciousness itself perceives when it affirms "I think, I exist" is its own activity, but this activity cannot be exercised if it is not through the opportunity of a given perception. "Without any empirical representation, which provides the material for thinking, the act I think would not take place".[45] Although the *I think* is an intellectual representation, it presupposes the relation with something given to sensitivity in general.[46] Thus, transcendental apperception, even as the plain recognition that my existence is given in the mere fact of thinking, requires perception to be able to execute the activity through which the self affects itself. And it is through this activity that the transcendental apperception takes notice of its own existence.

Although through this section we have spoken of the necessity to have representations in general for the exercise of pure apperception, it is worth mentioning that perceptions, before other representations, have primacy here. Of course, the unity of consciousness puts all representations under itself. However, it is not necessary to have conceptual representations or representations of determined objects for the self-consciousness of apperception. However, perceptions are essential, because without them there would be no material for thinking, without which the act *I think* would not take place.[47] Moreover, since pure apperception does not refer to indeterminate intuition, it is not necessary to establish determinate objects of the senses, but simply to aim to perception.

I conclude this section with a brief summary: pure apperception is not knowledge, since through it I do not know myself nor anything else. But through it, I am aware of the unity that all my representations must have in a single consciousness, which is what is expressed in the principle "the I think must be able to accompany all my representations". Now, in so far as I am aware of my own thinking and, therefore, of the synthetic unity of consciousness, I am aware of my own existence. But this existence cannot be taken as knowledge in

---

[43] KrV A346 / B404.

[44] KrV B417.

[45] KrV B423 note.

[46] Baher, "La relación entre autoconciencia pura y existencia en la segunda edición de la Crítica de la razón pura", 216; Jáuregui and Vigo, "Algunas Consideraciones Sobre La 'Refutación Del Idealismo'", 33.

[47] KrV B423 note.

the proper sense, since it is always indeterminate. In this way, the self-consciousness that is given in this act of consciousness is, above all, consciousness of the unity of my representations and, through it, awareness of my existence. But the consciousness of my existence does not occur without the consciousness of the unity of my representations since the act by which I unify my representations is the act that gives me notice of my existence. In this way, without perceptions to unify, there would be no transcendental apperception.

6. Empirically determined self-consciousness

Thus far, we have talked about self-consciousness as pure apperception. However, Kant points out that there is another way of understanding consciousness. For example, in the *Anthropology from a pragmatic point of View* he distinguishes between a consciousness given by an act of reflection that is a consciousness of the understanding (pure apperception), and another one given through apprehension and that is an empirical apperception:

> In psychology we investigate ourselves according to our ideas of inner sense; in logic, according to what intellectual consciousness suggests. Now here the "I" appears to us to be double (which would be contradictory): 1) the "I" as subject of thinking (in logic), which means pure apperception (the merely reflecting "I"), and of which there is nothing more to say except that it is a very simple idea; 2) the "I" as object of perception, therefore of inner sense, which contains a manifold of determination that make an inner experience possible.[48]

With this distinction, Kant opens a door that had been closed in the treatment of pure apperception: taking the self as an object of knowledge. However in this case, the *I think* does not know itself as a mere logical function, but as an object of perception. Since intuition takes part here, it is possible to determine existence and, therefore, the actual knowledge of it is also possible. But this implies that self-knowledge is knowledge of itself as a phenomenon and not as a thing in itself[49]:

> But how the I that I think is to differ from the I that intuits itself (for I can represent other kinds of intuition as at least possible) and yet be identical with the latter as the same subject, how therefore I can say that I as intelligence and thinking subject cognise myself as an object that is thought, insofar as I am also given to myself in intuition, only, like other

---

[48] AA 7:134 note.
[49] KrV B430, AA 7: 142.

phenomena, not as I am for the understanding but rather as I appear to myself, this is no more and no less difficult than how I can be an object for myself in general and indeed one of intuition and inner perceptions.[50]

These two ways of understanding self-consciousness restrict the pretension of accessing the self as it is in itself. Pure apperception cannot take the *I think* as an object of knowledge. Empirical apperception, which presents itself as self-knowledge, requires something more than just thinking, that is, it requires intuition. It is the knowledge we have about our own self through the representations that are given to us in the inner sense, that is, in time. Consequently, the self is known, in this case, only as it appears to itself, not as it is in itself. In other words, self-knowledge is phenomenal.

That we can distinguish these two senses of consciousness does not imply that the self itself is double (which would be contradictory, as Kant points out in the passage of the *Anthropology*). On the contrary, as indicated in the passage just quoted from the *Critique*, they are identical. Rather than a distinction between two senses of the self, Kant distinguishes the points of view from which the subject is considered. In the *Anthropology*, for example, Kant describes pure apperception as the consciousness of one's activity, that is, what the human being *does*, and the inner sense as the consciousness of what he *undergoes*, in so far as he is affected by the play of his own thoughts.[51] Ultimately, Kant states that the empirical unity of apperception is derived from the original unity of consciousness.[52] We can speak of the self as an object of perception according to our representations of the inner sense only because there is already a certain unity that cannot be given by those same representations.[53] This relationship between pure apperception and empirical apperception can be observed in some passages in which Kant expresses the possibility of determining the indeterminate consciousness of the existence of the *I think* in so far as it is put in relation with what is given to the inner sense.[54]

We should now show, then, how self-consciousness can be empirically determined and what the conditions of possibility of this determination are. But, before that, I think it is pertinent to briefly explain what I think Kant means by an empirically determined self-consciousness.

On the one hand, as we appreciated when analysing the existential content of the proposition "I think", it is not possible to understand existence there as

---

[50] KrV B155.
[51] AA 7: 161.
[52] KrV B140.
[53] KrV B134.
[54] KrV B157 -158, B406-407, B420.

a category, because the experience that gives rise to that proposition is an indeterminate intuition. On the other hand, since we now speak of an empirically determined consciousness, it is necessary to take the existence of which we have consciousness categorially. Therefore, we must also take the intuition that is an occasion of this consciousness as a determinate intuition (or as one that is to be determined in this act) given to the inner sense. This does not mean that pure apperception can do without something given to the inner sense, but that it has no need to determine intuitions. For pure apperception, a rhapsodic succession of representations in the inner sense that can be taken, all of them, as mine is enough. It is not necessary to determine these representations in a specific order under categorical links: as we have pointed out before, what gives rise to the consciousness of the *I think* is the self-affection that takes place on the inner sense in the act by which the understanding gives unity to these representations. This unity does not need a previous act of liaison, it is a condition of it.

Furthermore, if the consciousness of one's own existence is to be determined, there must be something on which an act of determination can be exercised. This cannot be the *I think*. The only thing on which an act of synthesis can be exercised is, then, the representations that I have in the inner sense. In this way, I understand that what is determined cannot be, obviously, the self as a noumenon nor the synthetic unity of apperception, but the inner sense, putting a given place in time to each one of the representations that are otherwise given to me as a rhapsodic succession. To put it another way: what is determined is the stream of my consciousness.

This is what I understand Kant wants to point out when he relates the knowledge I have of myself as the object of intuition and of my internal perceptions with the act by which I draw a line. [55] In this example, Kant explains that we represent time by drawing a line, and in the drawing of the line we know the unity of its dimension, the determination of its temporal extension and the places that occupy the internal perceptions in time.[56] Now, the act of drawing the line (in our mind) is an action of the subject by which the manifold of the inner sense is synthesised, determining the latter.[57] Thus, the empirically determined consciousness entails self-affection once more. However, in this case, the self-affection does not have an opportunity for its action the recollection of a manifold in the original unity of consciousness, but the determination of the order in the representations of the inner sense, that is, the production of a link in the manifold. Through this action, we intuit ourselves

---

[55] KrV B155-156.
[56] KrV B156.
[57] KrV B154-155.

through the inner sense insofar as we are internally affected by ourselves. And what we intuit about ourselves is the order that we produce in the determinations of the inner sense, as phenomena, in time.[58] This intuition of myself allows what was forbidden in the transcendental apperception: "I cognise myself not by being conscious of myself as thinking, but only if I am conscious to myself of the intuition of myself as determined in regard to the function of thought".[59] Thus, the empirically determined consciousness of my own existence is, in the proper sense, self-knowledge. Phenomenal self-knowledge, of course, and not knowledge of the self as a thing in itself.

7. Knowledge and self-knowledge

In the example we discussed in the previous section, it is not irrelevant for Kant to choose the line as an external representation of time. It is by drawing the line, which is properly a spatial object, that the inner sense is determined. The drawing of the line, as the action of the subject, exerts a synthesis of the manifold in space. But in this action, the inner sense is also determined.[60] This should not surprise us if we consider that, according to Kant, every object of the external sense is necessarily also the object of the inner sense.[61] In any case, the underlying thesis is that the determination of the inner sense cannot be exercised if representations are not given to the external sense. Thereby Kant writes:

> [...] we must always derive the determination of the length of time or also of the positions in time for all inner perceptions from that which presents external things to us as alterable; hence we must order the determinations of inner sense as appearances in time in just the same way as we order those of outer sense in space.[62]

It is not possible, thus, to establish an order in the representations of the inner sense without reference to the order of spatial objects.

This last idea, that the order of the representations of the inner sense needs the order of the objects of the external sense, can be approached referring again to the discussion with rational psychology. The fourth paralogism of rational psychology, as presented in the first edition of the *Critique*, holds that the consciousness of one's existence is immediate, while the existence of external phenomena must be inferred as the cause of our perceptions. According to this,

---

[58] KrV B156.
[59] KrV B406.
[60] KrV B155.
[61] KrV A34 / B52.
[62] KrV B156.

the existence of external objects is doubtful.[63] In the second edition of the *Critique*, Kant describes this same stance in other terms: I distinguish my own existence as a thinking entity from other things outside of me. Therefore, I could exist as a thinking entity independently of those other things.[64] To this second formulation of the paralogism, Kant answers with something that we have already discussed in this work: the consciousness of one's existence in the *I think*, as a consciousness of a synthetic unity, is not possible without the representations on which the unity is exerted. Therefore, one cannot deduce the existence of the self as a thinking entity from the consciousness of existence given in apperception. However, what I am interested in discussing now is the idea that underlies both formulations of the fourth paralogism: the conviction that self-knowledge is immediate and knowledge of external objects is mediate. This conviction of the rational psychologist converges with another stance that Kant also tries to refute: problematic idealism. If knowledge of external objects is mediated, their existence must be inferred and, therefore, it is doubtful and indemonstrable.

Kant offers proof of the existence of external objects in a passage of the second edition of the *Critique* entitled "Refutation of idealism".[65] I cannot undertake here a detailed reconstruction of the argument,[66] but reviewing the central points of Kant's strategy can be fruitful in understanding the relation between self-knowledge and knowledge of external objects.

The theorem that Kant intends to prove is: "the mere, but empirically determined, consciousness of my own existence proves the existence of objects in space outside me".[67] By taking self-consciousness as the premise, Kant establishes as a starting point for the argument the only knowledge that the problematic idealist accepts as doubtless. It should be noted, however, that Kant is not talking of self-consciousness as transcendental apperception, but of the consciousness of my existence as determined in time, that is, of empirical apperception.

---

[63] KrV A355-367.
[64] KrV B409.
[65] KrV B274-279.
[66] Different attempts at a reconstruction can be found in: Henry Allison, *Kant's Transcendental Idealism. An Interpretation and Defense* (New Haven: Yale University Press, 2004), 121–125; Efraín Lazos, *Disonancias de La Crítica. Variaciones Sobre Cuatro Temas Kantianos* (UNAM: Instituto de investigaciones filosóficas, 2014), 196–199; Jorge Ornelas, "La disolución kantiana del idealismo," *Revista de filosofía DIÁNOIA* 50, no. 55 (November 3, 2005), https://doi.org/10.21898/dia.v50i55.354, 101–104.
[67] KrV B275.

But would the problematic idealist be willing to grant this starting point? Or would he argue that the certainty of self-consciousness is exhausted in the *I think* of transcendental apperception? It seems to me that he must accept Kant's premise: by saying "I think", the problematic idealist is presupposing more than he would recognise.[68] Only empirical apperception allows the possibility of self-knowledge. Denying it and admitting only the *I think* of transcendental apperception would nullify self-knowledge, something that the problematic idealist does not do.[69] That said, it might seem that Kant can only use the self-consciousness determined in time as the premise of his argument because the problematic idealist does not want to give up self-knowledge. But what would happen if the idealists were willing to do it and accept only the *I think*? The question is rather if he can do it. Accepting "the empirically determined consciousness of my own existence" is not more than accepting that there is a certain temporal order in the representations of my inner sense (that is, that the "stream of my consciousness" is not just a rhapsodic flow of representations). Being able to question this premise already implies that my internal representations have a certain order. Only someone who did not know the order of their mental states could legitimately doubt this. But such a person would not be able to raise such a doubt. To say that self-knowledge is the existence determined in time is simply to accept that the knowledge of one's existence implies a sequence of representations among which a certain order can be established.

After stating his premise, Kant affirms that all temporal determination presupposes something permanent in perception.[70] So, if there is order in the representations of the inner sense, there must be something permanent. This premise, which is the cornerstone of the argument, is based on the first analogy. There it is established that, given that our apprehension of the manifold of appearance is always successive and changing, it does not allow itself to establish an objective order in the succession of our representations. Therefore, something permanent is needed as a criterion of the objective order of succession.[71] But, the proof continues, I do not find anything permanent in my internal experience, because it is precisely what is to be determined. If I accept: a) that my internal experience is determined, *i.e.*, that it is not rhapsodic, b) that something permanent is required as a criterion for that determination and

---

[68] Alejandro Escudero Pérez, "El idealismo transcendental y el problema del mundo externo," *ENDOXA*, no. 18 (January 1, 2004), https://doi.org/10.5944/endoxa.18.2004.508 5, 143.

[69] Lazos, *Disonancias de La Crítica. Variaciones Sobre Cuatro Temas Kantianos*, 200.

[70] KrV B275.

[71] KrV A182 / B225-226.

c) that there is nothing in my internal experience that is permanent, then one should conclude, as Kant wants, that the determination of my inner sense is only possible if there are external objects that provide me with the perception of the permanent that serves as a criterion of determination. The empirically determined consciousness of my existence would then imply the immediate awareness of the existence of external objects.[72]

In this proof, Kant does not demonstrate inferentially from my self-knowledge the existence of external objects. It shows, rather, that self-knowledge, the experience that I have of myself, is only possible if I have immediate experience of external objects. Thus, the culmination of the test is not the demonstration of the existence of objects, but of the immediate experience we have of them. I cannot examine this argument thoroughly here. But the above is enough to clarify the thesis with which we began this section: self-knowledge is not possible without knowledge of external objects. It is necessary to emphasise that perceptions are not enough here (in contrast with what we said about transcendental apperception). The empirically determined consciousness needs knowledge of objects to which it can attribute permanence and, therefore, objects which can be determined under categories of relation. And insofar as it can execute these determinations on the objects, it determines accordingly the order and place that representations of the inner sense occupy in time. Therefore, without knowledge of external objects, there will be no self-knowledge.

Bibliography

Allison, Henry. *Kant's Transcendental Idealism. An Interpretation and Defense.* New Haven: Yale University Press, 2004.

Baher, Alejandra. "La relación entre autoconciencia pura y existencia en la segunda edición de la Crítica de la razón pura." *Revista de Estudios Kantianos* 3, no. 2 (October 30, 2018): 208–23. https://doi.org/10.7203/REK.3.2.12776.

Beiser, Frederick C. *German Idealism: The Struggle Against Subjectivism, 1781-1801.* Cambridge: Harvard University Press, 2002.

Henrich, Dieter. *The Unity of Reason. Essays on Kant's Philosophy.* Cambridge: Harvard University Press, 1994.

Hume, David. *A Treatise of Human Nature.* Oxford: Clarendon Press, 1975.

Jáuregui, Claudia, and Alejandro Vigo. "Algunas Consideraciones Sobre La 'Refutación Del Idealismo.'" *Revista de Filosofía* II (1987): 29–41.

Kant, Immanuel. "Anthropology from a Pragmatic Point of View." In *Anthropology, History, and Education,* edited by Günter Zöller and Robert B. Louden, translated by Robert B. Louden. Cambridge: Cambridge, 2007.

---

[72] KrV B275-276.

————. *Critique of Pure Reason.* Translated by Paul Guyer and Allen W. Wood. Cambridge: Cambridge University Press, 1998.

————. *Gesammelte Schriften.* Berlin-Leipzig: Georg Reimer & Walter de Gruyter, 1900.

Kitcher, Patricia. "Kant on Self-Identity." *The Philosophical Review* 91, no. 1 (1982): 41–72. https://doi.org/10.2307/2184668.

Lazos, Efraín. *Disonancias de La Crítica. Variaciones Sobre Cuatro Temas Kantianos.* UNAM: Instituto de investigaciones filosóficas, 2014.

Longuenesse, Béatrice. "Kant's 'I Think' versus Descartes 'I Am a Thing That Thinks'." In *Kant and the Early Moderns,* edited by Béatrice Longuenesse and Daniel Garber, 9–31. Princeton: Princeton University Press, 2008.

Ornelas, Jorge. "La disolución kantiana del idealismo." *Revista de filosofía DIÁNOIA* 50, no. 55 (November 3, 2005): 95–117. https://doi.org/10.21898/dia.v50i55.354.

Pérez, Alejandro Escudero. "El idealismo transcendental y el problema del mundo externo." *ENDOXA,* no. 18 (January 1, 2004): 141–70. https://doi.org/10.5944/endoxa.18.2004.5085.

Stepanenko, Pedro. *Unidad de La Conciencia y Objetividad. Ensayos Sobre Autoconciencia, Subjetividad y Escepticismo En Kant.* UNAM: Instituto de investigaciones filosóficas, 2008.

Chapter 8

Moral Conscience in Kant's Late Philosophy: Is it Relevant for the Concept of Radical Evil?

Jimena Portilla González

Universidad Panamericana

Abstract: In this chapter, I discuss moral conscience as the faculty in charge of evaluating practical reason's judgement of moral actions. The second part presents a discussion about the concept of radical evil in the *Religion* and its link to self-deception. In the third section of this article, I will show the arguments for an interpretation that leaves space for the moral conscience as a faculty whose exercise must be cultivated (as Kant mentions in the *Doctrine of Virtue*). Finally, I will present my arguments for the plausibility of a link between conscience and radical evil.

Keywords: Kant, problem of evil, practical reason, conscience, deception.

***

Several problems arise from the Kantian analysis of our maxim's motivations. It is well known that Kant is especially aware of the self-deception present in the motives of our moral election of maxims and actions. Part of the correct way to evaluate an action's morality consists in the objective work of practical reason through the categorical imperative. But the human tendency towards self-deception still risks that unnoticed impure elements are taken as grounds of our moral choice.

In this chapter, I discuss moral conscience as the faculty in charge of evaluating practical reason's judgement of moral actions. This kind of judgement does not focus on the objective side of moral evaluation but on its subjective and reflective activity. In his late philosophy, Kant turns to this notion of moral conscience. The special *caution* needed in this kind of judgement is intended to bring some *certainty* on the subjective act of holding our maxims to be true, and therefore morally good. This notion of a second-order judgement is presented in the first part of the chapter.

The second part presents a discussion about the concept of radical evil in the *Religion* and its link to self-deception. Propensity to evil entails impurity on the grounds of our actions, as well as self-deception and frailty in the choice of our main choice. Such opacity in our maxim formation is a great obstacle to a clear judgement from the moral conscience. We must consider this and question if moral conscience is powerful enough to overcome this difficulty.

In the third section of this chapter, I will show the arguments for an interpretation that leaves space for the moral conscience as a faculty whose exercise must be cultivated (as Kant mentions in the *Doctrine of Virtue*). The last section concerning the duty of self-knowledge clears some ways that the moral conscience must consider for its self-assessment. We will see that these duties cannot be separated, because self-knowledge is needed at different levels of the moral judgement.

Finally, I will present my arguments for the plausibility of a link between conscience and radical evil. I do not pretend to show a direct connection between these two concepts in Kant's texts. I rather point out the convenience of the moral conscience as a tool to prevent our moral disposition (*Gesinnung*) from mixing or using a completely immoral ground for our subsequent maxims. In a broad sense, the guidance of moral conscience may form our motivations in a more correct, duty-based and virtuous way.

1. Moral Conscience: a subjective faculty of judgement

Kant's moral pre-critical works, such as his *Lectures on Ethics* consider moral conscience as an instinct and as a tribunal or internal forum[1]. The notion of instinct depicts the unavoidability of the presence of conscience in all human beings. A more robust and relevant concept of moral conscience began to be developed since his writing *On the Miscarriage of all Philosophical Trials in Theodicy* in 1791.[2] There is a change in the nature of the tasks of conscience.

---

[1] Immanuel Kant, "On the Miscarriage of All Philosophical Trials in Theodicy (1791)," in *Religion and Rational Theology*, ed. Allen W. Wood and George di Giovanni, The Cambridge Edition of the Works of Immanuel Kant (Cambridge: Cambridge University Press, 1996), 19–38, https://doi.org/10.1017/CBO9780511814433.004. References of Kant's works are cited by the page numbers of the edition of the Royal Prussian Academy of Sciences, currently the German Academy of Sciences. (27: 351.22, 353.25).

[2] G. Felicitas Munzel, *Kant's Conception of Moral Character: The "Critical" Link of Morality, Anthropology, and Reflective Judgment* (Chicago: University of Chicago Press, 1998).

Conscience is no longer just a tool that evaluates actions directly. Human beings must be conscious in two different ways: through a material consciousness and a formal consciousness. The former depicts the common use of the term moral conscience and is broadly the same that he uses in his Lectures. Kant holds that the understanding is the faculty that judges objectively, *i.e.* whether an action follows the moral law. The categorical imperative is the principle with which this evaluation is made, but conscience needs analysis of the subjective conditions of our judgements. That is why a subjective conscience is necessary. Formal consciousness is properly the moral conscience. It evaluates "*whether I in fact* believe to be right (or merely pretend it)".[3] In contrast with his earlier notion of moral conscience, Kant affirms for the first time that conscience cannot err. This will be repeated in his later works:

> An erring conscience is an absurdity. "I can indeed err in the judgement in which *I believe* to be right, understanding which alone judges objectively (rightly or wrongly), but in the judgement *whether I in fact* believe to be right (or merely pretend it) I absolutely cannot be mistaken, for this judgement, or rather this proposition — merely says that I judge the object in such-and such- a way.[4]

Truthfulness is a condition that every declaration must have. In my opinion, this is a matter of both epistemology and will. Self-deception can be traced as influencing our closest maxims, and even sometimes we can notice it from actions. But most of the time our subjectivity is reluctant to show its true motives even within ourselves. Kant is always aware of this difficulty, even as he observes self-love as forming incentives for action in sophisticated ways of self-deception. In his work on *Theodicy*, he says that the propensity to falsehood and the impurity is the principal affection of human nature. As he will continue in the *Religion*, Kant holds that there lies an impurity that remains hidden, "where the human being knows how to distort even inner declarations before his own conscience"[5] and the lie (referring to the lie about our true belief in our declaration) "undermines the ground of every virtuous intention".[6]

---

[3] 8:268.

[4] 8:268. For a detailed research on the logical and epistemological importance of the infallibility of conscience, see Franz Knappik and Erasmus Mayr, "'An Erring Conscience Is an Absurdity': The Later Kant on Certainty, Moral Judgment and the Infallibility of Conscience," *Archiv Für Geschichte Der Philosophie* 101, no. 1 (March 1, 2019): 92–134, https://doi.org/10.1515/agph-2019-1004.

[5] 8:270.

[6] 8:269.

Following a chronological order, I will continue the analysis of moral conscience in the *Religion within the Boundaries of Mere Reason*.[7] Kant states: "Conscience is a consciousness which is of itself a duty", this proposition opens a new view of the concept. This reflective judgment must be especially careful in its exercise. "We ought to venture nothing where there is a danger that it might be wrong (*quod dubitas, ne feceris!*, Pliny)".[8] Is Kant asking for a quasi-passive attitude to prevent us from acting in incorrect ways?[9] Such a command would be contradictory to Kant's interest for a reason that can and must be practical. According to the previous notes, we can answer to the question. The conclusion of our judgements must lie on solid grounds. We must be *certain* that we sincerely hold a maxim to be true. That does not imply that *objectively* we cannot err. Of course, we can judge an object of choice to be moral when it is not. But we can examine the honesty of our intentions while judging our declarations.

Kant uses as an example the case of the inquisitor who judges that a subject ought to be condemned over his religious beliefs. The main problem is that the source of his judgement cannot be objective. Being certain that an action is right, implies not having a mere opinion, but a genuine conviction:

> conviction in this matter has no other grounds of proof except historical ones, and in the judgement of the people (if they subject themselves to the least test) there is always the possibility that an error has crept into these (proofs).[10]

My interpretation of this example is that an important part of the problem goes back to the contingent/necessary distinction in Kant's moral philosophy. Beliefs that merely rely on contingent facts and whose true motivations are hard to find are not fit to ground moral decisions. What instead could have been a correct motivation, would be a command compatible with pure reason. I think that the evaluation of the categorical imperative is fundamental in these cases (like in any contemporary example of dogmatism). This step prevents taking something subjective as objective or taking a persuasion for a conviction. Still, the judge must make another judgement to examine if he really takes that as a true and a good (rational) command.

---

[7] James J. Dicenso, *Kant's Religion Within the Boundaries of Mere Reason: A Commentary* (New York: Cambridge University Press, 2012).

[8] 6:185.

[9] Jens Timmermann, "Quod Dubitas, Ne Feceris : Kant on Using Conscience as a Guide," *Studi Kantiani : XXIX, 2016*, no. XXIX (2016), https://doi.org/10.19272/201602901010, 168.

[10] 6:187.

Once again, Kant makes clear that conscience passes a judgement upon itself (upon practical reason): "Rather, here reason judges itself, whether it has actually undertaken, with all diligence, that examination of actions (whether they are right or wrong) and it calls upon the human being himself to witness *for* or *against* himself whether this has taken place or not".[11]

2. The opacity of moral maxims, self-deception and radical evil

Before further analysis of moral conscience, I will consider some difficulties concerning radical evil and maxim formation. The opacity thesis is not new in Kant's ethics, but the *Religion* scrutinises this problem in detail. The first issue is that maxims, the subjective guides of our practical actions, cannot be seen. They are hidden and their motives or incentives are opaque. We have also a very pervasive propensity towards evil, that is, radical evil.

The theory of radical evil entails an incorrect subordination of our main maxim. Kant affirms that our interests in actions can be pathological or practical. The former refers to the principles dependent on sensibility, *i.e.*, inclinations; whereas the latter takes interest in actions themselves since these are duties. Maxims contain either kind of motivation, but there is also a moral disposition under the name of *Gesinnung*. Even though some commentators translate it as intention, it has a deeper meaning. Just like actions have maxims as their rules, maxims are dependent on a moral subjective principle that directs them. Kant tends to depict *Gessinung* as the right order of intentions that constitutes such a principle. In it, both moral a non-moral motivation is present, but one is subordinated to the other. The disposition of a good *Gesinnung* has the moral law as its priority and places the non-moral intentions under the rule of the moral principle.

Even though a good *Gesinnung* must be possible for human beings, this order is rarely observed among us. This kind of right order in some ways resembles that of good will. The former may be thought of as an idea, it is a will that has absolute worth because it is independent of consequences. A subject's *Gesinnung* accepts the role of non-moral rules in our general attitude towards morality. It may be more open because here Kant is aware that we need to satisfy other kinds of wishes and rules, besides morality. But we also need to order the maxims so that they have the moral law as their centre. Humans are capable of virtue, to act in accordance and motivated by the moral law is possible for us because we are free, and we feel respect for the moral law. But in the *Religion*, Kant also holds that all human beings have a propensity towards evil.

---

[11] 6:186.

The concept *radical evil* refers to a tendency held freely to corrupt our moral choices, and put more briefly, our *Gesinnung*. The root of our maxims is corrupted by our own choice to treat material and non-moral intentions as if they were the moral law. Even when nature prepares aspects of our subjectivity of morality through dispositions such as animality, humanity and personality,[12] we freely and willingly turn that guidance away. To have a bad *Gesinnung* then means that we prefer non-moral incentives (self-love and inclinations) instead of the moral law. We may act legally right, *i.e.*, in accordance with the moral law, and so the object of the duty is done. But when non-moral intentions ground the reasons for acting in conformity to a duty, there is evil involved. The subject has not placed in a correct order the principles of all his choices. As the highest moral subjective principle, *Gesinnung* is "the disposition by which our life is to be judged (life as a whole)".[13]

Kant's depiction of the order between our *Gesinnung*, maxims and actions could infer a way to trace back a subject's true intentions. This kind of theory would be helpful for moral conscience. Moral conscience could have control over the different kinds of intentions and so it would identify if the moral law or self-love is predominant over the other. But there is yet another difficulty to be noticed. Kant's thesis of *radical evil* comes with explanations on how there is an opacity beyond our maxims and a tendency to self-deception on every subjectivity. Even if we can show that there is an order and a guide of the maxims that rule our actions, we cannot be certain of its content and formality (the way in which both principles have been placed by us).

Radical evil (*das radikal Böse*) is a propensity, "the subjective ground of the possibility of an inclination (habitual desire, *concupiscentia)* insofar as this possibility is contingent for humanity in general".[14] Natural predispositions to good are necessary, human beings are constituted that way. But evil is a noumenal choice (not made in a specific moment), and so nothing in space or time could have been its cause. That is why it is a free act, and contingent for humanity. We are free to choose whether we form and follow a corrupted *Gesinnung* or not.

This propensity or radical evil has three degrees: frailty, impurity and depravity or corruption of the human heart.[15] Frailty is our weakness in following the good maxim that we have adopted. The second degree; impurity, has the power to follow its maxim. But it does not follow duty only from the moral law, it "needs still other incentives besides it in order to determine the

---

[12] 6:26.
[13] 6:77.
[14] 6:29.
[15] 6:30.

power of choice, in other words, actions conforming to duty are not done purely from duty".[16] Self-deception is present at this level. On the first level, the subject is clear on the maxim wanted. She struggles to do what is right, but her inclinations are stronger as incentives and so she fails to make it a principle of action. But impurity implies that even if we know that morality needs a *true commitment* to the moral law, we want it to be subordinated to other principles. We may as well believe that we are doing our duty because of our own worth, but that, deep down in our intentions, it is not true.

At last, corruption, depravity or perversity of the human heart is the power of free choice that subordinates incentives of the moral law to non-moral ones. Here it is not a matter of mixing incentives like the impurity does. Kant implies here that we damage our *Gesinnung* on this level, (in spite of the legality of the good actions): "yet the mind's attitude is thereby corrupted at its root (so far as the moral disposition is concerned) and hence the human being is designated as evil".[17] This is important for the present essay because truthfulness and honesty should be present in our maxims. As we have seen above, conscience must trace those qualities in moral judgement in order to evaluate it.

Later in the *Religion* Kant stresses the dishonesty and self-deceit of radical evil. Perversity of the heart[18] not only has natural frailty, but it is *dishonest* in not screening incentives in accordance with the moral guide. More importantly, it deceives itself by considering itself *justified* before the law.[19] We can relate this propensity to the inquisitor, who already believes he is right and does not want to take his judgement under an objective principle, namely reason. That same practical reason, in the form of conscience, must also verify if his conviction is real, or if it is only a persuasion (personal security of one's belief, with no objective proof). The effect *dishonesty* has on our moral (good) disposition is unavoidable, it "hinders the establishment in us of a genuine moral disposition".[20] Finally, dishonesty is an unworthiness that rests on the radical evil, which "(inasmuch as it puts out of tune the moral ability to judge what to think of a human being, and renders any imputability entirely uncertain, whether internal or external) constitutes the foul stain of our

---

[16] 6:30.
[17] 6:30.
[18] Kant usually uses this term as a metaphor for our deepest intentions, *i.e.* our moral disposition. That is why he says moral regeneration is possible through a "revolution of the heart".
[19] 6:37.
[20] 6:38.

species".[21] Moral judgement becomes more difficult when we become aware of the various ways radical evil intervenes in our election of maxims.

Conscience plays a very close role in the examination of intentions. Kant says in the *Religion* that the voice of conscience calls for *diligence*[22] and *sincerity* when coming across an error.[23] Diligence, as an effort to be careful with our judgements, and sincerity with our own intentions are important devices against radical evil. Radical evil has at its centre techniques of self-persuasion. Along with systematic distraction, moral conscience can deteriorate, so "the receptiveness for moral claims the gradually decreases".[24]

The inner attitude (*Gesinnung*) is the proper object of the application of morality to nature. Its effect is the moral formation of the subject, the moral formation of his character. "Although moral law (causality by freedom) certainly lacks objective theoretical reality, "it has (...) a real application which is exhibited *in concreto* in dispositions [*Gesinnungen*] or maxims".[25]

3. Moral conscience in the *Doctrine of Virtue*: *Gewissen's* cultivation as a duty and the tribunal of conscience

In 1797, Kant published the *Metaphysics of Morals*, where he made some important additions to his critical moral philosophy. The *Doctrine of Virtue* includes different ends that are also moral duties. Kant also reinterprets the position of some feelings that form the receptivity of duty in the subject, he calls them aesthetic preliminary concepts[26]. One of those aesthetic preconditions for duty is moral conscience. It is a "natural predisposition of the

---

[21] 6:38.

[22] 6:185.

[23] 6:187.

[24] Andrea Esser, "The Inner Court of Conscience, Moral Self-Knowledge, and the Proper Object of Duty," in *Kant's "Tugendlehre": A Comprehensive Commentary*, ed. Oliver Sensen, Jens Timmermann, and Andreas Trampota (Berlin/New York: Walter de Gruyter, 2013), 280.

[25] 5:56.

[26] The aesthetic pre-notions of the receptivity of duty reinforce the hypothesis that they are a series of natural conditions that are pre-given and "that are the subjective dimension that makes possible the *Faktum* of reason" We will see that conscience is "the *forum* in which we recognise ourselves as moral, and thus, being free." (Cf. Fasching, *Zum Begriff der Freduschaft bei Aristoteles und Kant*. Quoted in Vicente De Haro Romo, *Duty, Virtue and Practical Reason in Kant's Metaphysics of Morals*, trans. Erik Norvelle (Hildesheim: Olms, 2015), 168).

mind for being affected by concepts of duty".[27] It is our duty to exercise or cultivate this already given faculty in us:

> The duty here is only to cultivate one's conscience, to sharpen one's attentiveness to the voice of the inner judge, and to use every means to obtain a hearing for it (hence the duty is only indirect).[28]

Even though it is each subject's duty to cultivate this precondition throughout life, it is not a matter of mere irreflexive repetition. This notion of moral conscience is linked to Kant's interpretation of the classic internal court of judgement. It entails that we are not to leave our intentions in charge of only one side of our subjectivity. The relation between moral law, our maxims, and our deeds must go through an exercise of reflective moral deliberation. Kant sometimes seems to mix both concepts of moral judgement: as an objective judge of deeds (material consciousness), and as a subjective evaluator of practical reason as a judge (formal consciousness). Such is the case in the following passage, even when he tries to ensure that conscience is only the latter:

> For, conscience is practical reason holding the human being's duty before him for his acquittal or condemnation in every case that comes under a law. This is not directed to an object but merely to the subject (to affect moral feeling by its act), and so it is not something incumbent on one, a duty, but rather an unavoidable fact.[29]

Conscience as an "unavoidable fact" is as present in us as the conscience Kant had called in his pre-critical ethics an instinct. The voice of conscience always speaks when the faculty of the understanding (or practical reason, he uses both faculties in different parts of his works) has already come to a deed, applying the rule of the categorical imperative.[30] Just like practical reason is always prepared to remind us of our duties, moral conscience follows us like a shadow, in the form of internal judgement. Kant is aware that we may try to make it disappear through "pleasures and distractions". However, its voice cannot be shut.[31] From this proposition, we can infer that even the worst criminal has a moral conscience. It is already present in us, just as our reason. That is why we

---

[27] 6:399.
[28] 6:401.
[29] 6:400.
[30] 6:400.
[31] 6:439.

do not have a duty to have a moral conscience, what is in our power is to listen to it or to *try* to avoid hearing it. [32]

There is a question related to the last point that remains unanswered. What happens when a *passion (Leidenschaft)* takes over a subject's will? [33] In the *Doctrine of Virtue*, Kant addresses passions as a "sensible desire that has become a lasting inclination". It is interesting that the philosopher from Könnigsberg holds passion to permit reflection, because of the calm with which we give ourselves to it. That roots up deeply and it takes up *what is evil into its maxim*. "And then evil is then *properly* evil, that is, a true *vice*".[34] It seems that passions are like an inverted mirror of how we should subordinate our maxims or even our *Gesinnung*. However, we could ask how it is possible to reflect when the passion is so strong that we may feel absolutely ruled by it. If it lets reason take it as the material of a maxim, can it be equally taken by reason and converted to virtue? In the *Religion* Kant argues for the possibility of a conversion or revolution of the heart. Can we relate passions to the perversity of the heart? How can we be detached from such a rooted kind and such a lasting inclination? How can conscience make it listen to its verdict? These questions would need another essay to be examined.

Conscience is no longer considered as objective consciousness. In the *Doctrine of Virtue*, "conscience does not directly contribute to moral orientation, but merely exhorts us to always subject our actions to moral reflection and criticism, and to appeal to the 'inner court of justice'".[35] The tribunal of conscience is a metaphor common before Kant's time. In his late philosophy, especially in the *Religion* and the *Doctrine of Virtue*, he refers to it more than once. Kant develops a sophisticated model where there is not just an accused and the voice of the moral law to judge actions and maxims (which had been the image he gave us in the former quotations).

> But the internal imputation of a deed, as a case falling under a law (*in meritum aut demeritum*), belongs to the faculty of judgement (*iudicium*), which, as the subjective principle of imputing an action, judges with rightful force whether the action as a deed (an action coming under a *lae*) has occurred or not. Upon it result with the action (condemnation or

---

[32] Kant also argues for the absurdity of an erring conscience, as he did on his essay on *Theodicy*. He concludes: "*Unconscientiousnss* is not lack of conscience but rather the propensity to pay no heed to its judgement"; 6:400.

[33] *Willkür.*

[34] 6:408.

[35] Esser, "The Inner Court of Conscience, Moral Self-Knowledge, and the Proper Object of Duty", 272.

acquittal). All this takes place before a tribunal *(coram indicio)*, which, as a moral person giving effect to the law, is called a court *(forum)*. Consciousness of an internal court in man ("before which his thoughts accuse or excuse one another") is conscience.[36]

First, condemnation or acquittal is expressed in every subject with feelings, and so we can react more efficiently to the judge's commands upon our actions. Then, Kant explains how every part of this court proceeds. The prosecutor in our conscience must show proof of the judge's sentence. He is there to prevent the accused from believing the dishonest and self-conceiting excuses of the attorney or solicitor. These come from self-love, they may even, as Kant says in the *Religion,* turn to human nature's frailty to convince ourselves about an evil maxim. Overall, his "duty is to verify whether he (the accused) can be absolved of any guilt or whether he is to be sentenced or condemned for his conscious negligence of a particular duty".[37]

On the other hand, the inner judge (who has already the knowledge of the objective judgement) pronounces a sentence for the accused. Kant identifies him with the concept of God. Only God can sentence happiness or misery. This capacity is logically grounded on a relation between our actions and the effects they have on the world. Only God can make virtue or vice correspond to happiness or misery. Kant is indirectly referring to his *Summum Bonum.* What confers God (the mere idea of him for the sake of a moral conscience) this great capacity? He must be "a scrutiniser of hearts, since the court is set up within the human being" The underlying opacity of our intentions can only be thought of as clear to the concept of a divine being. [38]

God is both the origin of the legislation, the judge and the only capable of causing the effects of his laws. In this way "conscience must be thought of as the subjective principle of being accountable to God for all one's deeds".[39] The accused must listen to the whole trial, but he is the only one who can make a choice from it if the conscience is prospective or accept or reject it if it is retrospective. Kant also explains[40] that in this trail both *homo noumenon and*

---

[36] 6: 439.

[37] Esser, "The Inner Court of Conscience, Moral Self-Knowledge, and the Proper Object of Duty", 279.

[38] This does not mean that we ought to lose autonomy and give an external authority the power over our judgements. We must evaluate ourselves in accordance to such a practical postulate. Then, we can be certain that we can hold our beliefs as true. The moral law (with its objectivity) and the impartiality in the justice of an all-knower must help us with the guidance of moral judgement.

[39] 6:440.

[40] 6:440, footer.

homo phenomenon are represented. The former "is subject to the concept of freedom and he is subject to a law he that he gives himself, as another from the human being as a sensible being endowed with reason, only in a practical respect".[41] It is of great importance that Kant recognizes both kinds of "men" coexisting in our subjectivity. As we can relate to both a noumenal and a phenomenal world, both perspectives should also communicate.

If we were just rational beings, acting only from practical interests, there would be no need for a conscience. Our acts would always correspond and be originated in duty. But we would not properly be moral beings. In a way, it is fundamental that we are free to choose our intentions even if we have the risk of being *evil*. Nevertheless, it is also necessary to take as moral principle reason in its purity, the ideal of a sacred being whose intentions are always identical to the moral law.[42] If we, on the other hand, were endowed with a reason whose only possible task is the regulation of pathological interests, morality would be impossible. Just as Kant concluded in the *Groundwork*, we need to see humanity from both perspectives. The court of justice divides in its juridical exercise these different tendencies and capacities of humanity. Only then, can we have a universal and objective principle judging our deeds.

There is one last comment about moral conscience as it appears in the *Doctrine of Virtue*. It warns us before we act, and it sentences a judgement of culpability or innocence after we act.[43] Claudia Blöser[44] considers the relation between this quote, a quote where prospective conscience is established in the *Religion*[45] and a notion of the *Gewissen* in the first *Critique*.[46] In it, Kant presents how the moral law connects an act with the feeling of regret. It does it independently of when this event happened as an event whose author is the subject. These quotes show a conscience both in relation to time (it has an effect before and after the act), and a conscience independent of time. These sides of *Gewissen* do the relation between empirical and intelligible character. In the *Gewissen* there are both aspects of a person: the intelligible, but also the empirical. In the empirical perspective, the acts are temporal phenomena, and so her acts are planned, performed and judged in retrospective.[47]

---

[41] 6:440.

[42] This is why in the *Religion* Kant studies Jesus as a moral archetype of a perfect *Gesinnung*.

[43] 6:440.

[44] Claudia Blöser, *Zurechnung Bei Kant* (Berlin: Walter de Gruyter, 2014).

[45] 6:186.

[46] 5:99.

[47] For a further research on character, see Munzel, *Kant's Conception of Moral Character: The "Critical" Link of Morality, Anthropology, and Reflective Judgment.* She relates

4. The Duty of Self-knowledge

The scrutiny of our hearts has proved to be very difficult. Moral conscience must make a considerable effort to clarify a subject's intentions. It is not the case that we can know its contents completely, rather subjectively, we can judge if we hold our maxims with *truthfulness*. This means that we have some security regarding our own conscience being exercised or cultivated. I think that Kant realises the need for positive ways of facing self-deception. It makes sense that after the first two parts of the *Religion*, Kant finishes his book with the possible and morally necessary battle of the good principle against the bad principle in human beings, and its actual capacity to overcome radical evil. But also, he develops a theory of virtue in the *Metaphysics of Morals*. Imperfect duties have an important role because they connect the subjectivity of sensibility and the objectivity of practical reason.

The duty of self-knowledge comes together with the indirect duty to cultivate moral conscience. We cannot conceive the latter without the former.

> This command is "know" (scrutinise, fathom) yourself" [...] in terms of your moral perfection in relation to your duty. This is, know your heart – whether it is good or evil, whether the source of your actions is pure or impure, and what can be imputed to you as belonging originally to the substance of a human being or as derived (acquired or developed) and belonging to your moral condition. [...] To remove the obstacle within (an evil will actually present in him) and then to develop the original predisposition to a good will with him, which can never be lost.[48]

Once again, we can ask how we can know our deepest intentions. The noumenal self we discussed above has some tools to according to our possibilities, judge like the "scrutiniser of the hearts". The last sentence in Kant's quotation above clearly refers to evil's interaction within our maxim formation and *Gesinnung*. Self-knowledge is the subjective duty that can and must be exercised against our subjective tendency towards self-conceit. The "original predisposition to a good will" is the *Gesinnung*. It cannot be lost because everything (practical reason, conscience, and the predispositions towards good) conforms to an important part of what human beings are. They are elements of our nature that leave germs on us to fight the *free* propensity

---

empirical character to the free power of choice, "the actualised synthetic unity of causality", as stated in GMunzel, *Kant's Conception of Moral Character: The "Critical" Link of Morality, Anthropology, and Reflective Judgment*, 143. This is the same choice that can be seen in time but has had in radical evil an origin independent from time.
[48] 6:442.

towards evil. Self-knowledge is understood this way and the *Gesinnung* may be in danger when we prefer to conduct our life with a false subordination of principles. However, they do not annihilate the possibility of the conversion of our hearts: a true guidance of our character towards good.

The cultivation of self-knowledge as a disposition makes practical the general condition of *truthfulness* that every judgement ought to have. It also marks a necessary limit between self-love from getting into morality's grounds. If we can recognise the force and position of our inclinations, we may control them in easier ways. The commandment to recognise oneself causes "impartiality in appraising oneself in comparison with the law, and sincerity in acknowledging to oneself".[49]

Self-knowledge not only precedes and constitutes the process in a tribunal of conscience. The first part of self-knowledge is "the recognition of the purity or impurity of the source and therefore, for the motivation for one's actions." The second element of self-duty is "the identification, within the sphere of what conditions the action, of what may be legitimately imputed to the agent, insofar as it is the fruit of a moral choice".[50] It is very interesting to consider self-knowledge so interpreted, as the limits and conditions of humanity. If we are aware for example, of the role we give to inclinations in morality, the recognition of purity or impurity of motivation can have great effects.

Finally, self-knowledge deals with two difficulties. The first one is a general psychological opacity of the soul: our motives are obscure. In addition, the knowledge of one's moral motives can only be inferred from the sensible to the super-sensible. It is through the manifestation of the *Gesinnung* that we know something about the quality of the *Gesinnung*.[51] To know oneself is in a certain way, an ideal that must be sought. "The examination of our representations and what we presume to be such —including our moral sentiments, or what we presume to be such —can contribute to a more apt and sharper moral judgement, and to the correction of our moral prejudices".[52]

5. Conclusion

My interpretation of moral conscience shows a connection with the concept of radical evil through the moral need to clarify moral intentions. There is not a

---

[49] 6:442.
[50] Claudio La Rocca, "Kant on Self-Knowledge and Conscience," in *Das Leben Der Vernunft. Beiträge Zur Philosophie Kants*, ed. Dieter Hüning, Stefan Klingner, and Carsten Olk (Berlin-Boston: De Gruyter, 2013), 365.
[51] La Rocca, "Kant on Self-Knowledge and Conscience", 369.
[52] La Rocca, "Kant on Self-Knowledge and Conscience", 370.

causal link between these two concepts, nor is it necessary to understand one of them to conclude the other. The kind of relation I want to show is that of a rational resource for fighting radical evil. If we take the tribunal of conscience into account, we understand that there is a bad action to be judged; that is the role of the accused. Furthermore, this chapter has shown that evil is really on our supreme maxim: the way we revert our *Gesinnung*. Then, we may infer something from our actions, in order to "observe" our *Gesinnung* or the noumenal moral character behind our actions. Nevertheless, we do not have a direct way of doing it, and *certainty* does not come from that step. Even if there are objective principles that work in that way from actions to maxims, (take the universality of the categorical imperative, for example), they cannot assure its moral perfection. Self-love is often hidden under the beautiful form of a good maxim (that is coherent with duty).

Then, how are we to reverse a corrupted *Gesinnung*? If moral dispositions contrary to radical evil are natural, they should play some role in the present moral research. Reason is practical in objective ways; we know that we are free because we can follow the categorical imperative's commands. But as we showed below, there is a propensity that nurtures itself with self-deception and dishonesty. The *Doctrine of Virtue* manages to satisfy subjective tools to constantly prevent radical evil from gaining domain over our maxim construction. The duties of self-knowledge and cultivating moral conscience have strong powers to *avoid* radical evil as a governing force. What we can do with them, may be interpreted as negative. Just as it is a duty to maintain ourselves healthy, that is, to protect our physical integrity, and to avoid sickness, we must avoid moral corruption through the reflective habit of our motives of action. The right way to do it is through *constant, diligent and cautions* evaluations of our moral choices. It is of great importance to remember that this judgement is of second-order. This means that it is reason evaluating itself, or in other ways, it is a subject corroborating if what he holds as a maxim is what she really believes to be *true and morally right*. That is if the motivation behind her maxims is the real reason why she wants to perform a moral action.

Bibliography

Blöser, Claudia. *Zurechnung Bei Kant*. Berlin: Walter de Gruyter, 2014.

De Haro Romo, Vicente. *Duty, Virtue and Practical Reason in Kant's Metaphysics of Morals*. Translated by Erik Norvelle. Hildesheim: Olms, 2015.

Dicenso, James J. *Kant's Religion Within the Boundaries of Mere Reason: A Commentary*. New York: Cambridge University Press, 2012.

Esser, Andrea. "The Inner Court of Conscience, Moral Self-Knowledge, and the Proper Object of Duty." In *Kant's "Tugendlehre": A Comprehensive*

Commentary, edited by Oliver Sensen, Jens Timmermann, and Andreas Trampota, 269–91. Berlin/New York: Walter de Gruyter, 2013.

Kant, Immanuel. *Lectures on Ethics*. New York: Cambridge University Press, 1997.

Kant, Immanuel. *Critique of Practical Reason*. Translated by Lewis White Beck. Indianapolis: H. W. Sams, 1956.

———. "On the Miscarriage of All Philosophical Trials in Theodicy (1791)." In *Religion and Rational Theology*, edited by Allen W. Wood and George di Giovanni, 19–38. The Cambridge Edition of the Works of Immanuel Kant. Cambridge: Cambridge University Press, 1996. https://doi.org/10.1017/CBO 9780511814433.004.

———. *The Metaphysics of Morals*. Translated by Mary Gregor. Cambridge: Cambridge University Press, 1996.

Knappik, Franz, and Erasmus Mayr. "'An Erring Conscience Is an Absurdity': The Later Kant on Certainty, Moral Judgment and the Infallibility of Conscience." *Archiv Für Geschichte Der Philosophie* 101, no. 1 (March 1, 2019): 92–134. https://doi.org/10.1515/agph-2019-1004.

La Rocca, Claudio. "Kant on Self-Knowledge and Conscience." In *Das Leben Der Vernunft. Beiträge Zur Philosophie Kants*, edited by Dieter Hüning, Stefan Klingner, and Carsten Olk. Berlin-Boston: De Gruyter, 2013.

Munzel, G. Felicitas. *Kant's Conception of Moral Character: The "Critical" Link of Morality, Anthropology, and Reflective Judgment*. Chicago: University of Chicago Press, 1998.

Sticker, Martin. "When the Reflective Watch-Dog Barks: Conscience and Self-Deception in Kant." *The Journal of Value Inquiry* 51, no. 1 (March 1, 2017): 85–104. https://doi.org/10.1007/s10790-016-9559-4.

Timmermann, Jens. "Quod Dubitas, Ne Feceris: Kant on Using Conscience as a Guide." *Studi Kantiani: XXIX, 2016*, no. XXIX (2016). https://doi.org/10.192 72/201602901010.

Torralba, José M. "The Three-Fold Function of the Faculty of Judgement in Kant's Ethics: Typic, Moral Judgment and Conscience." In *Libertad, Objeto Práctico y Acción: La Facultad Del Juicio En La Filosofía Moral de Kant*, edited by José M. Torralba, 423–45. Hildesheim: Olms, 2009.

Chapter 9

Kant, Peirce, and the Rationality of Natural Science

Daniel R. Herbert

The University of Sheffield

Abstract: In "Kant, Peirce, and the Rationality of Natural Science", Daniel Herbert analyses Peirce's criticisms of Kant's concept of synthetic reasoning and his lack of explanation of the possibility of synthetic a posteriori judgments. The first part of the chapter is a contribution in its own right offering new perspectives on Kant's analysis. However, the use of Peirce's critique in the second part locates this discussion in a wider constellation of thinkers, something that adds up to a glimpse of how it is possible to get out of the dichotomy of theory and practice. The difference regarding the need for a philosophical explanation of synthetic a posteriori judgments, according to Herbert, explains why Kant and Peirce are led to pursue significantly distinct inquiries with respect to the grounds of scientific knowledge. Whereas Kant takes it that a Transcendental Deduction is called for in order to satisfy the demand for an explanation of the a priori grounds of those synthetic a priori judgements without which natural science would be impossible, Peirce makes it his objective to explain the enabling conditions of the possibility of scientific knowledge as a long-running process of inquiry making use of synthetic inference.

Keywords: Kant, Peirce, inference, practical reason, theoretical reason.

***

In his 1869 paper, 'Grounds of Validity of the Laws of Logic', Peirce wrote that:

> According to Kant, the central question of philosophy is 'How are synthetical judgements *a priori* possible? But antecedently to this comes the question how synthetical judgements in general, and still more generally, how synthetic reasoning is possible at all. When the answer to the general problem has been obtained, the particular one

will be comparatively simple. This is the lock upon the door of philosophy[1].

As such, Peirce accuses Kant of overlooking two questions of fundamental importance in providing an account of the possibility of human knowledge. Just as Kant himself objected to the speculative metaphysicians of the Leibnizian rationalist tradition for not first explaining the grounds of the possibility of synthetic a priori judgements (a problem the solution of which, he thinks, demands a transcendental deduction of the categories), Peirce criticises Kant for neglecting two even more fundamental questions. Firstly, how is it possible to gain knowledge through judgements based on the content of experience? Secondly, and most fundamentally of all, how is it possible to extend our knowledge by making non-deductively valid inferences?

That Kant did not recognise any demand for an explanation of the possibility of synthetic a posteriori judgements seems apparent from a passage from the Discipline of Pure Reason, in which he claims that:

> There is no difficulty as to how, by means of experience, I can pass beyond the concept which I previously have. Experience is itself a synthesis of perceptions, whereby the concept which I have is obtained by means of a perception is increased through the addition of other perceptions[2].

As a consequence of these differing outlooks regarding the need for a philosophical explanation of the possibility of synthetic a posteriori judgements, Kant and Peirce are led to pursue significantly distinct investigations with respect to the grounds of scientific knowledge. Whereas Kant takes it that a Transcendental Deduction is called for in order to satisfy the demand for an explanation of the a priori grounds of those synthetic a priori judgements without which natural science would be impossible, Peirce makes it his objective to explain the enabling conditions of the possibility of scientific knowledge as a long-running process of inquiry making use of synthetic inference. Moreover, since Peirce argues that all of our synthetic knowledge results from our capacity for synthetic inference, he is of the view that an explanation of the possibility of synthetic inference, which is possible without appeal to the use of transcendental arguments, is sufficient to explain the

---

[1] Charles S. Peirce, "Grounds of Validity of the Laws of Logic: Further Consequences of Four Incapacities," in *The Essential Peirce*, ed. Nathan Houser and Christian J. W. Kloesel, vol. 1 (Indianapolis: Indiana University Press, 1992), 78. From here on, "EP1".
[2] Immanuel Kant, *Critique of Pure Reason*, trans. Paul Guyer and Allen W. Wood (Cambridge: Cambridge University Press, 1998). From here on, "KrV". (KrV, A764/B792).

grounds of our entitlement to any of those judgements which Kant mistakenly labels as synthetic a priori. As such, Peirce's investigation into the grounds of the possibility of synthetic inference is of great importance in his attempts to explain the grounds of the possibility of scientific knowledge, while refusing to make any commitment to having to give a counterpart to Kant's Transcendental Deduction.

1. Analytic and Synthetic

There can be little doubt that Kant's question about the possibility of synthetic a priori judgements occupies a central place in his philosophical project. He repeatedly stresses the importance of this question, referring to it as "the proper problem of pure reason"[3] and the "general problem of transcendental philosophy"[4]. It is also clear that Kant thought that this problem has a particular significance in accounting for the possibility of a viable metaphysics since he claimed that "[m]etaphysics stands or falls with the solution to this problem; its very existence depends upon it"[5]. According to Kant, "[a]ny knowledge that professes to hold *a priori* lays claim to be regarded as absolutely necessary"[6]. In respect of their apriority then, synthetic a priori judgements must be true *necessarily*, and the question about their possibility is therefore a question about the possibility of judgements expressing necessary truths of a certain kind. In addition to *synthetic* a priori judgements, Kant recognises as necessarily true the further class of *analytic* judgements, the possibility of which he regards as entirely unproblematic. As Hanna states, Kant counts a judgement or proposition as analytic "if and only if it is necessarily true by virtue of its conceptual form or content alone"[7]. The class of analytic judgements therefore includes all and only those judgements the truth of which is guaranteed by the principle of non-contradiction together with the meaning of the terms in the judgement, for instance "every bachelor is an unmarried male". Since the negation of any such judgement entails a contradiction, the possibility of analytic judgements is not open to question.

Because of their syntheticity, however, synthetic a priori judgements cannot be shown to be true simply by conceptual analysis. Since the negation of a synthetic judgement, e.g. "London is the most highly populated city in England", does not entail a contradiction, the truth-value of such a judgement must depend on something more than the conceptual relations between its

---

[3] KrV B19.
[4] KrV A66/B91.
[5] KrV Prol.276.
[6] KrV Axv.
[7] Robert Hanna, *Kant and the Foundations of Analytic Philosophy* (Oxford: Clarendon Press, 2001), 239.

terms. One way in which one might try to determine the truth-value of a synthetic judgement is by appealing to empirical evidence. In that case, however, it would seem that the judgement in question does not express a necessary truth, but rather a contingent truth. As Kant maintains, "[e]xperience tells us, indeed, what is, but not that it must necessarily be so and not otherwise"[8]. Evidently, then, Kant acknowledges experience as a source of true belief and also regards the possibility of synthetic *a posteriori* judgements as unproblematic[9]. Nonetheless, the merely contingent status of truths discoverable by experience means that the possibility of synthetic a priori judgements cannot be explained by the possibility of empirical knowledge any more than it can by the principle of non-contradiction.

Briefly put then, Kant's question about the possibility of synthetic a priori judgements is the question of how it is possible for a judgement to be necessarily true without being true by definition. This question merits our attention, in Kant's view, because judgements of this sort feature not only in metaphysics (a branch of knowledge the possibility of which has to be argued for), but also in the established fields of mathematics and natural science, the scientific credentials of which are not in question. In each of these fields, Kant thinks, we rely on judgements which are held as necessary, without being analytic. The truths of mathematics, for Kant, while necessary, are not mere statements about conceptual entailment. He denies, for instance, that the concepts of the numbers '4' and '2', together with the concept of addition, entail the concept of the number '6', and therefore maintains that the truth of mathematical statements must depend on something other than simply definition and deductive logic. Moreover, since definitions alone convey no information about the actual world, our knowledge of natural phenomena cannot rest upon analytic judgements. While many of our judgements about the natural world express merely contingent truths based on experience, however, Kant insists that natural science also makes claim to knowledge of necessary truths and therefore requires a source of non-empirical knowledge. Hence Kant writes:

> *Natural science (physics) contains* a priori *principles.* I need cite only two such judgements: that in all changes of the material world the quantity of matter remains unchanged; and that in all communication of motion, action and reaction must always be equal. Both propositions, it is

---

[8] KrV A1.
[9] For further evidence see KrV A764-5/ B792-3.

evident, are not only necessary, and therefore *a priori*, but are also synthetic[10].

Kant makes a distinction within natural science between 'pure' and 'empirical' natural science. The two judgements mentioned in the passage above are examples of pure natural science insofar as they assert certain *logically* possible states of nature to be, *in fact*, impossible. The first of these judgements, for instance, can be rephrased in the following terms: "if there is a change of the material world then, necessarily, the quantity of matter remains unchanged", or, the equivalent judgement: "it is impossible, in a change of the material world, for the quantity of matter to change". Pure natural science therefore specifies limits of possible states of natural phenomena. Empirical natural science, meanwhile, helps determine which of the possible states of affairs allowed by pure natural science in fact obtain. The distinction between pure and empirical natural science is central to Kant's conception of natural science and is representative of his belief that the possibility of a principled body of rational knowledge presupposes a priori norms the legitimacy of which is beyond doubt. He repeatedly stresses the need for such a priori principles in the *Metaphysical Foundations of Natural Science*, claiming, for instance, that "proper science requires a pure part lying at the basis of the empirical part, and resting on *a priori* cognition of natural things"[11] and that "[a] rational doctrine of nature thus deserves the name of a natural science, only in case the fundamental natural laws therein are cognised *a priori*, and not mere laws of experience"[12].

One way in which Kant attempts to motivate his question about the grounds of the possibility of synthetic a priori judgements therefore relates to the need for an explanation of an otherwise mysterious fact about the knowledge we possess in the established sciences of mathematics and natural science. In each of these fields, Kant maintains, we possess knowledge which cannot possibly result either from experience or conceptual analysis. Although the actuality (and therefore, trivially, the possibility) of synthetic a priori judgements, at least in mathematics and pure natural science, is not in question, there nonetheless remains a question about the *grounds* of the possibility of judgements of this sort. As such, we are committed to giving an explanation of the grounds of the possibility of synthetic a priori judgements insofar as it is incumbent upon us

---

[10] KrV B17-18.

[11] Immanuel Kant, "Metaphysical Foundations of Natural Science (1786)," in *Theoretical Philosophy after 1781*, ed. Gary Hatfield et al., The Cambridge Edition of the Works of Immanuel Kant (Cambridge: Cambridge University Press, 2002), 171–270, https://doi.org/10.1017/CBO9780511498015.004. From here on, "MF". (MF:470).

[12] MF:468.

to achieve a full understanding of the conditions which enable the possibility of mathematical and scientific knowledge.

2. The Problem of Metaphysics

By Kant's own admission, however, the theoretical aspect of his Critical philosophy is concerned not only with the grounds of the possibility of mathematics and natural science but also with the more contested area of metaphysics. Whereas Kant does not seem to seriously entertain doubts about the scientific credentials of mathematics and natural science, he thinks that the extent to which metaphysicians express disagreement with one another casts doubt upon the status of metaphysics as a field of human knowledge subject to rational principles. Scepticism or complacent indifference to metaphysics, although natural responses to the lack of progress in this domain, are not real options in Kant's view, since our knowledge of natural phenomena depends upon metaphysical assumptions. As Gardner puts it: "What makes scepticism about metaphysics unsustainable is that metaphysics cannot be repudiated in isolation from cognition in general. Metaphysical enquiry employs the same cognitive power as is employed in commonsense and scientific judgements about the world of experience..."[13].

The extent to which metaphysical assumptions inform our claims to knowledge of the natural world is, in Kant's view, amply demonstrated by Hume's critical discussion of the notion of a causal relation. As is evident from the Preface to the *Prolegomena*, Hume's sceptical empiricism was of monumental significance in the development of Critical philosophy. Of all the early modern philosophers, Kant credits Hume with having come closest to recognising the importance of the problem of accounting for the possibility of synthetic a priori judgements[14]. Focussing in particular upon the concept of a causal relation, Kant presents Hume as a critic of metaphysics who nonetheless contributed significantly towards its development by calling attention to a problem of decisive importance for determining the grounds of possibility of legitimate metaphysical claims, maintaining that:

> Since the *Essays* of Locke and Leibniz, or rather since the origin of metaphysics so far as we know its history, nothing has ever happened which could have been more decisive to its fate than the attack made upon it by David Hume. He threw no new light on this kind of knowledge; but he certainly struck a spark from which light might have

---

[13] Sebastian Gardner, *Kant and the Critique of Pure Reason* (New York: Routledge, 1999), 21.
[14] See KrV Prol.277.

been obtained, had it caught some inflammable substance and had its smouldering fire been carefully nursed and developed.[15]

The intention of the theoretical part of the Critical system is therefore very much informed by Hume's contributions to metaphysics and epistemology, and it is Kant's intention to take full account of these sceptical challenges to the justificatory credentials of our use of synthetic a priori judgements and to respond to them in a manner which will show such judgements to rest upon a priori rational grounds.

According to Kant's discussion in the *Prolegomena*, Hume deserves recognition for having shown conclusively that the concept of causality, conceived as a "necessary connection" between spatio-temporally contiguous events; cannot be shown to apply to objects either by simple logical analysis of the terms involved in assertions about causal relations, or by reference to the content of empirical evidence. Defending Hume against the criticisms of certain adherents of the Scottish common-sense realist school of philosophy (amongst whom he includes Reid, Oswald, Beattie, and lastly, Priestley)[16], Kant remarks that Hume's intention was never to challenge the utility of the concept of a necessary connection, but only to show that it has its origins in a subjective faculty which is ultimately non-rational, and hence that our judgements of causality, while perfectly sensible for anyone who wants to live through to next week, are not justified according to strict standards of rationality. Hence, for Hume, it is not just rational subjects that we make judgements about necessary connections between events, but rather in our capacity as natural biological kinds acting under the influence of customary habits adopted for their utility in preserving our existence and furthering our projects. As Kant writes of Hume's problem: "it was a question concerning the *origin* of the concept, not concerning its indispensability in use"[17]. This problem merits our attention, in Kant's view, because the origins of a concept are relevant to determining the proper scope of its employment and its function in cognition. Assuming, for instance, that a certain concept is somehow derived a posteriori, by inference from the contents of a finite set of past experiences, we may be led to question the legitimacy of applying that concept to objects we have yet to observe since the conditions occasioning the formation of the concept in question have nothing to do with

---

[15] KrV Prol.257.

[16] KrV Prol.258. Kant's assessment of the Scottish commonsense realist response to Hume is, however, somewhat uncharitable and is particularly implausible in Reid's case. See, for instance, A. D. Woozley, ed., "Introduction," in *Essays on the Intellectual Powers of Man*, by Thomas Reid, vol. 17 (Cambridge University Press, 1942).

[17] KrV Prol.259.

such objects. Again, assuming that a certain concept arises from a subject's capacity for such acts as imagining, desiring, hoping or willing, we may suspect that the concept in question has no legitimate application to objects since the concept is not *about* objects, but rather certain subjective states. According to Kant, therefore, the objective validity of a concept (*i.e.* its application to objects) depends to a significant degree upon the specific cognitive operations by virtue of which we are able to employ that concept in a judgement.

Hume's denial of the apriority of the causal relation rests on the observation that the concept of such a relation involves the difficult notion of a necessary connection between objects which are nonetheless conceivable as obtaining separately. According to Waxman[18], Hume raises a twofold challenge to the apriority of causality, involving both a conceptual and an epistemological doubt. The first of these casts suspicion upon the very possibility of thinking a causal relation by claiming to identify an inconsistency in the conceptual form of such a relation. In presenting this conceptual doubt, Hume, as Kant puts it:

> ...challenged reason, which pretends to have given birth to this concept of herself, to answer him by what right she thinks that anything could be so constituted that if that thing be posited, something else must also be posited, for this is the meaning of cause[19].

According to Kant's portrayal, the concept of causality involves a rule expressible in the form of a hypothetical judgement, to the effect that "if x is given then y follows necessarily". For the relation in question to be properly causal, however, the terms of this relation must, according to Waxman's elegant reconstruction of Hume's reasoning, be conceivable as distinct objects, such that there is no necessary relation between them discoverable by simple conceptual analysis. Whereas, for instance, the obtaining of a valley is inconceivable without that of a mountain, the same cannot be said of the relation between spatio-temporally contiguous events, such as the movement of one billiard ball which follows its impact by another. Our ability to conceive of the events of the latter kind of relation obtaining independently of one another therefore undermines the suggestion that they are necessarily connected in thought.

The epistemological phase of Hume's challenge to the apriority of the causal relation is closely related to the conceptual phase, since Hume maintains that the only a priori knowledge available to us is that afforded by analysis of the

---

[18] Wayne Waxman, "Kant's Humean Solution to Hume's Problem," in *Kant and the Early Moderns*, ed. Daniel Garber and Béatrice Longuenesse (Princeton: Princeton University Press, 2008), 174-181.

[19] KrV Prol.257.

relations of ideas, *i.e.* conceptual analysis. Here, however, his purpose is to challenge our entitlement to claim to know of objects, a priori, that they must have a necessary and sufficient cause for their obtaining. Hence, Hume means to challenge the apriority of the "general maxim in philosophy, that *whatever begins to exist, must have a cause of its existence*"[20]. Such a principle is a statement about a matter of fact, but Hume maintains that it is impossible to conceive of matters of fact being necessary and therefore denies that they can be known to obtain a priori:

> The converse of every matter of fact is still possible, because it can never imply a contradiction, and is conceived by the mind with the same facility and distinctness, as if ever so conformable to reality[21].

Since the converse of the general causal principle stated above does not imply a contradiction, it is not true necessarily and therefore is not knowable a priori. As such, the limitation of a priori knowledge to relations discoverable by conceptual analysis carries the sceptical consequence that no rational grounds can be offered for our belief in causal relations. Kant summarises Hume's legacy to metaphysics as follows:

> He demonstrated irrefutably that it was entirely impossible for reason to think *a priori* and by means of concepts such a combination as involves necessity. We cannot at all see why, in consequence of the existence of one thing, another must necessarily exist, or how the concept of such a combination can arise *a priori*. Hence he inferred that reason was altogether deluded with reference to this concept, which she erroneously considered as one of her children, whereas in reality it was nothing but a bastard of imagination, impregnated by experience, which subsumed certain representations under the law of association and mistook a subjective necessity (custom) for an objective necessity arising from insight[22].

However, the sceptical implications of Hume's challenge to the rational basis for our judgements about causal relations are not limited to metaphysics but extend to the natural sciences. Hume remarks on the sceptical implications of

---

[20] David Hume, *A Treatise of Human Nature* (Oxford: Clarendon Press, 1975). From here on, "THN". (THN:57).

[21] David Hume, *An Enquiry Concerning Human Understanding*, ed. Peter Millican, Oxford World's Classics (Oxford, New York: Oxford University Press, 2008). From here on, "EHU". (EHU:25).

[22] KrV Prol.257-8.

his discussion of causality for the practice of natural science when he claims that:

> The only immediate utility of all sciences is to teach us, how to control and regulate future events by their causes. Our thoughts and enquiries are, therefore, every moment employed about this relation: yet so imperfect are the ideas which we form concerning it, that it is impossible to give any just definition of cause, except what is drawn from something extraneous and foreign to it[23].

In order to defend the dignity of human reason against such a sceptical conclusion, Kant thinks, we must explain our entitlement to such synthetic a priori judgements as the principle of causality, thereby showing metaphysics to be possible as a science. In so doing, however, it will be necessary to offer a transcendental deduction of the objective validity of pure concepts, such as that of a causal relation.

3. The Necessity of Causal Knowledge

Kant agrees with Hume in regarding causal relations as, by definition, deterministic, and maintains that to assert that an event, x, is the cause of a subsequent event, y, is to assert that, if x obtains then, *necessarily*, y will obtain. Since he also denies that necessary and strictly universal rules can be derived by means of induction, Kant therefore holds that an entitlement to regard empirical phenomena as subject to deterministic causal laws can only be provided a priori. At the same time, however, Kant is sensitive to Hume's criticisms of attempts to base knowledge of causal relations in supposed rational insights by means of a priori intellectual faculties and in complete abstraction from the subject's capacity for sensible experience. It is central to the Critical philosophy that, although knowledge is impossible without the use of general concepts, these are only able to relate to their objects by the mediation of spatio-temporal intuitions; representations which are given in sensible experience and which relate to objects immediately. As such, by denying any role for the subject's capacity for sensible experience in explaining our entitlement to the "objective" use of the concept of causality, Kant thinks, the pre-Critical rationalist fails to give due consideration to a necessary feature of any cognitive relation between subject and object, and therefore cannot make a principled distinction between their own metaphysical speculations and the dubious visionary testimony of mystics. An adequate proof of our entitlement to regard

---

[23] EHU:76. By this 'something extraneous and foreign' Hume of course means a customary habit of associating events after repeated observation of their conjunction.

causal relations as really operative in nature ought, therefore, to be possible a priori, while remaining compatible with the fundamental Kantian principle that knowledge of objects is a priori conditional upon sensible intuition.

In the Aesthetic, Kant argues that if x is a possible object of human knowledge, then x must occupy a position in time, and, if it is an "external object", space as well. The same point can be expressed by saying that space and time are transcendental conditions of the subject-object relation, or that the very possibility of a subject's being cognitively related to an object rests upon the a priori condition that the object occupies a location in a manifold of spatio-temporal intuition. With the Deduction of the categories, Kant aims to show that the pure concepts of the understanding, including substance, causality and interaction, have a similarly transcendental function, enabling the possibility of the subject-object relation a priori, and necessarily determining the general form of the objects of possible cognition. By means of the Deduction, then, Kant intends to show that, in addition to being subject to the a priori *sensible* condition of occupying a spatio-temporal location, the objects of possible human knowledge are necessarily subject to further a priori *conceptual* conditions set by those pure concepts of the understanding identified in the Metaphysical Deduction. The transcendental status of the concept of causality, for instance, entails that if x is a possible object of human knowledge, then x is necessarily subject to deterministic causal laws.

Kant indicates this general strategy near the beginning of the *A Deduction*, claiming at A95 that although pure concepts of the understanding "cannot indeed contain anything empirical; yet none the less they can serve solely as *a priori* conditions of a possible experience". Moreover, Kant maintains that this is the only possible basis for the objective validity of the categories, and consequently claims that:

> If, therefore, we seek to discover how pure concepts of understanding are possible, we must enquire what are the *a priori* conditions upon which the possibility of experience rests, and which remain as its underlying grounds when everything empirical is abstracted from appearances. A concept which universally and adequately expresses such a formal and objective condition of experience would be entitled a pure concept of understanding[24].

Kant makes a similar point in the B Deduction, claiming that experience is necessarily subject to the conceptual norms contained in the categories

---

[24] KrV A95-6.

because "the categories contain, on the side of the understanding, the grounds of the possibility of all experience in general"[25].

The knowledge that objects-for-us are necessarily subject to the conceptual norms of the pure understanding is not yet sufficient, however, to ground any specific synthetic a priori judgements. For this, the pure concepts must actually be applied, in an act of judgement, to the temporal form of intuition characteristic of our specifically human mode of sensibility, an operation which presupposes the identification of distinctively temporal counterparts for the categories, by means of the Schematism, which are then able to act as rules for enacting synthetic unity in a manifold of temporal intuition so as to enable the possibility of achieving cognition of an object. While the Schematism specifies the specific temporal conditions under which the pure concepts may be applied as general rules, and the System of Principles identifies the synthetic a priori judgements which result from subsuming temporal intuitions under the pure concepts, the Deduction is nonetheless essential to Kant's argument in the Analytic, insofar as it provides the original proof that the categories are applicable to objects-for-us, and hence that empirical reality necessarily conforms to the conditions required for us to be able to make synthetic a priori judgements.

Kant's response to Hume's sceptical naturalism about the grounds of our knowledge of causal relations, and other purportedly necessary features of any possible world of human experience, is therefore characteristically 'transcendentalist' insofar as it aims to show, by means of conclusive arguments, that certain representations (intuitions, concepts, judgements, etc.) are objectively valid a priori as necessary conditions of the very possibility of the subject-object relation found in experience. The Deduction of the categories provides a fundamental example of this general strategy by showing that, unless it conformed to certain a priori conceptual forms, there could not possibly be any such thing as an object of human experience. The same transcendentalist strategy can be found in the Analogies of Experience, that section of the System of Principles in which Kant argues for the transcendental, 'object-enabling', or, as Allison has put it 'objectivating'[26] status of specific synthetic a priori judgements associated with each of the relational categories of substance, causality and interaction. In each case, Kant argues that one or another feature of a temporal manifold would be impossible were it not for the necessary truth of a particular synthetic a priori judgement.

---

[25] KrV B167.

[26] Henry Allison, *Kant's Transcendental Idealism. An Interpretation and Defense* (New Haven: Yale University Press, 2004), 11.

For instance, in the Second Analogy, the section dealing specifically with the proof of the synthetic a priori judgement that every event necessarily results from a previous event according to deterministic causal laws, Kant argues that it would be impossible to recognise a temporally successive arrangement of phenomena as ordered independently of subjective volition unless such phenomena were subject to deterministic causal laws. In order, for instance, to recognise the succession of phenomena $a1$, $a2$, $a3$,...an, experienced in observing a boat floating downstream, as determined independently of one's own agency[27], it is necessary that the order of the sequence be determined by an objective rule of succession, according to which later phenomena result necessarily from earlier phenomena, or, in other words, a deterministic causal law. As such, causal laws necessarily condition the possibility of the experience of event sequences as objective, *i.e.* as determined independently of subjective agency. In this respect, our knowledge of the synthetic a priori principle that all possible events arise from previous events according to deterministic causal laws is justified a priori as a necessary condition of this feature of temporal experience. Hulswit comments on the anti-Humean significance of Kant's argument, noting that "Kant explicitly rejected Hume's view that we first perceive temporal succession between events, and then regard one as cause and the other as effect. The opposite is true: in order to establish an objective order in time, we need cause-effect relationships"[28]. Guyer also testifies to the transcendentalist method employed in the Analogies in general, describing Kant's strategy as:

> ...the strategy of arguing that certain fundamental assumptions about the structure of our experience, particularly its temporal structure, necessitate our assumption of certain synthetic *a priori* judgements that in turn use *a priori* concepts of the greatest concern to both traditional metaphysicians and sceptics- the concepts of substance, causation and interaction[29].

In summary, Kant regards an explanation of the grounds of the synthetic a priori knowledge we in fact possess as possible but as demanding a response to

---

[27] The contrast here is with arrangements which depend upon the subject's choices about the order in which to experience the members of the series. In viewing the parts of a house from top to bottom, for instance, the succession of phenomena is determined by the subject's choice to view the parts of the house in that particular order, rather than, say, from bottom to top.

[28] Menno Hulswit, *From Cause to Causation. A Peircean Perspective* (Dordrecht: Kluwer Publishers, 2002), 38.

[29] Paul Guyer, *Kant* (New York: Routledge, 2006), 105.

Humean scepticism about the capacity of human reason to uncover the legitimating conditions of our knowledge of empirical matters of fact. As Kant himself acknowledged, Hume's ultimate intention was not to deny that we in fact possess empirical knowledge of nature, but rather to deny that the enabling conditions of such knowledge can possibly themselves become objects of knowledge by any rational means.[30] Allison's case for the importance of transcendental idealism in distinguishing Kant from his early modern predecessors seems highly informative here, insofar as a Kantian diagnosis of Humean scepticism about the claims of rationality can appeal to Hume's characteristically realist approach to the transcendental (*i.e.* object-enabling) conditions of human knowledge as features of a subject-independent natural domain, rather than as immanent features capacity for cognition[31]. Whereas for Hume then, the subject-object relation is possible but operates "behind reason's back", so to speak, according to natural laws which elude all possibility of rational explanation, Kant, by treating objects as appearances, and therefore as necessarily subject to ideal norms discoverable by means of a reflexive investigation into the necessary conditions for a subjective encounter with an object of experience, avails himself of the resources for an explanation of the grounds of possibility of non-empirical synthetic knowledge of any possible object of human cognition. As Allison has argued[32], Kant's transcendental idealism, by distinguishing between appearances and things-in-themselves and making a cognitive relation to the former necessarily conditional upon a priori forms of representation originating in subjective faculties, represents a fundamental departure from the transcendental realist model of the subject-object-relation, of which Hume is a representative, and makes possible an understanding of the grounds of synthetic a priori knowledge by means of an inquiry into the a priori subjective conditions for cognition of objects. In the course of such an inquiry, Kant maintains, it will be shown, by means of the Deduction, that causality is one of twelve a priori concepts to which appearances necessarily conform, and also, in the Second Analogy, that the experience of objective event-sequences is necessarily conditional upon the synthetic a priori knowledge that every event results from a previous event according to deterministic causal laws.

---

[30] See, for instance, the above remarks concerning Kant's defence of the significance of Hume's scepticism concerning causality against the dismissive manner in which, he claims, it was received by the Scottish Common Sense realist school of philosophy.

[31] Allison, *Kant's Transcendental Idealism. An Interpretation and Defense*, 25-7.

[32] Allison, *Kant's Transcendental Idealism. An Interpretation and Defense*, 20-49.

4. Synthetic Judgements and the *A Priori*

It is interesting to note that, in the summary account presented in the *Prolegomena*, of the topics discussed in the Analytic, this material is offered in answer to the question, "How is pure natural science possible?" thus suggesting that the conclusions of the Analytic are directly relevant to grounding the claims of natural science, at least in what Kant calls its 'pure' part. We have already seen that Kant takes certain specific examples of scientific knowledge as illustrative of the possession of synthetic a priori knowledge, the grounds of which stand in need of philosophical explanation. Further evidence of a role for the Analytic in explicating the possibility of natural science is provided in the *Metaphysical Foundations of Natural Science*, in which Kant offers, as synthetic a priori judgements of physics, a number of principles of 'phoronomy', 'dynamics', 'mechanics' and 'phenomenology', each of which represents a field of synthetic a priori knowledge concerning bodies subject to motion in space, in respect of their conformity to the four basic categorial divisions- quantitative, qualitative, relational and modal.

Kant, like Hume before him, was considerably impressed by the remarkable achievements of Newtonian physics. In his *History of England*, Hume speaks of Newton with admiration, claiming that "[i]n Newton this island may boast of having produced the greatest and rarest genius that ever arose for the ornament and instruction of the species"[33]. Nonetheless, Hume also remarks that "[w]hile Newton seemed to draw off the veil from some of the mysteries of nature, he showed at the same time the imperfections of the mechanical philosophy, and thereby restored her ultimate secrets to that obscurity in which they ever did and ever will remain"[34] [ibid.]. According to Millican, Hume considered Newton to have provided accurate descriptive laws of natural phenomena but also to have highlighted the basic incomprehensibility of nature by concluding that mechanistic principles are inadequate to explain gravity[35]. In Kant's diagnosis, however, it is not Newtonian physics as such, but mistaken philosophical assumptions (the assumption of transcendental realism as a model of the subject-object relation for instance) which are responsible for giving empirical reality the appearance of unintelligibility. In fact, Kant tells us, an a priori warrant and explanation is possible for the necessary truth of many of the synthetic judgements of Newtonian physics once it is recognised that the objects of any possible experience are themselves subject to a priori norms set by the a priori structure of human cognition itself.

---

[33] David Hume, *The History of England*, vol. 6 (Indianapolis: Liberty Fund, 1983), 542.
[34] Ibid.
[35] EHU:228.

In addressing the *Metaphysical Foundations of Mechanics*, Kant offers as a synthetic a priori judgement the "Second Law of Mechanics", according to which "Every change in matter has an external cause (every body persists in its state of rest or motion, in the same direction, and with the same speed, if it is not compelled by an external cause to leave this state)"[36]. In the proof of this law of natural phenomena, he remarks that "[f]rom general metaphysics we take as basis the proposition that every change has a *cause*, and here it is only to be proved of matter that its change must always have been an *external cause*"[37]. Here we find evidence for Friedman's claim that the first *Critique* "provides the overarching philosophical context for the more specific issues in natural science and natural philosophy with which Kant is occupied in the *Metaphysical Foundations*" [38]. The proof of the second law of mechanics relies upon the Second Analogy, which depends in turn upon the Deduction of the categories. Kant's proof of the first and third laws of mechanics are similarly dependent upon the First and Third Analogies, and therefore also upon the Deduction. Since Kant also maintains that no synthetic a posteriori judgement may be admitted as part of natural science unless it receives some kind of support from synthetic a priori judgements of natural science, and since the latter is impossible without a Deduction of the categories, Kant's philosophy of natural science ultimately depends upon a proof that certain a priori concepts precede the possibility of experience. In answer to Hume's scepticism about the rational basis for natural science, Kant replies that natural science is made possible by synthetic a priori judgments which have their grounds in the a priori structure of the rational understanding of a manifold of temporal intuition.

5. Peirce and the Necessity of Ampliative Reasoning

In *The Probability of Induction* (1878), Peirce repeated a claim he had made about the Critical philosophy nine years earlier in *Grounds of Validity of the Laws of Logic*. He writes:

> Late in the last century, Immanuel Kant asked the question, 'How are synthetical judgements *a priori* possible?' By synthetical judgements he meant such as assert positive fact and are not mere affairs of arrangement; in short, judgements of the kind which synthetical reasoning produces and which analytic reasoning cannot yield. By *a priori* judgements he meant such as that all outward objects are in space, every event has a cause, etc., propositions which according to

---

[36] MF:82.
[37] MF:83.
[38] MF:xxix.

him can never be inferred from experience. Not so much by his answer to this question as by the mere asking of it, the current philosophy of that time was shattered and destroyed, and a new epoch in its history was begun. But before asking *that* question he ought to have asked the more general one, 'How are synthetical judgements at all possible?' How is it that a man can observe one fact and straightway pronounce judgement concerning another different fact not contained in the first?[39].

Here Peirce seems to commend Kant for addressing the question of the conditions of possibility of knowledge while criticising him for not pursuing his inquiry with a sufficient degree of generality. Whereas for Kant the only kind of judgement which demands philosophical explanation is the synthetic a priori judgement, Peirce maintains that an explanation must be forthcoming for the possibility of synthetic a posteriori judgements, which, as the passage above suggests, he believes to be, in every case, a result of 'synthetical' (*i.e.* non-reductive or 'ampliative' reasoning). As such, Peirce regards Kant's 'critical' project as insufficiently general, insofar as it does not address the question of the possibility of synthetic posterior judgements, an undertaking which, according to Peirce, must be preceded by an investigation into the possibility of extending our knowledge by means of two kinds of synthetical inference, or 'reasoning'- abduction and induction.

There can be little doubt that the Critical philosophy does not recognise any need to pursue an investigation into the possibility of synthetic posterior judgements. Kant makes this clear in the *Prolegomena* when, after having claimed that the possibility of analytic judgements is readily accounted for by the principle of non-contradiction, he asserts that "[t]he possibility of synthetic *a posteriori* judgements, of those which are gathered from experience, also requires no special explanation; for experience is nothing but a continual joining together (synthesis) of perceptions"[40]. It might nonetheless be thought that Kant is too dismissive of problems concerning the grounds of empirical knowledge though. After all, the very possibility of what Kant, mistakenly, calls 'pure' natural science depends upon an appeal to specifically posterior concepts such as motion and mass[41]. Insofar as it relies upon such concepts,

---

[39] EP1:167.

[40] KrV Prol:275.

[41] Kant's use of the term 'pure' to describe the claims of a natural science which depends upon the empirical concept of motion is inconsistent with his statement that: "*A priori* modes of knowledge are entitled pure when there is no admixture of anything empirical. Thus, for instance, the proposition 'every alteration has its cause', while an *a priori* proposition, is not a pure proposition, because alteration is a concept which can be derived only from experience" (KrV B3).

'pure' natural science is not really 'pure' at all, but rather an account of synthetic judgements which Kant alleges may be inferred a priori once it is already known that certain specific empirical concepts, such as motion and mass, apply to certain natural phenomena. A set of synthetic a priori judgements of mechanics, for instance, would be impossible without the prior knowledge that the a posteriori concept of motion has application to bodies in space.

Since motion is not an a priori concept, it must somehow be derived from the content of experience, in which case our ability to employ this concept will be conditional upon the ability to infer general kinds and relations from more particular experiences. Indeed, although Kant has relatively little to say about empirical concepts, his considered position seems to be that they result from inductive inference. We, therefore, find that Kant's account of 'pure' natural science in fact depends upon the synthetic a posterior knowledge that certain inductively inferred concepts apply to certain branches of natural phenomena and that without an explanation of why the use of induction may reasonably be expected to provide us with true beliefs about natural laws and kinds, Kant's explanation of the possibility of 'pure' natural science will be incomplete. What seems to be missing from Kant's position is an explanation of our entitlement to the objective use of a posteriori concepts, something which the Deduction, given its exclusive concern with the objective validity of purportedly a priori concepts, cannot possibly provide.

Whereas Kant gave comparatively little attention to the grounds of legitimacy of induction, however, Peirce devoted himself to the task of explaining how induction and abduction, which he presents as two distinct forms of synthetic inference, can be understood to contribute to the growth of human knowledge. What Peirce wants to see explained is our capacity to infer from one fact discovered to us by observation, another fact not conceptually entailed by the first. So fundamental to human cognition is the use of synthetic inference, in his view, that all possible synthetic knowledge is to be accounted for by means of the use of abduction and induction, thus making an investigation into the grounds of the possibility of synthetic a priori judgements redundant. Hence, Peirce maintains that the apparent need for synthetic a priori judgements will disappear with the provision of an adequate theory of synthetic inference. Contra Kant, it is not synthetic a priori judgements which require a special explanation but rather synthetic inferences.

6. The Problem of Inductive Reasoning

In *The Probability of Induction*, Peirce remarks upon a distinction between 'analytic', or deductive, reasoning and synthetic reasoning, claiming that only the former can establish the exact numerical value of a probability, or as Peirce calls it 'definite probability'. He writes, for instance, that:

> When we draw a deductive or analytic conclusion, our rule of inference is that facts of a certain general character are either invariably or in a certain proportion of cases accompanied by facts of another general character. Then our premise being a fact of the former class, we infer with certainty or with the appropriate degree of probability the existence of a fact of the second class[42].

So, for instance, equipped with the knowledge that all men are mortal, we can know that for any x, if x is a man, then the probability of x also being mortal is 1. Again, if we begin with the knowledge that of the total population of beans in a bag, 70% are purple, then we can know that for any x, if x is a bean drawn from the bag in question, then the probability of x also being purple is 0.7. In each of these examples, deductive inference results in a conclusion with a possible application in making predictions about future outcomes. In the first case, for instance, I am able to predict, with absolute certainty, that the man in question shall die one day, while in the second, my knowledge of the probability of drawing a purple bean from the bag in question is 0.7, enables me to make an educated guess about the likely colour of the next bean I draw from that bag.

However, Peirce thinks that conclusions of this sort cannot be provided by means of synthetic inference, claiming that:

> When we sample a bag of beans we do not in the least assume that the fact of some beans being purple involves the necessity or even the probability of other beans being so. On the contrary, the conceptualistic method of treating probabilities, which really amounts simply to the deductive treatment of them, when rightly carried out leads to the result that a synthetic inference has just an even chance in its favor, or in other words is absolutely worthless. The color of one bean is entirely independent of that of another [43].

---

[42] EP1:168.
[43] EP1:168-9.

By "the conceptualistic method of treating probabilities"[44], Peirce means the view that probability is "simply the degree of belief which ought to attach to a proposition"[45]. When probability is thought of in conceptualistic terms, the probability of a proposition will vary between 0 and 1, according to the degree to which one should be confident of the truth of that proposition. For a conceptualist then, a proposition with a probability of 1 should be regarded as certainly true and a proposition with a probability of 0 as certainly false. Since the evidence one has for the truth of a proposition will vary according to circumstances, the conceptualist is likely to hold, that the probability of that proposition will also vary according to the present state of evidence.

Peirce maintains however that conceptualism cannot explain how the use of induction can entitle us to believe in the probable truth of a proposition. Since facts about the future are not conceptually entailed by facts about the past, inference from our knowledge of the latter to the probability of a given future outcome cannot result in conclusions with any probability value other than 0.5. As such, we cannot reason deductively from past experience to the claim that a certain future outcome is any more or less likely than any of its possible alternatives. But in that case, we do not seem to be able to infer the numerical value of the probability of a possible future outcome of type α at all, since to make such an inference we must already know the ratio of outcomes of type α to outcomes of all other types, whereas all we can possibly know is the ratio of past events of type α to past events of all other types. One's knowledge of the probability of drawing an ace from a normal deck of cards, depends for instance on prior knowledge of the ratio of aces to non-aces in a normal deck of cards, whereas such prior knowledge is not often available to us in forming predictions about nature.

Peirce does in fact deny that we can know the exact numerical value of the probability of an inductive conclusion, and this leads him to ask how synthetic inference can reasonably be thought to add to our knowledge at all. That is, if it cannot tell us how likely it is that a particular inductive generalisation is true then what exactly can induction teach us? Peirce maintains that it is impossible for us to know how often the use of inductive inference will lead us to form false beliefs, in which case we must explain the connection between the use of induction and the formation of true belief, in order to provide a rational warrant for belief in inductive conclusions.

---

[44] Peirce borrows this terminology from John Venn, *The Logic of Chance* (London: MacMillan, 1876).
[45] EP1:156.

Although Misak has argued that Peirce "virtually ignores Hume's problem of induction", and that "he simply was not interested in it"[46], it seems that Peirce's discussion of conceptualism about probability and its failings in explaining the possibility of empirical knowledge by means of synthetic inference in fact bears directly upon the Humean problem of induction. That Hume can be described as a conceptualist about probability is suggested in the opening passage of section VI of the *Enquiry*, "Of Probability", in which he claims that "[t]hough there be no such thing as *Chance* in the world, our ignorance of the real cause of any event has the same influence on the understanding, and begets a like species of belief or opinion"[47]. This remark is interesting insofar as it shows that Hume's scepticism about the rational grounds for belief in causal relations is not an obstacle to his endorsing causal determinism, but it also suggests that he regards probability as relative to grounds for belief, and therefore as a merely subjectively valid, rather than objectively valid, notion. Hume's causal determinism commits him to deny that probabilities of any value other than 0 or 1 are attached to natural events, and he maintains that in making predictions about likely outcomes, we are limited to speaking of the relative evidence we have available for obtaining the outcome in question.

Hume's conceptualism is instrumental in his reaching a sceptical conclusion regarding the rational grounds for inductive conclusions, and for the very reasons Peirce identifies in *The Probability of Induction*. Indeed, it is rather surprising, given the similarity between Hume's problem of induction and Peirce's observations about the limits of conceptualism, that Peirce does not mention Hume by name in this context. Nonetheless, it is clear that when he asserts that the testimony of past experience cannot provide evidence concerning future outcomes, it is clear that Peirce is addressing the same problem that motivated Hume's scepticism about induction, and that by developing an alternative to the conceptualist approach to induction, Peirce is indeed, contrary to Misak's interpretation, responding to 'Humean' concerns about the grounds of induction.

7. Pragmatism and "Abductive" Reasoning

In explaining the possibility of synthetic inference extending or 'amplifying' our knowledge beyond its present state, Peirce insists that we cannot appeal to the norms of deductive reasoning. In *Deduction, Induction and Hypothesis* (1878)

---

[46] John Boler and C. J. Misak, "Truth and the End of Inquiry: A Peircean Account of Truth.," *The Philosophical Review* 102, no. 1 (January 1993), https://doi.org/10.2307/218 5663, 97.
[47] EHU:56.

he classifies as 'deductive' all arguments which infer a result from a rule and a case, giving the following example:

Rule. - All the beans from this bag are white.

Case. - These beans are from this bag.

[therefore] Result .- These beans are white [48].

Since reasoning in this manner cannot provide us with any knowledge which is not conceptually entailed by, and therefore implicit in, the knowledge we already possess of a rule and a case, Peirce labels deductive reasoning 'analytic' or 'explicative'. Deductive reasoning has an important application in making predictions about future outcomes, and Peirce presents the use of deduction as an essential feature of the scientific method, by means of which we are able to specify experimentally confirmable implications of the truth of our hypotheses. However, insofar as we are only able to reason deductively by appeal to our knowledge of rules and cases, deduction is not a self-sufficient element of scientific practice and is unable to properly perform its predictive function in the absence of rules (which Peirce presents as inferred inductively) and cases (which he maintains result from abductive inference).

As Peirce makes clear in his criticisms of conceptualist approaches to probability, attempts to assign probability values to possible future outcomes by inference from a finite set of past cases are simply faulty efforts at deductive reasoning. From the premise that any number of x are p, nothing can be inferred about whether a further x is more or less likely to also be p. Peirce is critical of thinkers such as J.S. Mill who attempt to remedy this situation by introducing a major premise (in Mill's case the principle that nature is uniform) by appeal to which inference from past cases could result in probable conclusions about the future. According to Peirce, proceeding in such a manner makes the validity of our reasonings about empirical phenomena dependent upon "a mere metaphysical formula"[49], whereas the conformity of our reasonings to logical norms ought to be possible before making any particular metaphysical claims.

Peirce therefore maintains that the logical form of inductive arguments, properly so-called, is not reducible to that of deductive arguments and that an

---

[48] EP1:188.
[49] EP1:179.

explanation of our entitlement to the use of induction must show how our knowledge can be increased by reasoning in the following general manner:

Case. – These beans are from this bag.

Result. – These beans are white.

[therefore] *Rule.* – All the beans in this bag are white.

Whereas deduction infers a result conceptually entailed by a rule and a case, induction 'amplifies' our present state of knowledge by inferring a rule from a case and a result *without* being conceptually entailed by them. Although the example given here draws the conclusion that a certain property is universal to all of the members of a certain general class, it is no less a case of inductive inference to a general rule to reason that, since a proportion of the beans from this bag, 70% say, are white, 70% of all of the beans in this bag are white. Since the truth of the premises of an inductive inference of either kind is no guarantee of the truth of its conclusion, however, inductive reasoning is a fallible process. Peirce nonetheless argues that the fallibility of inductively derived rules does not make it irrational for us to participate in inductive reasoning, claiming that the use of induction is warranted by the self-correcting character of this kind of inference in the long term, a consequence of which is that induction cannot fail to lead us to the truth as long as our inquiries are allowed to reach their furthest possible point of development.

In order to properly understand his defence of the long-term connection between true belief and the use of induction, it must be kept in mind that Peirce conceives of truth in pragmatist terms, as a property of the consensus achieved by the community of inquirers at the ideal limit of an empirical investigation carried out according to the normative standards of scientific research. Although the truth at which scientific inquiry aims must be understood in terms relative to the notion of a final consensus reached by a community of responsible inquirers, the use of induction makes it possible for such a consensus to be held in check by features of the natural world which obtain independently of any opinion about them. Indeed, it is the use of induction which distinguishes the scientific method from the a priori method Peirce criticises in *The Fixation of Belief* (1877). While science and a priori metaphysics share a common appeal to speculative hypotheses and proceed to infer deductive implications of the truth of such conjectures, science is set apart by its use of inductive methods in advancing claims about the general rules to which natural phenomena are subject. By requiring that our claims about general laws and kinds be warranted by inference from representative samples of empirical evidence, the inductive phase of what Peirce presents as "the method of science" demands that our hypotheses be able to answer to experience and make it possible for our results to be conditioned by contingently obtaining facts about the world.

In Peirce's view, it is not the testimony of past experience but the promise of an inquiry eventually converging upon a single final result that validates the use of induction. Inductive inference is legitimated by the fact that it performs a necessary contribution towards the eventual realisation of the final scientific consensus which is what the pragmatist, or rather the 'pragmaticist', understands by the pragmatic value of truth, insofar as by conceiving of truth in such terms inquirers are provided with an empirically significant target at which to direct their practical efforts in the course of active research. Peirce therefore presents as a rule of ampliative logic the principle that "if there is a truth about whether x, then inquirers would eventually converge upon the truth about whether x by using induction for long enough and with representative samples of evidence".

8. Hypothetical Reasoning and Ampliative Knowledge

According to Peirce's defence of induction, although we cannot use past experience to directly justify belief in the probable truth of our inductive conclusions, we can nonetheless provide an indirect justification for such belief, in consequence of a destined long-term connection between the use of inductive methods and the formation of true belief. As such, the justification for our inductive beliefs results not from the relation they bear to past experience, but rather from the fact that they represent the furthest stage of progress in an inquiry, which, if allowed to continue for long enough, is destined to alight upon the truth. We are therefore entitled to belief in the probable truth of our inductive conclusions, in spite of the fact that we cannot possibly know how great the possibility of their being false because these conclusions result from a method which is 'fated' to take us to the truth in the long run.

Peirce expresses the self-correcting character of induction in *The Doctrine of Chances*, a paper from slightly earlier in 1878, as follows:

> But in the long run, there is a real fact which corresponds to the idea of probability, and it is that a given mode of inference sometimes proves successful and sometimes not, and that in a ratio ultimately fixed. As we go on drawing inference after inference of the given kind, during the first ten or hundred cases the ratio of successes may be expected to show considerable fluctuations; but when we come into the thousands and

millions, these fluctuations become less and less; and if we continue long enough, the ratio will approximate towards a fixed limit[50].

Since there is a fact about, for instance, the ratio of purple to non-purple beans in a particular bag, this fact will exercise an influence over the results of our sampling of the contents of that bag. As we continue our sampling, the fact about the ratio of purple to non-purple beans will exercise a greater and greater influence over the conclusions of our inductive arguments, so that the room for error becomes smaller and smaller until we arrive at an accurate conclusion about the ratio in question. Of course, we can never be in a position to know for sure that the latest inductive conclusion to which our sampling has led us will not need to be corrected in the light of further evidence, or, in other words, that there is not still further to go in the process of convergence, but since the repeated confirmation of our latest conclusion is just what we would expect to find at the point at which inquiry has converged upon the true hypothesis, this is all the evidence that the Peircean pragmatist requires to justify belief in the truth of an inductive conclusion.

Peirce compares his explanation of the possibility of synthetic inference to Kant's account of the possibility of synthetic a priori judgements by borrowing from Kant the principle that "whatever is universally true is involved in the conditions of experience". For Kant, the universal truth of the principle of causal determinism is a consequence of its status as a transcendental condition of the possibility of experience. For Peirce, the truth of a generalisation is a consequence of a fact which conditions our specific experiences of sampling for general patterns. For instance, what makes true the generalisation that "70% of the beans in this bag are purple" is that our experiences of sampling the contents of the bag in question are conditioned, or determined, by the fact that 70% of the beans in that bag are indeed purple. In this case, of course, it is a fact not about our cognitive faculties, but rather about the natural world, which conditions the experience in question, and, in this respect at least, Peirce therefore presents a realist account of the possibility of inductive inference.

9. Hypothesis, Abduction and Science

While Peirce's account of the long-term validity of inductive inference is essential to his position on the methods to be employed in the pursuit of scientific knowledge, he is insistent that induction is not sufficient for our investigative purposes, and that there is an irreducible role for deduction and abduction (or what he sometimes calls 'hypothesis' or 'retroduction') in our

---

[50] EP1:146.

inquiries at discovering truth. Peirce presents the distinction between abduction, induction and deduction as conditional upon the classification of arguments according to the categories of Firstness, Secondness and Thirdness, respectively, and, insofar as the inference is a sign, upon the corresponding semiotic distinction between icons, indices and symbols. Presented in these terms, induction stands as a case of Secondness because it involves a direct encounter between a representational state of the inquirer and something other than that representational state. The inductive stage of an inquiry admits of the possibility of surprise on our part, for it is here that we directly encounter, in what Peirce calls the 'outward clash'[51] of experience, a world that is thus and so, irrespective of what we may happen to think about it, and which therefore has the capacity to defeat our expectations by behaving in ways which we do not yet understand. Since induction involves immediate contact between the inquirer (or, rather, some representational state thereof) and some state of the world, an event must always involve a forceful reaction wherein the inquirer is affected by the object by having their perceptual states determined by the object (but which may also often involve an experiment whereupon the object is forcefully determined by a deliberate action on the inquirer's part) the sign which stands for the object here will be an index. As such, in consequence of its being grounded, in respect of its relation to its object, on a direct forceful encounter in which it is directly affected by its object, the inference drawn at the inductive stage of an inquiry is an indexical sign.

The inductive stage of an inquiry must be preceded, however, by a deductive stage, which must, in turn, be preceded by an abductive stage. The importance of abductive inference, not only to Peirce's philosophy of science but to his philosophy in general, is difficult to overstate[52]. In Peirce's theory of inquiry, the abductive stage precedes the use of deduction and induction, as the stage at which a hypothesis is formed and selected for subsequent empirical testing. Since the abductive stage is prior to the inductive, the hypothesis or abductive inference is not forcefully determined by any immediate contact with any state of the physical world, and must therefore be other than indexical, because its status as a sign does not obtain in consequence of its having been affected by some state of the world. Instead, Peirce maintains, the abductive inference is an icon, that is, a sign of a merely possible, but not necessarily actual, state of affairs. If inductive testing of the hypothesis gives us reason to suppose that the

---

[51] EP1:233-4.

[52] Davis is particularly enthusiastic about the significance of Peirce's theory of abduction and its role in scientific inquiry. See William H. Davis, "Hypothesis or Abduction: The Originative Phase of Reasoning," in *Peirce's Epistemology* (Dordrecht: Springer, 1972), 22–86.

hypothesis is true, this does not entail that it is no longer an icon (but, rather, an index) because the hypothesis itself is not at any stage forcefully affected by any state of the physical world. As an icon, the hypothesis does not stand for an object by standing in an actual force-transferring relation with it, but rather by there being a resemblance between the relational structure of the object represented in the hypothesis and that state of the world of which the icon happens to be a sign. Since it is only required, for something to be an iconic sign, that it has for its object some possible structure of relations (which need not, for non-mathematical purposes, be merely formal), there is no requirement that there should actually obtain anything which that structure resembles.

Because the icon need not stand in relation to anything and has for its object only a possible structure of relations, or schema, it is therefore a monadic relation and an instance of Peirce's category of Firstness. Peirce outlines the form of the abductive inference, that class of argument which results in an abductive sign, as follows:

The surprising fact, C, is observed

But if A were true, C would be a matter of course

Hence, there is reason to suspect that A is true[53].

As such, abduction is similar to induction, and dissimilar from deduction by being a form of synthetic (rather than analytic), probable (rather than apodeictic) and ampliative (rather than explicative) inference. At the same time, however, abduction differs from induction by being an inference to a case, rather than to a rule. Whereas the inductive argument has a conclusion of the form 'all x are y', the abductive inference argues to conclusions of the form 'x is y'.

Before proceeding to elaborate upon the status of abduction in Peirce's theory of inquiry, it may be appropriate to outline how deduction is held to contribute to this position. According to Peirce, the deductive stage of an inquiry mediates between the abductive and inductive stages, and therefore, with respect to this mediating function, stands as an instance of the category of Thirdness. The role of deduction in inquiry is to infer from a hypothesis various corollaries which follow necessarily from that hypothesis, such that we may be provided with an idea of what to encounter at the inductive stage of our inquiry if various specified conditions are obtained and the hypothesis in question is not in error.

---

[53] Charles S. Peirce, "Pragmatism and Abduction," in *The Essential Peirce*, ed. Peirce Edition Project, vol. 2 (Indianapolis: Indiana University Press, 1998), 231. From here on, "EP2".

As such, the corollaries identified at the deductive stage of the inquiry provide the conditions necessary for us to be able to recognise the results of an experiment conducted at the subsequent inductive stage as corroborating a hypothesis formed at the initial abductive stage. Such corollaries are classifiable as symbols because they are signs by means of which it is possible to interpret an icon (delivered by abduction) and an index (delivered by induction) as having the same object, or as being related in terms of meaning.

However, although the purely explicative or analytic nature of the deductive inference ensures that there is little risk of error at this stage of our inquiry (so long, of course, as one is not subject to certain idiosyncrasies which impair one's capability to make deductively valid inferences), there is a much greater likelihood of our making errors at the abductive stage, by forming and selecting for subsequent empirical testing, a hypothesis which would not be corroborated at the inductive stage. Peirce does not allow us to have any a priori entitlement to expect, of any hypothesis, we decide to submit for subsequent empirical testing, that it would be corroborated at the inductive stage of an inquiry. As Peirce remarks, abduction is 'ultimately nothing but guessing'[54], although fallible inference from the results of other inquiries carried through to the inductive stage avail us of a posteriori grounds upon which to make more or less 'educated' guesses.

As such, there is no possible a priori guarantee of the validity of abductive inference, even in the long run, and Peirce suggests as much in claiming that the only ground of our entitlement to make use of abductive inference is that it is only by doing so that we allow ourselves even a *chance* of satisfying our epistemic responsibility to discover truth. However, if as Peirce maintains, there can be no a priori guarantee that the use of abductive inference would lead us to select hypotheses that would be corroborated at the inductive stage of an inquiry, then, since the success of the inquiry depends upon the initial selection of a correct hypothesis at the abductive stage, it follows that there cannot be any a priori guarantee that participation in *any* inquiry would lead us to discover any fact about the world. Moreover, since the inductive stage of any inquiry is subsequent to the abductive stage, Peirce's claim that the continued use of induction *would*, in the long run, lead to the discovery of truth, should be interpreted as something of an abstraction from his complete account of the investigative process and as being qualified by the assumption that we are at such a world that is hospitable to our efforts at achieving knowledge by means of the inductive testing of abductive hypotheses.

---

[54] EP2: 107.

This is not at all to suggest that Peirce's claims about the long-term validity of induction are somehow inconsistent with his views about the lack of an a priori guarantee for the validity of abductive inference. Induction is a form of inference distinct from abduction and is not responsible for the errors which arise at the abductive stage of an inquiry. All that can be meant by asserting that induction is valid in the long run is that, if enough tests are carried out at the inductive stage of an inquiry, then, eventually, perhaps only given more time than the human race may continue to last, the inductive stage of the inquiry would eventually come to the correct conclusion about whether the hypothesis is true. While induction is a fallible form of inference and mistakes may often be made in carrying out observational experiments, Peirce maintains that if the hypothesis on trial has a truth-value then the continued use of induction *would* eventually result in the discovery of that truth-value. However, while they may be responsible for short-term mistakes arising from observational errors, or drawing premature conclusions about the results of an experiment, scientists operating at the inductive stage of an inquiry do not have to answer for the premises which have been handed down to them by scientists operating at the earlier abductive and deductive stages.

10. Inquiry and Regulative Hope

While he is therefore correct to maintain that Peirce holds the use of inductive reasoning to be valid in the long-term[55], Apel is nonetheless mistaken in thinking that this commitment to the eventual self-correction of induction entails a commitment, first, to the claim that *were* our inquiries to be sufficiently well-conducted and for a sufficient length of time, *then* they would result in the discovery of truths about reality, and, second, to the transcendental conditions of the truth of this claim, including the reality of the categories. Induction is only the final stage of the three-part process which leads to the inference to a conclusion based upon observational evidence, and while it is able to "put its own house in order", so to speak, by correcting those errors for which it is responsible (if allowed enough time and effort for the self-correcting process to develop sufficiently), it cannot stand alone in the process of inquiry but relies upon premises inferred by means of deduction and, ultimately, abduction. Since abduction is neither a form of necessary inference (and is therefore unlike deduction) nor is it self-correcting (and is therefore unlike induction), there is no a priori guarantee of a connection between the use of abductive inference and the eventual discovery of truths about reality. It

---

[55] K.-O. Apel, *Charles S. Peirce: From Pragmatism to Pragmaticism*, trans. John Michael Krois (New York: Prometheus Books, 1995), 36.

is Peirce's position, however, that the success of the whole inquiry is conditional upon the selection of a correct hypothesis at the abductive stage.

As such, contra Apel, Peirce does not suppose that there is any a priori guarantee that the continued following-out of the three-stage process of scientific inquiry would eventually lead to the discovery of truths about reality. Since the inductive stage of any such process could not possibly result in such discoveries unless the hypothesis identified at the abductive stage happened to be correct, the possibility of scientific knowledge is a priori conditional upon obtaining the conditions necessary for the possibility of our forming correct hypotheses at the abductive stage of our inquiries. However, the absence of any a priori grounds for a connection between the use of abductive inference and the formation of true hypotheses about reality entails that any grounds for our entitlement to claim that there is such a connection must be a posteriori. In that case, however, there cannot be any possibility of a Peircean counterpart to the Transcendental Deduction, which would attempt to infer the objective validity of the categories from their status as a priori necessary conditions of the possibility of scientific knowledge, together with the a priori categorical premise that we are at such a world where scientific knowledge is possible. While the use of abductive inference is necessary for us to stand even a chance of making empirical discoveries, it also introduces into the process of scientific investigation a degree of fallibility which we have no a priori entitlement to assert would eventually be removed by the pursuit of a sufficiently well-conducted inquiry over any amount of time.

As a matter of fact, Peirce did think that history has provided more than sufficient inductive grounds for an a posteriori entitlement to infer the probable truth of the hypothesis that there obtain the conditions necessary for the possibility of scientific knowledge, including the reality of the categories and the ability of the inquirer to submit correct abductive hypotheses for inductive testing. Peirce describes our assurance of the possibility of scientific knowledge, not as a priori, but rather, as 'empirical confidence'[56], thus undermining Apel's case for there being a Peircean counterpart to the Transcendental Deduction. Whereas Apel attributes to Peirce a transcendental argument to satisfy the Kantian demand for a priori grounds of our entitlement to the classification of empirical phenomena according to a list of categories necessarily presupposed in any claim about such phenomena, it is in fact entirely compatible with Peirce's stated position that future developments in our inquiries could present us with empirical evidence for supposing that most of our presently held empirical beliefs are mistaken, and that there are therefore far less compelling a posteriori grounds than we had originally

---

[56] EP1:234.

thought for supposing there to obtain the conditions necessary for the possibility of scientific knowledge.

However, Peirce allows that our non-negotiable duty to pursue the discovery of truths about reality provides sufficient grounds for an a priori entitlement to hope that they obtain the necessary conditions for scientific knowledge. Since we have an a priori duty to act towards a goal which could not possibly be achievable unless such conditions are obtained, and since, as is often assumed, we cannot take ourselves to have a responsibility to realise some state of affairs unless we also assume that there is at least some possibility of our being able to do so, we are therefore a priori permitted not to accept any a posteriori grounds as sufficient to commit us to reject the possibility of scientific knowledge. Such an a priori entitlement to carry on *hoping* for better things to come, whatever the present state of our inquiries, provides a sufficient defence against a posteriori sceptical challenges (of which the so-called 'sceptical meta-induction' may provide an example) which allege that we have an epistemic responsibility which commits us to *doubting* the possibility of scientific knowledge. Contrary to transcendentalist interpretations of Peirce's position, however, and unlike Kant himself, Peirce does not assume that our assurance against scepticism is entailed by our having a priori entitlements to claim knowledge even of the possibility of scientific discovery.

Although Apel does recognise an important role for hope in Peirce's positions, he takes it what we are to hope for is not the obtaining of the a priori necessary conditions for the possibility of scientific knowledge (this having already been established, in Apel's view, by means of a Peircean counterpart to the Transcendental Deduction), but rather that the pursuit of our inquiries *will* eventually result in the discovery of truths about reality, by being allowed sufficient time and effort for them to reach their natural end. In fact, however, the role of hope in Peirce's position extends somewhat further than Apel gives credit for, and includes the claim that we have an a priori entitlement to hope that there obtain such conditions that the continued pursuit of inquiry *would* result in scientific knowledge under certain conditions, and not just that it *will* in fact. In other words, much as Kant denies that we have any a priori *knowledge* to the effect that it is even *possible* for our actions to contribute towards the eventual realisation of the highest moral good, so Peirce denies that we have any a priori *knowledge* to the effect that it is even possible for our actions to contribute to the eventual realisation of the discovery of truths about reality. Moreover, in Kant's case as well as Peirce's, the absence of any a priori guarantee for the possible realisation of our a priori duties, results from the absence of any a priori guarantee that there obtain the conditions necessary for the world to be hospitable to the possible satisfaction of our responsibilities. As such, Kant maintains that we have an a priori entitlement to hope that the conditions in question obtain, and, in Peirce's case, this means that we are a priori entitled to hope both that the categories are objectively valid and that it is possible and, moreover, 'destined' that our continued participation in scientific inquiries, making use of abductive, deductive and inductive reasoning, would and, furthermore, shall, result in the discovery of truths about reality.

11. Fallibilism and Scientific Knowledge

While both Kant and Peirce are similarly occupied with providing philosophical explanations of the grounds of scientific knowledge, they differ significantly with respect to the kinds of scientific knowledge to be explained and the manner of explanation appropriate for these purposes. Although Kant recognises a valuable (indeed, indispensable) role for induction and 'analogy' (which is similar to Peirce's 'abduction') in the pursuit of scientific knowledge, he does not uphold the view that a philosophical justification may be offered to explain the a priori grounds of our entitlement to make use of these forms of synthetic inference. Instead, Kant maintains, that the role of philosophical explanation with respect to scientific knowledge is to show how synthetic a priori judgements of natural science are possible, and this requires the Transcendental Deduction.

Peirce's thoroughgoing fallibilism prevents him, however, from acknowledging any place for synthetic a priori judgements in science, and he therefore endeavours to explain how scientific knowledge is possible by means of synthetic inference. Although his belief in the intrinsically self-correcting character of induction shows Peirce to be more optimistic than Kant about the possibility of a philosophical explanation of the grounds of our entitlement to make use of this form of synthetic inference, he maintains that the success of our inquiries depends upon our choice of correct hypotheses at the abductive stage of an investigation, and that we have no a priori entitlement to anything more than a hope that it is even *possible* for us to be able to select hypotheses which would be corroborated at the inductive stage of the inquiry. As such, Apel's attribution to Peirce of a transcendental argument to prove that there obtain the necessary conditions, including the reality of the categories, which would make possible the eventual success of our inquiries, does not account for the important role which Peirce assigns to our a priori entitlement to hope for that possibility.

Bibliography

Allison, Henry. *Kant's Transcendental Idealism. An Interpretation and Defense.* New Haven: Yale University Press, 2004.

Apel, K.-O. *Charles S. Peirce: From Pragmatism to Pragmaticism.* Translated by John Michael Krois. New York: Prometheus Books, 1995.

Boler, John, and C. J. Misak. "Truth and the End of Inquiry: A Peircean Account of Truth." *The Philosophical Review 102*, no. 1 (January 1993): 110. https://doi.org/10.2307/2185663.

Davis, William H. "Hypothesis or Abduction: The Originative Phase of Reasoning." In *Peirce's Epistemology*, 22–86. Dordrecht: Springer, 1972.

Gardner, Sebastian. *Kant and the Critique of Pure Reason.* New York: Routledge, 1999.

Guyer, Paul. *Kant.* New York: Routledge, 2006.

Hanna, Robert. *Kant and the Foundations of Analytic Philosophy.* Oxford: Clarendon Press, 2001.

Hulswit, Menno. *From Cause to Causation. A Peircean Perspective.* Dordrecht: Kluwer Publishers, 2002.

Hume, David. *A Treatise of Human Nature.* Oxford: Clarendon Press, 1975.

———. An Enquiry Concerning Human Understanding. Edited by Peter Millican. Oxford World's Classics. Oxford, New York: Oxford University Press, 2008.

———. *The History of England.* Vol. 6. Indianapolis: Liberty Fund, 1983.

Kant, Immanuel. *Critique of Pure Reason.* Translated by Paul Guyer and Allen W. Wood. Cambridge: Cambridge University Press, 1998.

———. "Metaphysical Foundations of Natural Science (1786)." In *Theoretical Philosophy after 1781*, edited by Gary Hatfield, Henry Allison, Michael Friedman, and Peter Heath, 171–270. The Cambridge Edition of the Works of Immanuel Kant. Cambridge: Cambridge University Press, 2002. https://doi.org/10.1017/CBO9780511498015.004.

Peirce, Charles S. "Grounds of Validity of the Laws of Logic: Further Consequences of Four Incapacities." In *The Essential Peirce*, edited by Nathan Houser and Christian J. W. Kloesel, 1:56-82. Indianapolis: Indiana University Press, 1992.

———. "Pragmatism and Abduction." In *The Essential Peirce*, edited by Peirce Edition Project, 2:226-240. Indianapolis: Indiana University Press, 1998.

Venn, John. *The Logic of Chance.* London: MacMillan, 1876.

Waxman, Wayne. "Kant's Humean Solution to Hume's Problem." In *Kant and the Early Moderns*, edited by Daniel Garber and Béatrice Longuenesse, 172–92. Princeton: Princeton University Press, 2008.

Woozley, A. D., ed. "Introduction." In *Essays on the Intellectual Powers of Man*, Vol. 17. Cambridge University Press, 1942.

Chapter 10

The Limits of Self-Legislation

Tom O'Shea
University of Edinburgh

Abstract: Tom O'Shea questions the limits of self-legislation and some forms of constructivism that can be formulated from some modern approaches, like the Kantian and Humean conceptions of normativity. In order to do so, O'Shea outlines and critiques two neo-Hegelian forms of constructivism that present alternatives to the Kantian and Humean positions. The author takes the reader directly into the crux of the issue they wish to discuss. In doing so the author also provides an excellent historical framing and contextualisation of the problems involved in self-legislation.

Keywords: Hegel, Kant, Hume, normativity, self-legislation.

***

1. Introduction

Modernity confronts us with a distinctive challenge. The decline of a shared religious metaphysic deprives us of common landmarks by which to orient our thoughts and actions. We cannot look to God or a divinely-ordered nature for guidance on what to believe or do. So too, the disenchanted nature that has followed in the wake of modern science puts pressure on appeals to other kinds of natural teleology. Yet, simply thinking and acting as we each like—following whatever desires we happen to possess—appears to condemn us to a capricious existence incompatible with human freedom. Rousseau suggests in this respect that "the impulse of mere appetite is slavery".[1] Furthermore, believing as well as acting as we like is a recipe for delusion and fantasy (not to mention that powerful social and economic actors are able to shape our desires for their own gain). How then do we cope with such normative disorientation?

---

[1] Jean-Jacques Rousseau, *The Social Contract and First and Second Discourses*, ed. and trans. Susan Dunn (New Haven: Yale University Press, 2002), 167.

We might respond to this anomie by insisting on the primacy of theoretical rationality. This kind of rationality concerns the justification of our beliefs rather than the propriety of our actions—asking "What should we believe?" rather than "What should we do?" Theoretical rationality can be understood to be answerable to whatever normative standards are compatible with empirical science and the canons of mathematics. The manifest technical and experimental success of modern science would offer its own warrant for approaching doxastic inquiry with natural scientific norms in view. Practical rationality could then be reconceived more modestly as a faculty which tells us whether and how we can achieve our goals, but without telling us what those goals should be. That silence about ends could result from a strict non-cognitivism about practical normativity, which denied that judgements about what we should or should not do were truth-apt. Alternatively, it might arise from an error theory that held that all such judgements were false. Clipping the wings of practical rationality in this way renders it little more than an extension of theoretical reasoning, concerned with the most efficient causal mechanisms for achieving our given ends, or the possibility of realising multiple ends simultaneously. But the cost of doing so is profound: the loss of any substantial ethical, aesthetic, or political normativity.

Can we do better than this retreat for robust practical reasons? We will consider some broadly constructivist approaches to normativity which develop the Kantian appeal to self-legislation. In Kant's writings, self-legislation denotes the will's subjection to a law of which it can consider itself the author.[2] For contemporary Kantian constructivists, self-legislation serves as a metaphor underpinning their claim that normativity arises not from natural law, divinity, or desire, but rather from the self-disciplining structures of rational agency, which subjects itself to norms. These Kantian constructivists endorse transcendental accounts of lawgiving, which argue that there are some normative commitments that must be presupposed by every rational agent.[3] The promise of Kantian constructivisms is that they explain the obligatoriness of morality, as well as the origins of other forms of practical normativity, while

---

[2] Immanuel Kant, *Practical Philosophy*, trans. Mary Gregor (Cambridge: Cambridge University Press, 1999), 81.

[3] See Onora O'Neill, *Constructions of Reason: Explorations of Kant's Practical Philosophy* (Cambridge: Cambridge University Press, 1989); Onora O'Neill, *Towards Justice and Virtue: A Constructive Account of Practical Reason* (Cambridge: Cambridge University Press, 1996); Onora O'Neill, *Constructing Authorities: Reason, Politics and Interpretation in Kant's Philosophy* (Cambridge: Cambridge University Press, 2016); Christine M. Korsgaard, *The Sources of Normativity* (Cambridge: Cambridge University Press, 1996), https://doi.org/10.1017/CBO9780511554476; Christine M. Korsgaard, *Self-Constitution* (Oxford: Oxford University Press, 2009).

doing justice to both naturalist scruples and the autonomy of the will.[4] They also share a commitment to the primacy of a robust practical reason—whether in regards to our practical conduct alone or across both practical and doxastic domains. While some of these constructivist strategies are almost entirely concerned with practical normativity, others are more explicit in holding out the hope of unifying practical and theoretical reason under a common self-imposed principle.[5]

Constructivists regard us as legislators of the laws to which we are subject since we institute norms by binding ourselves. In short: we are subject to such norms only because we take ourselves to be subject. This does not imply we are accountable to all or only those norms which we think we are. Nevertheless, constructivist accounts of self-legislation incorporate *attitude-dependent* conceptions of normativity. While constructivists accept the attitude-dependence of norms, they disagree about the nature of this dependence. We can distinguish at least three families of constructivist approaches to the relationship between attitudes and norms in this respect. The Kantian constructivist claims that the attitudes towards norms that an agent adopts will commit them to the moral law irrespective of the content of these attitudes. This is an extraordinarily strong claim which is typically underpinned by a transcendental strategy. For example, Christine Korsgaard[6] has sought to show that a necessary condition of the possibility of acting is taking ourselves to have some specific reasons and that by endorsing any specific reasons we ultimately commit ourselves to valuing the rational natures of ourselves and of others. Thus, from the constitutive conditions of rational agency, we are meant to find compelling reasons to cooperate and care for one another and to forswear exploitation and maltreatment. Such arguments have prompted many objections and more than a few incredulous stares. For our purposes, the significant feature of these Kantian approaches is that despite the normative force of the moral law being *attitude*-dependent, it remains *content*-independent with respect to the attitudes towards norms people actually adopt.

Some pressure to abandon this Kantian transcendental approach has been exerted by critics who have sought to show that there are no substantive normative commitments presupposed by rational agency as such, or that any such commitments cannot do the ambitious work of grounding moral or political

---

[4] Robert Stern, "Constructivism and the Argument from Autonomy," in *Constructivism in Practical Philosophy*, ed. James Lenman and Yonatan Shemmer (Oxford: Oxford University Press, 2012), 119–37.

[5] O'Neill, *Constructions of Reason: Explorations of Kant's Practical Philosophy*, chap. 1.

[6] See: Korsgaard, *Self-Constitution*; Korsgaard, *The Sources of Normativity*.

norms in particular.[7] Whatever the success of these objections, constructivists are increasingly endorsing a self-legislative conception of normativity without pursuing a broadly Kantian strategy of identifying certain normative commitments that are 'baked in' into the legislative process. In this respect, individualist accounts of self-legislation combine attitude dependence with a greater degree of content dependence—establishing a closer connection between the norms to which people are actually subject and those to which they take themselves to be subject. For individualist constructivists, it remains the attitudes of individuals towards norms that underpin what is legislated, with only minimal constraints on the legislative process concerning consistency, instrumentality, and empirical truth. This broadly Humean approach expresses "skepticism about the ability of 'pure' practical reason to tell us how to live", and moreover no commitment to morality or other substantive universal norms is presupposed.[8] We cannot explore this Humean strategy in depth other than to note that the minimal constraints it imposes upon self-legislation come with the danger of inoculating people from seemingly legitimate criticism. For instance, so long as he has made no empirical errors, the consistent and conscientious misogynist would seem to have reason to continue acting on his resentment and antipathy towards women, and cannot be subject to rational reproach.[9]

My main aim in this chapter will be to outline and critique two neo-Hegelian forms of constructivism that present alternatives to these Kantian and Humean positions. The socio-historical constructivist account of self-legislation supplements the attitudes of the individual towards norms with the attitudes

---

[7] G. A. Cohen, "Reason, Humanity, and the Moral Law," in *The Sources of Normativity*, ed. Christine Korsgaard (Cambridge: Cambridge University Press, 1996), 167–88; David Enoch, "Agency, Shmagency: Why Normativity Won't Come from What Is Constitutive of Action," *The Philosophical Review* 115, no. 2 (2006): 169–98; Kerstin Budde, "Constructivism All the Way down – Can O'Neill Succeed Where Rawls Failed?," *Contemporary Political Theory* 8, no. 2 (May 2009): 199–223, https://doi.org/10.1057/cpt .2008.41; Tom O'Shea, "A Law of One's Own: Self-Legislation and Radical Kantian Constructivism," *European Journal of Philosophy* 23, no. 4 (December 2015): 1153–73, https://doi.org/10.1111/ejop.12044.

[8] Sharon Street, "Coming to Terms with Contingency: Humean Constructivism about Practical Reason," in *Constructivism in Practical Philosophy*, ed. James Lenman and Yonatan Shemmer (Oxford: Oxford University Press, 2012), 40-59.

[9] For potential—although I believe ultimately insufficient—resources to rebut such objections, see Valerie Tiberius, *The Reflective Life: Living Wisely Within Our Limits* (Oxford: Oxford University Press, 2008), 189; Sharon Street, "In Defense of Future Tuesday Indifference: Ideally Coherent Eccentrics and the Contingency of What Matters," *Philosophical Issues* 19 (2009): 273–98, Street, "Coming to Terms with Contingency: Humean Constructivism about Practical Reason".

towards those norms of others whom they acknowledge in a community of recognition. Nevertheless, such legislation also need not generate the kinds of universal moral law that emerge from Kantian constructivism. The question that faces such socio-historical constructivisms is the same as that confronting the Humean approach: whether, in the absence of such robust universal laws, it is possible for them to account for a sufficient range of legitimate critical appraisal of people's conduct.

2. Brandom on Self-Legislation and Sociality

Can socio-historical constructivists support robust critical appraisal of human action? John Milton memorably describes Adam and Eve as "authors to themselves in all / Both what they judge and what they choose".[10] Robert Brandom's neo-Hegelian rationalist anthropology casts humanity in a similar light as beings responsible for their own fate through the commitments which they give to themselves in their beliefs and volitions. He understands the autonomy of rational agents in terms of a self-legislative model of discursive commitment. Initially, it seems that Brandom is in a strong position, because his attitude-dependent conception of normativity is less individualistic than both Humean and Kantian constructivisms, insofar as it incorporates a social and historical dimension. The attitudes of the individuals subject to norms are supplemented by the contribution of a community of recognition in determining their content. This allows greater scope for external critique than Humean individualistic self-legislation.

Brandom presents us not with a solitary self-legislator but a social division of labour in the institution of normativity.[11] Whether a norm has the authority to exercise a rational constraint upon an individual is determined by them. A norm binds someone if and only if they use a concept expressing it (or standing in an appropriate inferential relationship with a concept expressing it). This is a sufficiently broad understanding of self-legislation that promises to unite aspects of theoretical and practical rationality. That is because using a concept can either take the form of making a doxastic judgement or acting on a practical maxim in which the concept figures. However, what rational constraints the norm mandates are determined by a process of negotiation amongst other people that the individual acknowledges as having authority over the correct use of the relevant concept. The result is a social model of self-legislation. Norms are *self-legislated* because individuals undertake normative commitments by exercising

---

[10] John Milton, *Paradise Lost*, ed. Christopher Ricks (London: Penguin, 1968), 61.
[11] Robert Brandom, "Some Pragmatist Themes in Hegel's Idealism," in *Tales of the Mighty Dead: Historical Essays in the Metaphysics of Intentionality* (Cambridge: Harvard University Press, 2002), 219.

their own conceptual powers. Yet, these norms have *legislative* authority only because others enforce them and administer their content. If individuals were sovereign over both normative force and content—both whether and to what they bind themselves—then Brandom believes a Wittgensteinian objection would be decisive. Drawing on a reading of Wittgenstein's *Philosophical Investigations*, he says that, since in this case, "whatever *seems* right to me therefore *is* right, there can be no question of right or wrong".[12]

We might think this more social model of self-legislation is still too individualistic to support robust critical assessment, since a necessary condition of social constraints upon legislation being operative is the individual's own act of committing themselves, alongside their recognition of a community of deontic scorekeepers. If the individual always determines whether to bind themselves, then it seems that they can escape any normative commitments they feel inclined to. For example, social administration and enforcement of self-legislation can look like it would have no impact on the consistent misogynist who chooses not to impose norms relating to gender equality. However, this reading of social self-legislation risks being excessively decisionist. Brandom might stress that in a society where we communicate, interact with, and depend upon other people, we cannot help being caught up in various practices that require us to judge and act in ways that involve tokening our acknowledgement of norms in the eyes of others. We always already find ourselves within an existing social process of norm-negotiation and deontic scorekeeping, rather than simply creating norms *ex nihilo* through a deliberate decision. In the midst of such a process, we will inevitably discover that other people we recognise as authoritative judges take us have committed ourselves in ways we have not grasped the full implications of. Thus, moral and political critique would always be possible.

The always-already social and historical institution of normative authority has been spelt out in Brandom's more recent work through a supposedly Hegelian model of mutual recognition. The decidedly non-Hegelian example he uses to illustrate the process of norm-institution he has in mind is the development of Anglophone common law.[13] As he represents it, when a judge under common law is confronted with a novel case, they stand in relations of

---

[12] For the corresponding remark, see Ludwig Wittgenstein, *Philosophical Investigations*, trans. G. E. M. Anscombe (Oxford: Blackwell, 1953), pt. I §258.

[13] Brandom, "Some Pragmatist Themes in Hegel's Idealism", 230. For an application of this model to legal concepts themselves, see Robert Brandom, "A Hegelian Model of Legal Concept Determination: The Normative Fine Structure of Judges' Chain Novel," in *Pragmatism, Law, and Language*, ed. Graham Hubbs and Douglas Lind (Oxford: Routledge, 2014).

recognition with previous judges to whom they grant authority to determine whether their decisions are correct. This is the idea of legal precedent. Current judges stand in the same reciprocal relationship as future judges, who recognise their use of legal concepts as authoritative for them. But current judges are also responsible to future judges, insofar as the authority of their judgments must be recognised by those future judges in order to be real. Judges justify what to take as precedent by offering a rational reconstruction of the legal tradition, which both determines and reveals the content of the legal concepts that the judge is applying. This is said to depend upon

> the sort of rationality that consists in retrospectively picking out an expressively progressive trajectory through past applications of a concept, so as to determine a norm one can understand as governing the whole process and so project into the future.[14]

Of course, this appeal to a mutually recognisable historical community which is underpinned by a rational reconstruction of its own tradition is meant to sound a Hegelian note.

3. The Self-Legislative Trilemma

The common law analogy reveals that the sustained attitude- and content dependence that Brandom pursues cannot be workable. In real legal judgments, judges are rightly sensitive to what *ought* to be done, within the constraints of the law. This is in order to avoid the perverse outcomes which would arise from resolving the underdetermination of legal concepts in simply any narrowly permissible or pedantic fashion. For example, a recent case before the England and Wales Court of Appeal turned on the interpretation of a disclaimer for liability for certain financial losses "in any circumstances", which, construed literally, would unreasonably indemnify a contractor against their own fraud, malice, recklessness, or negligence towards another party.[15] In glossing such clauses, a competent judge needs some guiding sense of what would make a good judgment versus a bad one. This is partly determined by ethical and political norms which do not arise solely out of the legal tradition itself, insofar as they draw on wider understandings of justice, legitimacy, and felicitous results. However, this prior normative orientation is precisely what is not available to Brandom, because this is a global form of self-legislation which

---

[14] Brandom, "Some Pragmatist Themes in Hegel's Idealism", 13.
[15] See "Regus (UK) Ltd v Epcot Solutions Ltd - Case Summary," IPSA LOQUITUR, April 15, 2008, https://ipsaloquitur.com/contract-law/cases/regus-uk-v-epcot-solutions/.

attempts to account for all normativity. For his socio-historical constructivism, it is self-legislation all the way down.

We can sharpen this concern by observing how it results in a socio-historical version of the so-called Kantian paradox of self-legislation.[16] The problem can be presented as a trilemma. If we have not already legislated norms for ourselves, then there will be no basis for deciding how to legislate. Our legislative activity will be radically underdetermined—with no reason to legislate one way rather than the other. This makes self-legislation too arbitrary to be an expression of our freedom as rational agents: it becomes an unaccountable leap into the dark. But if we have already legislated norms that determine which other laws we ought to give to ourselves, then under the threat of a regress, there will be no grounds for legislating these higher-order norms. Thus, either self-legislation is effectively arbitrary at the first order, at higher orders, or else surreptitiously relies on another more fundamental and unexplained set of norms that are not legislated by us.[17]

Similarly, with respect to Brandom, without some norm to determine what a good rather than bad rational reconstruction consists in, then the process of norm-institution will be too arbitrary. Any reconstruction we happen to endorse that meets minimum standards of narrative intelligibility could thereby serve to justify the norms it valorises. Higher-order norms governing rational reconstruction itself will stand in need of their own justification, where attempts to justify them via another rational reconstruction will threaten a regress. But if there are independent normative standards governing the process, then rational reconstruction looks to be both pointless and self-defeating, because we ought to be able to appeal to these norms to orient our action directly, and therefore can conclude that there is an independent source of normativity. Therefore, Brandom finds himself confronted with a trilemma at the level of rational reconstruction.

---

[16] See Robert Pippin, "The Actualization of Freedom. In The Cambridge Companion to German Idealism," ed. Karl Ameriks (Cambridge: Cambridge University Press, 2000), 180–99; Robert Pippin, *Hegel's Practical Philosophy: Rational Agency as Ethical Life* (Cambridge: Cambridge University Press, 2008), 70-71; Terry Pinkard, *German Philosophy 1760-1860: The Legacy of Idealism* (Cambridge: Cambridge University Press, 2002), 60; and for critical discussion, Robert Stern, "Freedom, Self-Legislation and Morality in Kant and Hegel: Constructivist vs Realist Accounts," in *German Idealism: Contemporary Perspectives*, ed. Espen Hammer (London: Routledge, 2007), 245–66.

[17] For distinct but illuminating objections along these lines, see John McDowell, "Self-Determining Subjectivity and External Constraint," in *Self-Determining Subjectivity and External Constraint* (De Gruyter, 2005), 21–37, https://doi.org/10.1515/9783110179545. 21, and William F. Bristow, "Self-Consciousness, Normativity and Abysmal Freedom," *Inquiry* 49, no. 6 (December 2006), https://doi.org/10.1080/00201740601016197, 505.

Furthermore, the appeal to rational reconstruction from within this socio-historical model of legislation leaves little room for a whole society to be criticised. In discussing empirical concepts such as mass, Brandom allows that we "could all be treating as a correct application of the concepts involved what is objectively an incorrect one".[18] Yet, there are few resources to accommodate corresponding practical evaluation, other than failing to fulfil or understand the implications of norms we acknowledge as binding us. This creates problems when we allow for comprehensive social distortions in how people interpret their traditions or acknowledge the commitments undertaken by themselves or others. When a whole population is saturated with an ideology, then this would provide normative vindication and not merely social armature for it. Likewise, if we were to take seriously the possibility raised by critical theorists like Erich Fromm [19] that we might not live in a 'sane society', and thus that there may be widespread social pathologies, then this consequence appears especially troubling. In the absence of a more extensive apparatus for accommodating the effects of myriad forms of social power upon the legislative process, there are serious limits on any attempt to align Brandom's position with a critical approach to practical reason.[20]

4. Pippin's Institutionalism

Constructivists might turn to an alternative socio-historical use of self-legislation which is more institutional in character. Its most sophisticated advocate has been Robert Pippin, who is more attuned to the kinds of objection levelled here at Brandom, and insists that the "non-arbitrary nature of such self-legislating must find a place in any account."[21] The first major distinguishing feature of his account is a collective approach to self-legislation. Opera provides an illustration:

---

[18] Robert Brandom, *Making It Explicit: Reasoning, Representing and Discursive Commitment* (Cambridge: Harvard University Press, 1994), 53.

[19] Erich Fromm, *The Sane Society* (London: Routledge, 1955), chap. 2.

[20] For a critical-political reading of Brandom of this kind, see Thomas Fossen, "Politicizing Brandom's Pragmatism: Normativity and the Agonal Character of Social Practice," *European Journal of Philosophy* 22, no. 3 (2014): 371–95, https://doi.org/10.1111/j.1468-0378.2011.00504.x.

[21] In virtue of his counting himself among the 'card-carrying Hegelians' and his 'de re' interpretative methodology, I will refer to 'Pippin' here instead of 'Pippin's Hegel'. See Pippin, *Hegel's Practical Philosophy: Rational Agency as Ethical Life*, 33-4 & 90. Broadly similar accounts of Hegel can be found in Pinkard, *German Philosophy 1760-1860: The Legacy of Idealism*; and Larry Krasnoff, *Hegel's 'Phenomenology of Spirit': An Introduction* (Cambridge: Cambridge University Press, 2008), 14-5.

the proprieties of opera can obviously be said to be collectively self-legislated over time. They were not discovered, and there was no moment of constitution by fiat.[22]

No one individual is responsible, and instead, normativity becomes embodied in institutions which carry with them traditions and social roles in which authority coalesces. Ordinarily, there are no singular actions of self-binding which create norms, and instead, normativity is produced and enacted over time, sedimented by our forms of life.[23] No groundless arbitrary will launches individuals from a normless to a norm-governed state.

One of the potential problems with an institutional understanding of practical rationality is that it risks degenerating either into mere sociology or relativism. If it amounts to no more than a sociological account of the functioning of communal life, then we are left with a descriptivism that neglects normativity. In this case, we may do a good job of outlining how some institutions and their members tend to function but without demonstrating how they ought to do so. However, if what people are entitled and obliged to do becomes whatever a community happens to take to be so, then unattractive cultural positivism and relativism loom. Pippin rejects both such approaches.[24] For him, self-legislation is not a matter of internalising and following whatever any institution simply treats as a norm. Subjectively, the institutional norms must be ones which lead to actions with which individuals can identify themselves—not simply as rational agents but as the particular socio-historically shaped beings they are. Furthermore, the institutions involved must themselves be 'objectively rational', where the consistency and instrumental coherence of an institution's norms are not enough to secure such rationality.[25]

No absolute criterion for the objective rationality of an institution is invoked. Claims to rationality can be supported through the construction of narratives that present certain institutional forms as viable and progressive on their own terms when set against the backdrop of the problems of forebears and competitors—those which result in these alternative forms of life breaking down, such that we can no longer make them our own. The result is "a general theory of re-constituted positive normative authority out of such breakdowns", which seeks to avoid relativism by defending a developmental conception of the relevant objective rationality.[26]

---

[22] Pippin, *Hegel's Practical Philosophy: Rational Agency as Ethical Life*, 115.
[23] Ibid., 17.
[24] Ibid., 65.
[25] Ibid., 247 & 258.
[26] Ibid: 91; Pippin, *Hegel's Idealism: The Satisfactions of Self-Consciousness*, ch. 10.

5. Challenges to Pippin

Pippin combines collective self-legislation with a developmental understanding of the institutional norms orienting our practical reasoning. However, the far-reaching ambition of this approach to normativity causes major difficulties. Justification of institutions according to their successes in progressively overcoming breakdowns in forms of life presupposes that the identity of those breakdowns can be determined. To claim that a form of life encounters a particular fundamental problem is already to give a description in a normative vocabulary—one which identifies an obstacle to its proper functioning rather than an innocuous variation in that functioning. So, some normative framework must be implicitly introduced to diagnose a breakdown. Consequently, if norms arise in large part from within institutions which overcome breakdowns, but such breakdowns can only be individuated on the basis of normative evaluation, there appears to be no stable criterion for determining what either the breakdowns or solutions to them are.[27] If there is an appeal to an internal standard to identify the relevant breakdowns, which defers only to what the institution itself takes as the relevant problems to be overcome, then given there will often be disagreement about what these problems are, we still require some standard to conclude whose interpretations of the institution or form of life are most fitting.

The problems in terms of which objective rationality is measured might be made more determinate by identifying those which institutions *must* take seriously. For example, in order to simply subsist, the modern liberal-democratic state will encounter certain challenges, such as reproducing itself ideologically and guarding against internal and external security threats. However, these challenges are conditional: *if* the demise of liberal-democratic states is problematic, *then* they should avoid alienating their adherents and being obliterated by their enemies (*but* their demise might not be a problem). In the absence of a categorical imperative arising from pure practical reason, how might the missing antecedent premise be supplied?

We could look to constitutive conditions of institutions or forms of life in order to provide this premise. For example, an institution marked by sufficient authoritarianism or plutocracy might thereby fail to count as a liberal-democratic state, and so much authoritarianism and plutocracy are always

---

[27] For a similar objection to Pinkard, see Robert Stern, "Pinkard on German Idealism," *Hegel Bulletin* 25, no. 1–2 (January 2004): 1–17, https://doi.org/10.1017/S026352320000 197X.

potential problems it must overcome.[28] But this strategy inherits problems similar to those dogging Kantian constitutivism. How do we tell what is constitutive of this particular institution? For example, while a plutocratic state may fail to be liberal-democratic, the relevant institution might be interpreted not as a failed liberal democracy but as a successful plutocracy with superficial liberal-democratic features. If, in response, the authority to determine the constitutive properties of an institution or form of life is invested in its members, then assuming we can non-circularly identify these members and find sufficient agreement among them, what reasons will they have for what they take to be the essential purpose of their institutions and forms of life? Any reason would already presuppose the norm-giving institutional context which it is called upon to determine.

In place of identifying problems encountered by rational agents as such, or arising from constitutive features of institutions or forms of life, we might turn to socio-historically necessary problems and proprieties. Pippin suggests that Hegel's phenomenological method can help explain

> why essential features of a certain form of life, say essential features of modern moral and ethical and political identity, have come to have the grip they now do, why it would be difficult to imagine a liveable form of life, given such a history, assuming any other form.[29]

While self-legislation remains relative to our current form of life and its historical formation, it still imposes normative necessities insofar as the particular socially and historically shaped selves we are would be unable to avoid the breakdown of alternative forms of life and institutional orders that encode different norms. This brings back into view concerns about cultural positivism providing an imprimatur to the status quo. The objection might be defanged if we could show that legislation has force not simply relative to who we happen to have become but who we always already must have become, such that there never could have been viable alternatives. Yet, Pippin wisely demurs from the extremely strong necessitarian or teleological claims often associated with Hegelian philosophy.[30]

---

[28] Despite rejecting this approach as 'too formal', Pippin provides another helpful example: 'The police, considered as an object, are rational to the extent that they fulfil the role of the police, are the police, and not a private army used for the benefit of a tyrant, for example' (Pippin, *Hegel's Practical Philosophy: Rational Agency as Ethical Life*, 258).
[29] Ibid., 278.
[30] Ibid., 237 & 278.

What resources remain to escape a normative affirmation of the present? There are both objective-institutional and subjective-experiential openings for critical assessment. Objectively, institutions must accommodate "the true form of normative authority" being self-legislation.[31] Thus, they may fail to be structured so as to facilitate the relations to oneself and others necessary for normativity to be self-produced rather than legislated to us—primarily, 'mutuality of recognition', of the kind Hegel identifies in the modern state, and which is thought to enable the full range of self-determining agency.[32] Subjectively, alienation from legislation is possible, whereby "basic values begin to lose their grip on participants, requiring a re-orientation in communal norms".[33] For example, members of many advanced capitalist societies are arguably currently experiencing such a deepening alienation from the economic norms embedded in the domestic and global economic order that coalesced in the 1970s. Both objective and subjective shortcomings must be manifested in actual breakdowns rather than mere divergence from abstract philosophical ideals, but the possibility of these breakdowns occurring in the present provides a defence against normative acquiescence to the status quo.

There is a twofold problem, however, with grounding normativity in actual objective or subjective breakdowns. Some breakdowns are precipitated by factors only tangentially related to the activity and structure of the relevant institution or form of life. Consider the blow to feudalism delivered by the Black Death, which wrought dramatic social, economic, and political changes, including strengthening the bargaining power of surviving peasants relative to lords, and thereby greatly disrupting serfdom in Western Europe.[34] Such a shock is seemingly exogenous and orthogonal to the norms, institutions, and forms of life it undermines—arriving more like bad luck than a reflection of their own fundamental weakness. Pippin does distinguish "internal breakdowns from contingent failures while hinting that the latter is not decisive".[35] Yet, not only is this in tension with the claim that '*all that it means* for a practice or institution to fail is that it is no longer acknowledged as authoritative by a wide enough spectrum of a community', but he provides no criteria for making this distinction in practice—where, again, some standard of adjudication is needed when different interpretations of the nature of the

---

[31] Ibid., 260.
[32] Ibid., 261.
[33] Ibid., 221.
[34] Joseph Strayer, ed., *Dictionary of the Middle Ages*, vol. 2 (New York: Scribner, 1983), 257-67.
[35] Pippin identifies famine, decadence, and collective irrationality as examples of contingent failure (Pippin, *Hegel's Practical Philosophy: Rational Agency as Ethical Life*, 75).

breakdown are likely.[36] Conversely, other potential breakdowns *fail* to happen only due to felicitous circumstances that are equally tangentially related to the relevant institution or form of life. For example, the exploitation of huge reserves of natural resources like oil may shore up radically inegalitarian institutions by providing resources to sustain an extensive security apparatus and mollification of the wider population. Thus, the possibility of critical appraisal remains too beholden to the contingent successes of actually existing institutions and forms of life, such that the institutional model of self-legislation which Pippin provides falls short.

6. Conclusion

To recapitulate: I have argued that neo-Hegelian appeals to self-legislation that turn away from a content-independent Kantian transcendental strategy encounter serious difficulties in establishing normative standards for the evaluation of actions, individuals, and institutions[37]. Brandom's account of normativity, supported by his common-law analogy, is riven between a groundless and arbitrary justification of legislation, a higher-order regress, and presupposing the very normative order it seeks to explain. Pippin's institutional account also falters in its inability to identify both the *aporiae* that institutions and forms of life must overcome and the conditions under which objective and subjective breakdowns call for a reorientation of communal norms. Thus, both socio-historical versions of constructivism struggle to support more than relatively minimal normative resources in practical reasoning.

Why do such limits on our critical resources matter? Beyond the theoretical deficit in the inability to explain seemingly well-founded normative judgements—the further danger is that excessively anaemic constructivism would contribute to a wider intellectual and social climate in which we no longer had the skills, confidence, or inclination necessary to judge whether the social world is as it ought to be. In this vein, Kant proclaimed an 'age of criticism', such that "to criticism everything must submit".[38] Marx goes further still:

> there can still be no doubt about the task confronting us at present: the *ruthless criticism of the existing order*, ruthless in that it will shrink ne

---

[36] Ibid., 74. Emphasis added.

[37] In this chapter the topic of self-legislation did not directly considered the work of Axel Honneth on recognition, not due to a lack of interest but due to the limitations of space. But it is clear that considering the dialectic of recognition will add up important caveats to the issue of self-legislation, as Honneth has done in *The I in We* (2012).

[38] Immanuel Kant, *Critique of Pure Reason*, trans. Paul Guyer and Allen W. Wood (Cambridge: Cambridge University Press, 1998). From here on, "KrV". (KrV A xii).

ther from its own discoveries, nor from conflict with the powers that be.[39]

That task is no less vital today.

Bibliography

Brandom, Robert. "A Hegelian Model of Legal Concept Determination: The Normative Fine Structure of Judges' Chain Novel." In *Pragmatism, Law, and Language*, edited by Graham Hubbs and Douglas Lind, 19–39. Oxford: Routledge, 2014.

———. *Making It Explicit: Reasoning, Representing and Discursive Commitment.* Cambridge: Harvard University Press, 1994.

———. "Some Pragmatist Themes in Hegel's Idealism." In *Tales of the Mighty Dead: Historical Essays in the Metaphysics of Intentionality.* Cambridge: Harvard University Press, 2002.

Bristow, William F. "Self-Consciousness, Normativity and Abysmal Freedom." *Inquiry* 49, no. 6 (December 2006): 498–523. https://doi.org/10.1080/002017 40601016197.

Budde, Kerstin. "Constructivism All the Way down – Can O'Neill Succeed Where Rawls Failed?" *Contemporary Political Theory* 8, no. 2 (May 2009): 199–223. https://doi.org/10.1057/cpt.2008.41.

Cohen, G. A. "Reason, Humanity, and the Moral Law." In *The Sources of Normativity*, edited by Christine Korsgaard, 167–88. Cambridge: Cambridge University Press, 1996.

Enoch, David. "Agency, Shmagency: Why Normativity Won't Come from What Is Constitutive of Action." *The Philosophical Review* 115, no. 2 (2006): 169–98.

———. "Shmagency Revisited." In *New Waves in Metaethics*, edited by Michael Brady, 208–33. London: Palgrave Macmillan, 2011.

Fossen, Thomas. "Politicizing Brandom's Pragmatism: Normativity and the Agonal Character of Social Practice." *European Journal of Philosophy* 22, no. 3 (2014): 371–95. https://doi.org/10.1111/j.1468-0378.2011.00504.x.

Fromm, Erich. *The Sane Society.* London: Routledge, 1955.

IPSA LOQUITUR. "Regus (UK) Ltd v Epcot Solutions Ltd - Case Summary," April 15, 2008. https://ipsaloquitur.com/contract-law/cases/regus-uk-v-epcot-solutions/.

Kant, Immanuel. *Critique of Pure Reason.* Translated by Paul Guyer and Allen W. Wood. Cambridge: Cambridge University Press, 1998.

———. *Practical Philosophy.* Translated by Mary Gregor. Cambridge: Cambridge University Press, 1999.

---

[39] Karl Marx, *Letters from the Franco-German Yearbooks. Early Writings,* trans. Rodney Livingstone and Gregor Benton (London: Penguin Books and New Left Review, 1975), 207.

Korsgaard, Christine M. *Self-Constitution*. Oxford: Oxford University Press, 2009.

———. *The Sources of Normativity*. Cambridge: Cambridge University Press, 1996. https://doi.org/10.1017/CBO9780511554476.

Krasnoff, Larry. *Hegel's 'Phenomenology of Spirit': An Introduction*. Cambridge: Cambridge University Press, 2008.

Marx, Karl. *Letters from the Franco-German Yearbooks. Early Writings*. Translated by Rodney Livingstone and Gregor Benton. London: Penguin Books and New Left Review, 1975.

McDowell, John. "Self-Determining Subjectivity and External Constraint." In *Self-Determining Subjectivity and External Constraint*, 21–37. De Gruyter, 2005. https://doi.org/10.1515/9783110179545.21.

Milton, John. *Paradise Lost*. Edited by Christopher Ricks. London: Penguin, 1968.

O'Neill, Onora. *Constructing Authorities: Reason, Politics and Interpretation in Kant's Philosophy*. Cambridge: Cambridge University Press, 2016.

———. *Constructions of Reason: Explorations of Kant's Practical Philosophy*. Cambridge: Cambridge University Press, 1989.

———. *Towards Justice and Virtue: A Constructive Account of Practical Reason*. Cambridge: Cambridge University Press, 1996.

O'Shea, Tom. "A Law of One's Own: Self-Legislation and Radical Kantian Constructivism." *European Journal of Philosophy* 23, no. 4 (December 2015): 1153–73. https://doi.org/10.1111/ejop.12044.

Pinkard, Terry. *German Philosophy 1760-1860: The Legacy of Idealism*. Cambridge: Cambridge University Press, 2002.

Pippin, Robert. *Hegel's Idealism: The Satisfactions of Self-Consciousness*. Cambridge: Cambridge University Press, 1989.

———. *Hegel's Practical Philosophy: Rational Agency as Ethical Life*. Cambridge: Cambridge University Press, 2008.

———. "The Actualization of Freedom. In The Cambridge Companion to German Idealism." edited by Karl Ameriks, 180–99. Cambridge: Cambridge University Press, 2000.

Pippin, Robert B. "Brandom's Hegel." *European Journal of Philosophy* 13, no. 3 (2005): 381–408. https://doi.org/10.1111/j.1468-0378.2005.00235.x.

Rousseau, Jean-Jacques. *The Social Contract and First and Second Discourses*. Edited and translated by Susan Dunn. New Haven: Yale University Press, 2002.

Stern, Robert. "Constructivism and the Argument from Autonomy." In *Constructivism in Practical Philosophy*, edited by James Lenman and Yonatan Shemmer, 119–37. Oxford: Oxford University Press, 2012.

———. "Freedom, Self-Legislation and Morality in Kant and Hegel: Constructivist vs Realist Accounts." In *German Idealism: Contemporary Perspectives*, edited by Espen Hammer, 245–66. London: Routledge, 2007.

———. "Pinkard on German Idealism." *Hegel Bulletin* 25, no. 1–2 (January 2004): 1–17. https://doi.org/10.1017/S026352320000197X.

Strayer, Joseph, ed. *Dictionary of the Middle Ages*. Vol. 2. New York: Scribner, 1983.

Street, Sharon. "Coming to Terms with Contingency: Humean Constructivism about Practical Reason." In *Constructivism in Practical Philosophy*, edited by James Lenman and Yonatan Shemmer, 40–59. Oxford: Oxford University Press, 2012.

———. "In Defense of Future Tuesday Indifference: Ideally Coherent Eccentrics and the Contingency of What Matters." *Philosophical Issues* 19 (2009): 273–98.

Tiberius, Valerie. *The Reflective Life: Living Wisely Within Our Limits.* Oxford: Oxford University Press, 2008.

Wittgenstein, Ludwig. *Philosophical Investigations.* Translated by G. E. M. Anscombe. Oxford: Blackwell, 1953.

Index

A

A priori xii, 12, 46, 58, 78, 85, 93, 141-147, 149-158, 163, 165, 168-172

abduction vi, 157-158, 165-169, 172

action ix, xi, 1, 8, 11, 14, 19, 20, 23, 33-34, 44, 58, 60-61, 63-66, 68, 69-70, 83, 86, 88, 93-95, 97-99, 101-102, 113, 115, 119-120, 125-129, 130-131, 134-135, 137-139, 144, 166, 171, 176, 179, 182, 184, 188

aesthetic 132, 151, 176

aesthetics 15

amphibology 110

ampliative reasoning 156-157, 164, 167

analogy 21, 99, 102, 122, 153-154, 156, 172, 181, 188

analytic 143-144, 152, 155-157, 159, 162, 167-168

anatomy 24

animal perception 23, 41

anthropocentrism 90-91

anxiety vii, 24

Apel, Karl Otto 169-171, 173

apperception x-xi, 20, 37, 39-54, 57, 59-60, 66-69, 105-109 111-114, 115-123

Aquinas, Thomas 3, 6, 61

Arendt, Hannah ix, 14-15

Aristotle vii-viii, ix, 4, 13

atoms 13, 38, 60, 70

attention 38-39, 41-42, 47, 49-50, 53, 66-69, 144, 146-147, 158

authoritarianism 185-186

authority 98, 135, 179-181, 184, 186-187

autonomy xii, 10, 99, 135, 177-179

awareness 18, 22, 24, 27-28, 31, 34, 39-40, 42, 46-47, 52, 98, 109, 112, 116-117, 123

B

Bacon, Francis 9-10

belief x, 10-11, 17, 19, 24-25, 27, 31, 33-34, 38, 90, 95-96, 127, 131, 144-145, 149, 160-161, 163-165,172

Berkeley, George viii, x-xi, 11, 73-82

Biel, Gabriel 11

boar 42, 47, 49-50, 52, 60

Brandom, Robert 179-183

C

Calvinism 10

Categories
 - Aristotelian 6-7, 8
 - Kantian 8-9, 109-110, 123, 142, 151-152, 156, 169, 170
 - Peircean 166, 170, 172

cognition 25-26, 28-29, 31, 83, 86-89, 90, 92-93, 97-98, 145-147, 151-152, 154, 158

colours 26, 28, 51-52, 158

conscience xi, 42-43, 45, 125-139

conscientia x, 58-60, 67-69

consciousness x-xii, 13, 17, 34, 37-53, 57, 59-60, 66-69, 74-75, 81,

92-93, 96-97, 99-100, 105-123, 127-128, 133-135, 182
consecution 23-24, 34
constructivism xii, 175, 177-179, 182, 188
continuity ix, 1, 4-5, 38, 45-46, 51, 58-59, 62, 66
conviction 121, 128, 131
Critique of Practical Reason 99, 140
Critique of Pure Reason 85, 88, 97-99, 106, 114, 118-121, 136, 142, 146, 156, 188
Critique of the Power of Judgement 12, 15, 84-85

D

De Volder, Burchard 51, 61, 65-66
deduction xii, 150-152, 154, 156, 158, 161-163, 165-167, 169-172
Deleuze, Gilles 92
Descartes, Renée vii, 8, 10-11, 22, 30, 39, 86-88, 90, 93, 96, 99, 107, 109, 111
determinism 94, 98, 161, 165
diligence 129, 132
distinction ix-xii, 1-6, 11-12, 14, 18, 21, 28, 39-40, 43, 45, 47, 49-50, 52-54, 58-59, 66, 77, 83, 85-87, 98, 100, 105, 117-118, 128, 145, 150, 159, 166, 187
dogmatism 90, 128
double-truth 85
Duns Scotus, John 3, 6, 13, 61
duty 126, 128, 130-139, 171
dynamics 21-22, 155

E

emotions 86-88

empirical knowledge 17, 144, 154, 157, 161
Empiricism viii, 12, 73-76, 146
Enlightenment 85, 100-102
ethics viii, 6, 15, 38, 83, 85-88, 90-96, 100-101, 126, 129, 133
evil ix, xi, 14, 100, 125-126, 129-132, 134-139
experience viii-x, 1, 3, 7, 9, 11, 17-20, 22, 24-27, 29, 74-76, 78-79, 88, 96-97, 106, 108-109, 112, 115, 117, 119, 122-123, 142, 144-147, 149-158, 160-161, 164-166

F

faculty 12, 30, 42, 75, 81, 85, 113, 125-127, 133-134, 147, 176
faith 4, 8, 10, 88, 90
fallacy 110
fallibilism 172
fatalism 98
fideism 8, 88
firstness 166-167
freedom xii, 12, 14, 83, 85-86, 88-89, 93-94, 96-102, 132, 136, 175, 182-183
Fromm, Erich 183, 189

G

geometrical figure 20
geometry 11, 73-75, 77-79, 81
Gillespie, Michael Allan 4, 9-10

H

Hegel, George Wilhelm Friedrich x, 1, 12-14, 175, 182-183, 185, 187
Hobbes, Thomas viii, 10

Hume, David viii, 11-12, 108, 146-150, 154-155, 161, 175

hypothesis 6, 13, 17, 132, 161, 165-170

hypothetical 74, 148, 164

I

icons 20, 166

identity x, 12, 38, 57-65, 67-70, 94, 108, 110, 114, 185-186

imagination 12, 22, 30-32, 100, 149

immanence 85, 104

imperative 125, 127-128, 133, 139, 185

indices 166

indispensability 99, 147

induction 9, 150, 156-161, 163-169, 171-172

innate ideas 69, 75

inquiry xii, 5, 14, 141-142, 154, 157, 161, 163-172, 176

introspection 44, 49-50, 53

intuition xii, 89, 99, 106-107, 110-112, 114-120, 151-152, 156

instinct 126, 133

J

judgement xii, 33-34, 78, 127-128, 132, 135, 141-147, 149-150, 152-153, 155-158, 165, 172, 176, 188

K

Kepler, Johannes 18

Kolakowski, Leszek 96

Korsgaard, Christine 176-178

L

legislation xii, 12, 85, 135, 175-180, 181-188

Locke, John viii, 11, 39, 53, 58, 75, 146

Luther, Martin 8, 10-11

M

Malebranche, Nicholas 11, 84

Marx, Karl ix, 188

materialism 98

mathematical knowledge 73-74, 81, 144, 146

mathematics xi, 73-74, 77-78, 81, 86, 144-146, 176

maxim 99, 126, 128-131, 134-135, 137, 139, 149 , 179

McDowell, John 24, 182

medical 21, 35

memory 19, 23-24, 39, 48, 53-54, 58-59, 66-69

metaphysics 3, 6, 13, 15, 37-38, 49, 53, 60, 83, 86-89, 97-99, 101-102, 132, 137, 143-144, 146-147, 149-150, 156, 163, 179

Milton, John 179

mind ix-x, 5-6, 13, 17-18, 21, 24, 31, 34, 41-42, 60, 74-75, 77-78, 80-82, 83, 87, 90-96,100, 102, 119, 133, 149, 163, 180

Molyneux problem 75

Monadology 19, 23, 40, 43-48, 64

morality viii, 10, 83, 86-91, 99, 125, 129-132, 136-138, 176, 178

N

nature vii-ix, 1-2, 9, 11-13,17-19, 23, 25, 29, 34, 40-43, 45-48, 53, 59-68, 76-77, 79-80, 85-91, 94, 96-102, 109, 111, 115, 126-127, 130, 132, 137, 145, 151, 154-155, 160, 162, 168, 175, 177, 183, 187 necessity 94, 116, 149-150, 156, 159

Newton, Isaac viii,155

normativity xii, 88, 175-179, 182-185, 187-188

norms 87, 145, 151-152, 154-155, 161-162, 176-88

notio completa 63-64

noumenal 110, 130, 136-137, 139

noumenon 112, 119, 135

O

Ockham, William of x, 1-2, 4, 6-8, 11

omnipotence 7

omniscience 89

optics 74, 77-79

organ x, 21-24, 57, 59

P

panpsychism 93

pantheism 84

paralogism 110, 120-121

Peirce, Charles Sanders xii, 14, 20, 141-143, 153, 156-172

perception x-xii, 11, 17-34, 37-54, 57-61, 63-65, 68, 73-81,105-109, 111-118, 122-123, 142

phenomenology xi, 13, 29, 155, 183

phenomenon 33, 78, 110, 112, 117, 136

philosophy vii-xii, 1-4, 6, 8-9, 11-15, 17, 24, 37-38, 50, 58, 83, 85-90, 93, 96, 100-101, 110, 125, 128, 132, 134, 141, 143, 146-147, 149-150, 154-157, 166, 186

practical reason (*see reason*)

pragmatism 14, 167, 173, 183

pre-established harmony 11, 17, 38, 46, 62, 66

principle of continuity 45, 51, 54

principle of heterogeneity of sensible ideas 76-77, 79

principle of identity of indiscernibles x, 38, 57, 60,

principle of individuation 13, 61

principle of minimal perception 81

principle of nature and grace 40, 43

principle of non-contradiction 143-144, 157

principle of parsimony 7

principle of pure apperception 105-106, 114

principle of the equipollence of cause and effect 22

probability 156, 159-162, 164

proposition 29-30, 33, 62, 92, 95, 109, 111-114, 118-119, 127-128, 133, 143, 156-157, 160

propositional 24-25, 28, 31, 33-34

Q

qualities 7, 25-28, 34, 81, 131
- Primary 11, 18, 78
- Secondary 11, 18

R

rational psychology 105-106, 109-111, 114-116, 120

rationalism 8, 102

rationality 147, 153-154, 176, 179, 181, 184-185

reason viii-xii, 5-15, 18, 23-24, 27-28, 31, 34, 41, 70, 74, 82, 83-90, 97-101, 111, 125-139, 141-172

- Practical viii-xii, 1-2, 9-15, 34, 83-90, 97-101, 125-139, 141-145, 176-178, 183, 185-188
- Theoretical viii, ix, xii, 1-2, 9-15, 34, 58, 83-90, 97-101, 141-145, 176-177

reflection ix, xi, 1, 9, 38, 39-45, 47-48, 60, 67, 69, 117, 134, 187

regulative hope 169

Reid, Thomas 147

religion viii, 84, 90, 125-129, 131-132, 134-137

renaissance 10

retinal image x, 18

S

scepticism x, 17, 19, 21, 27, 88, 98, 146, 154, 156, 161, 171, 178

secondness 166

sentience 23-24

skepticism (see scepticism)

soul 8, 24, 31, 39-41, 43, 47, 53, 65-68, 87, 97, 109, 138

Spinoza, Baruch xi, 83-98, 100-102

Stern, Robert 13, 177, 182, 185

substance vii-viii, 3, 6-8, 11, 13, 17, 20, 29, 37, 40-41, 44, 47-48, 57-65, 84, 87, 89-91, 93, 95-96, 110-111, 137, 147, 151-153

Summum Bonum 135

symbols 166, 168

synthetic *judgement* 143-144, 155, 158

synthetic unity 105-106, 108, 113-115, 119, 121, 137, 152

T

Taylor, Charles 102, 104

theoretical reason (*see reason*)

thing-in-itself 64, 89, 98, 112, 120

thirdness 166-167

transcendental deduction xii, 106, 141-143, 150, 170-172

transcendental dialectic 109

transcendental idealism 89, 98, 121, 123, 154

tropes 8

truth 8, 61-62, 78-79, 85, 100-101, 143-144, 152, 154, 160-166, 168-170, 176, 178

U

universals ix-x, 1-8, 9-14

V

validity 141-142, 148, 150-151, 156, 158, 162, 165, 168-170

Via Antiqua 4

Via Moderna 4-5, 15

virtue 59, 62, 125-126, 129, 132, 134-137, 139, 176

W

wisdom 87

Wittgenstein, Ludwig 180